BIRDING TRAILS™
TEXAS

INCLUDING **GPS**

GULF COAST

261 Birding Trails for the Avid Birder
With GPS Coordinates for All Locations

FROM THE COVER - THE WHOOPING CRANE

An emblem of what can be done with an endangered species when one is devoted to the task, the whooping crane count has gone from below 50 in the 1940s to well over 200 thanks to several decades of careful and worthwhile use of the Endangered Species Act. Breeding and nesting in Canada, the adults with their young fly south to Texas each fall wintering on the Texas Gulf Coast. They are viewed by visiting birders from around the world.

Other titles from Sandhill Crane Press™

Birding Trails™

Birding Trails™ Texas Panhandle, Prairies and Pineywoods

Upcoming titles from Sandhill Crane Press™

Birding Trails™

Birding Trails™ Montana

Birding Trails™ Wisconsin

Birding Trails™ Eastern Oregon

BIRDING TRAILS™
TEXAS

GULF COAST

**261 Birding Trails for the Avid Birder
With GPS Coordinates for All Locations**

By Jim Foster

Birding Trails Series™

Sandhill
Crane
Press™

Birding Trails™ Series

Published by Sandhill Crane Press ™,
An imprint of Wilderness Adventures Press, Inc.™
45 Buckskin Road
Belgrade, MT 59714
866-400-2012
Website: www.wildadvpress.com
email: books@wildadvpress.com

First Edition 2014

Printed in South Korea

ISBN 978 -1-932098-91-4 (8-09206-98914-6)

Table of Contents

DEDICATION

This book is dedicated to Betty Landreth.

ACKNOWLEDGEMENTS

It would have been very hard to complete this book without the help of people listed here, and the help and encouragement of fellow author Nancy Millar and the McAllen Chamber of Commerce, Ann Vaughn and the Port Aransas Chamber, Diane Phrobst and the Rockport Chamber. I must commend the South Padre Island people at the Convention Center and boardwalk, keeping the birding areas open, especially Scarlet and George Colley.

Many thanks go out to all the good people and birders in the Corpus Christi area and their Chamber of Commerce. Ann and Diane have been very helpful for well over a couple of decades. As for farther south, I must give a big thanks to the Brownsville Audubon group and the Arroyo Colorado Audubon chapter. Quite a bit of help was given by the Garmin Company and especially Ted Gardner, whose help on this and the next book have been invaluable.

There are so many people outside the birding community who have added their input for this book, like my old friends of more years than I want to mention, John and Dorothy Artz, Dick Martin and all the good people and birders of Galveston Island and the Moore Museum, Texas. Mary Jo Bogatto at her Cactus Creek Ranch and Education Center, Ron and Linda Johnston, David Johnston, Linda and Gordon Landreth. Last but by no means least, the Texas Parks Department for their help and for providing the outdoor and birding experience to thousands over the years.

INTRODUCTION

As most birders know, or have discovered, Texas is a very large state with its coastal areas stretching from north to south, in spite of the fact that the Texas Gulf Coast consists of roughly only six percent of the state.

The coastline stretches from the Louisiana state line to Boca Chica Beach – a distance of 732 miles. Boca Chica is where the Rio Grande empties into the Gulf of Mexico, separating Texas from Mexico.

At one time I stepped across the mighty river while photographing terns and pelicans. Yes, the river stopped emptying into the Gulf of Mexico for a brief time while the river was filled with invasive water plants and reduced to a trickle.

Adjacent to the gulf are islands, bays, estuaries, salt flats, dunes, and marshes. Inland from the gulf was originally tall grass prairie, but is now largely devoted to farming, some ranching, and several concentrations of heavy industry and urbanization. The elevation of the region increases very gradually northwestward from sea level to about 150 feet. This was the land of the prairie chicken that filled many a stomach of early pioneers.

Densely wooded sections of live oak and other species are found along the many slow-moving rivers, creeks, bayous, and sloughs. This occurs where the surface is elevated and has adequate drainage. The area around Sea Rim State Park, High Island, and Galveston Island are good examples of this type of terrain.

In the coastal cities of Rockport and Fulton some of these live oaks have been bent over the years by the prevailing winds. This gives birders an idea of how strong and how long these winds have been blowing along this portion of the Texas Coast. It will also hint as to what migrating species must endure on their flights to and from winter to spring and fall to winter.

Many species of birds will nest along the Texas Coast that will not nest in any other location or parts of the state. Among these are the mottled duck, willet, white-faced and white ibis, roseate spoonbill, brown and American white pelicans, reddish egret, American oyster catcher, clapper rail, Wilson's plover, laughing gull, Forster's, royal, sandwich, and Caspian terns, black skimmer, boat-tailed grackle, and seaside sparrow.

The greater prairie chickens are unique inland nesters and are listed on the endangered species list. These birds once numbered in the hundreds of thousands before meat hunting and habitat loss took its toll.

As we move further into the future we must recognize the new dangers facing the birds of Texas and of the world. One of the largest dangers threatening birds is the feral cat. Each year these cats, some owned and some that have been wild for generations, kill millions of birds. Owners of cats should keep them inside and not let them roam outside either in daytime or during the night. These animals do NOT belong in the wild and must be removed. Spay, neuter, and release does not and will not work, now or ever.

The next and growing danger is the wind farm that is the cause of death of more birds; some on the endangered species list, such as the bald eagle, our national bird. The problem is being addressed, but I am afraid it's way too little too late.

Traveling farther south, the coastal areas of the King Ranch and Port Mansfield, and the Arroyo Colorado open new worlds to migrating species as they travel over the gulf and find rest and nourishment after making landfall.

So if visiting some of the most well-known coastal birding sites in Texas sounds appealing to you read on; or if you would rather visit some off-the-beaten-path local birding hotspot, this book will get you there.

The coastal birding trail or trails has it all, plus conveniences such as boardwalks, parking pullouts, observation platforms, and landscaping to attract native wildlife, allowing you to get closer to see many more birds.

Symbols Legend

 BICYCLING

 BLINDS

 BOAT ACCESS

 CAMPING

 FISHING

 HANDICAPPED ACCESS

 HIKING

 HUNTING

 PICNICING

 FEE

 RESTROOMS

Ethical Practices For Birdwatchers

Traveling throughout the state of Texas, birdwatchers will find that every place is unique and should be respected with all care possible.

Here are just a few of the ideas and practices that should occur while birdwatchers are in the field observing the many species of bird life Texas has to offer.

It is best if birders will learn the patterns of bird behavior so as not to interfere with life cycles or nesting practices of the species observed. This can be hard to accomplish because we, as a group, are always looking for something new, something special and unique.

Using the best equipment like binoculars and spotting scopes, we should try to not distress the birds while visiting their habitat – taking care to blend in with the environment while moving as little as we can and being quiet.

Respect and do your best not to interrupt the routine of the birds you're watching. Don't move into their feeding area just for a better view or a closer photograph.

Photographers should use the appropriate lens to photograph wild birds from a distance so as not to disturb or frighten the bird.

If while you are watching a bird and it starts to show stress, it is advised that you move farther back or use a longer lens to photograph the subject. This is also where spotting scopes and a good pair of binoculars will aid in observing and not disturbing the species.

Before entering any type of habitat you should acquaint yourself with the area and the fragility of any ecosystem. Stay on the trails that were put there to help lessen the impact on the area. In areas of endangered species, do not frighten or try to get too close. Texas has several endangered birds, so please observe all regulations and area rules.

If possible or appropriate, inform the managers or other authorities of your presence and the purpose of your visit. Most places will be aware of birders, their equipment, and the activities needed to pursue a certain birder species.

Birders should familiarize themselves with the rules and regulations of the areas where they will be, and abide by these rules strictly. In areas where fees are required, birders should pay these fees in advance before entering an area, or put money in the appropriate boxes. In the absence of any authority, birders should always use good judgment.

Birders should remember that they are the guests in these locations, and should treat them as if they are the homes of people they visit.

In regard to other birders and area visitors - the golden rule applies to birds as well as the people watching the birds.

Treat others courteously, and remember to ask before joining others in an area where they are already photographing or observing wildlife. This is an important issue, because at times birders and those photographing birds have spent considerable time gaining that position slowly and cautiously in order not to stress the bird. The appearance of a new individual could cause the bird to either leave the area or move farther away. You will disturb the bird and birder if you move in quickly or ask loudly.

Try to be a good role model, both as a photographer birdwatcher and as a person. Try to educate others by your actions in order to enhance their understanding of the situations and rules of the area.

Regarding state parks and wildlife management areas, these are special places offering people a chance to explore the outdoors and enjoy the wildlife. They have special rules and regulations covering their individual locations. In most state parks and wildlife management areas, the rules are easily understood and mostl are strictly enforced.

It is also true that state parks are places where families gather and give their youngsters a pleasing outdoor experience. Kids will be kids, so if some are too loud or boisterous, take it in stride and temper you comments, remembering you were once that age and all was fresh and new.

BIRDING TRAILS: TEXAS GULF COAST

East Texas Loop

The landscape in the eastern portion of Texas is one of small rolling hills covered with large pines, hardwood draws, and several large lakes.

Skirting the banks of Lake Sam Rayburn and following Highway 96 into Jasper can be the beginning of a great birding adventure on the East Texas Loop. Texas Parks and Wildlife has marked many of the birding locations with the familiar brown signs, as the numbers on this map will show.

This trail will take you from the Piney Woods of the East Texas forest to locations near Trinity Bay and on to Port Arthur where a drive down Highway 87 will take you along the Bolivar coast and East Bay to the Bolivar Ferry taking you to Galveston Island.

Interstate 10 will also take you to several birding locations on your way west and then north on Interstate 69 to the eastern shores of Lake Livingston. Driving slowly and taking your time at these locations will allow you to spot and watch the birds that are common to East Texas, like the red-headed woodpecker and even the elusive palliated woodpecker.

During the fall and winter months, millions of waterfowl fly from their northern nesting areas to the open waters of this area. Numerous shore and wading birds may be found by the birder who spends the time driving the many roads bordering the East Texas wetlands.

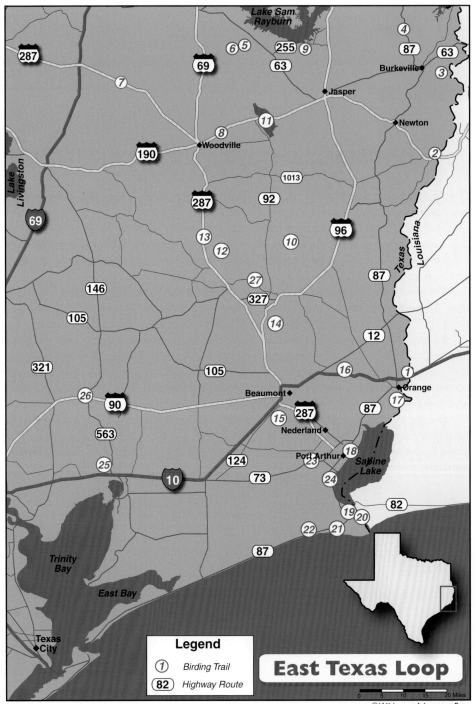

Legend

① Birding Trail

⑧② Highway Route

East Texas Loop

0   5   10   15   20 Miles

© Wilderness Adventures Press

East Texas Loop Locations

1. Tony Houseman State Park/Wildlife Management Area
2. Kera East Wildlife Management Area (Bon Wier)
3. Wild Azalea Canyons
4. Champion Canyon Rim Woodlands Trail
5. Angelina NF Boykin Springs Recreation Area
6. Angelina NF Upland Island Wilderness, Bouton Lake, and Sawmill Trail
7. Champion Woodland Trail
8. LPC Dogwood Trail
9. Jasper Sate Fish Hatchery
10. Martin Dies State Park
11. West BA Steinhagen Reservoir
12. Big Thicket National Preserve
13. Gore Store Road and Turkey Creek
14. Village Creek State Park
15. Tyrell Park and Cattail Marsh
16. Claiborne West Park
17. Lower Neches Wildlife Management Area and Bailey's Fish Camp
18. Pleasure Island
19. Sabine Pass
20. Sabine Pass Battleground SHP and Texas Point
21. Sabine Woods
22. Sea Rim State Park
23. JD Murphree Wildlife Management Area
24. Taylor Bayou
25. Lake Charlotte
26. Liberty
27. Roy E. Larson Sandyland Sanctuary

Spotted Sandpiper

EAST TEXAS LOOP

#1 Tony Houseman State Park/ Wildlife Management Area

GPS 30.123, -93.713

LOCATED JUST WEST OF THE SABINE RIVER ON I-10

KEY BIRDS
Tree nesters, woodpeckers, and shore birds

BEST SEASON
Migrations, summer, fall

AREA DESCRIPTION
Gulf coastal plains, eastern forests, and central plains share space with areas indicative of swamps and bayous

Tony Houseman State Park and Wildlife Management Area gives birders a great place to bird in a combination of an area near the Pineywoods and also birds that are found near the Gulf of Mexico.

This Wildlife Management Area is managed by the Texas Department of Transportation and Texas Parks and Wildlife. The Travel Information Center located in the area provides interpretive displays for visitors.

Birders will enjoy the 600-foot boardwalk that takes birders from the center into the marshlands.

Birders should look for waterfowl during migration and in winter, as well as a scattering of loons, grebes, gulls, terns, tree nesters, and woodpeckers.

Access is restricted at this time, but TPW is in the planning stages for developing a nature trail in the near future. Presently, these bottomlands may be entered through the Texas Department of Travel Information Center located on the north service road of I-10.

DIRECTIONS
Located just west of the Sabine River (which represents the border between Texas and Louisiana) on I-10.

CONTACT INFORMATION
Site open for day use only and a fee is charged.
8096 FM 2782
Nacogdoches, TX 75964
936-569-8547

EAST TEXAS LOOP

#2 Kera East Wildlife Management Area

GPS 30.747, -93.615

LOCATED JUST WEST OF LOUISIANA STATE LINE IN NEWTON COUNTY

KEY BIRDS
Brown-headed nuthatch and Bachman's sparrow

BEST SEASON
Summer

AREA DESCRIPTION
Longleaf pine forests in an upper coastal environment

Kera East is a private wildlife management and recreation area, owned and operated by the Louisiana-Pacific Corporation (LPC). There are times when LPC will allow entry, but by reservation only. Calling ahead is recommended.

The longleaf pine forests within this site contain some of the Pineywoods species, such as the brown-headed nuthatch and Bachman's sparrow which are found here. In late spring, swallow-tailed kites may be seen gliding above the trees bordering the Sabine River.

DIRECTIONS
From Orange, TX travel west on I-10 to its intersection with TX 87 (about two miles). Travel north on TX 87 to FM 1416. Travel east on FM 1416 to US 190 and Bon Wier. Continue east on US 190 to the state line and the bridge that crosses the Sabine River. About 0.5 mile before the river there is an old section of the highway where parking is available.

CONTACT INFORMATION
Information may be obtained by calling LPC at 409-384-5422. Site is open for day use only.

EAST TEXAS LOOP
Wild Azalea Canyons

GPS 30.539, -93.63

LOCATED ON FM 1414, NORTHEAST OF NEWTON, TEXAS

KEY BIRDS
Pileated woodpecker, wood thrush

BEST SEASON
Spring, summer

AREA DESCRIPTION
Pine forests, rock canyons, and thickets of wild azaleas

The area is owned and maintained by Temple-Inland Forest Products Corporation. Wild Azalea Canyons is noted for its pine forests and rock canyons. In mid- to late March, large thickets of wild azaleas come into bloom and are a favored attraction at this site. The surrounding pine forests are host to pileated woodpeckers, wood thrushes, hooded and Swainson's warblers, and summer tanagers.

Except for blooming season, there are no water or restroom facilities available. Some of the area paths are also steep and can be slippery. Please do not disturb any plants in this sensitive area.

DIRECTIONS
From Bon Wier, travel west on US 190 to FM 2626, then north on FM 2626 until it merges with TX 87. Continue north on TX 87 to FM 1414, then east on FM 1414 to Wild Azalea Canyons and Temple-Inland Wilderness Park.

CONTACT INFORMATION
Site open for day use only. If staying in the Newton area, contact Hinestead Ranch (409-379-3405) for information about "bed-and-bird" lodging within the 690-acre ranch. If staying in the city of Newton, visit Caney Creek Nature Park (one block east of the courthouse square in Newton), and Sylvan Nature Trail (four miles southeast of Newton on US 190, directly opposite the TxDOT roadside park).

Red-breasted Nuthatch

EAST TEXAS LOOP
Champion Canyon Rim Woodlands Trail

GPS ⊕ 31.069, -93.437

LOCATED JUST OFF TX 87 NEAR R255

KEY BIRDS
Red-eyed vireo, Louisiana waterthrush

BEST SEASON
Spring, summer

AREA DESCRIPTION
Wooded areas with open semi-grassland and some improved clearings

This is a great site for the birder as well as the photographer with well-marked and maintained trails.

Owned and maintained by Champion International Corporation, this wooded area attracts many species. Champion has constructed a trail around the rim of the canyon, and a number of breeding birds may be easily seen here during the late spring.

The area includes an old logging road last used by mule and ox-drawn wagons over a century ago, and a cannon range used by Fort Polk trainees during World War II.

The whole trail is a comfortable 1.6 miles and is marked in three sections - 1 - Easy Walking; 2 - Moderate to Strenuous Walking; 3 - Difficult Walking.

It is very convenient to get to and it has nice, well-marked trails. As stated, most of the trails do not require a great deal of exertion.

Louisiana waterthrush have been known to nest along the creek that flows through the bottom of the canyon, and blue-gray gnatcatchers, yellow-throated and red-eyed vireos, and black-and-white warblers are often observed here.

Continue north on TX 87 and you will come across a red-cockaded woodpecker group that straddles the highway near the Newton/Sabine County line.

DIRECTIONS
From Newton, TX drive north on TX 87 to R255 and Champion Canyon Rim Woodlands Trail.

CONTACT INFORMATION
Site open for day use only.

Red-eyed Vireo

EAST TEXAS LOOP

#5 Angelina NF Boykin Springs Recreation Area

GPS 31.0591, -94.2775

LOCATED ON BOYKIN SPRINGS ROAD – FR 313 – OFF OF TX 63

KEY BIRDS
Henslow's sparrow, red-cockaded woodpecker, chipping sparrow

BEST SEASON
Spring, summer

AREA DESCRIPTION
Diversity of woodland, bluestem grasslands

Originally constructed by the Civilian Conservation Corps in 1937, Boykin Springs still maintains its rustic charm, including a very large picnic shelter. There is a rich diversity of woodland birding in this area.

As you enter along Boykin Springs Road (FR 313), you will cross a fire-maintained longleaf pine forest. Birders and photographers will be glad to learn there are a number of red-cockaded woodpecker groups in this area, and one accessible group has been marked. Look for the signs as you enter along FR 313.

The bluestem grasslands within the forest are the preferred habitat for Bachman's sparrows. In the winter, the wetter grasslands attract a few Henslow's sparrows.

Brown-headed nuthatches prefer the dense pine stands all year through, while yellow-breasted chats, painted buntings, and Kentucky warblers like to nest in the yaupon thickets. Late spring and summer is the time to find chipping sparrows.

DIRECTIONS
Drive west on R255 from Sam Rayburn Reservoir to TX 63. Then drive northwest on TX 63 to Angelina National Forest (NF) and Boykin Springs Recreation Area.

CONTACT INFORMATION
Angelina National Forest, 111 Walnut Ridge Road, Zavalla, Texas 75980, or call: 936-897-3406
E-mail: mailroom_r8_texas@fs.fed.us
Site open daily. Developed camping available. Fee charged.

House Sparrow

EAST TEXAS LOOP
Angelina NF Upland Island Wilderness, Bouton Lake and Sawmill Trail

GPS 31.027, -94.317

BOUTON LAKE AND CAMPGROUND ARE LOCATED IN THE ANGELINA NATIONAL FOREST ON FR 303

KEY BIRDS
Louisiana waterthrush, bald eagle, red-cockaded woodpecker

BEST SEASON
Fall, spring, summer

AREA DESCRIPTION
Bottomland hardwoods, cypress trees, and mixed pine

One of the best-kept secrets about the 153,179-acre Angelina National Forest is Bouton Lake Campground. Completed in 1963, this area provides visitors with some excellent birding. Louisiana waterthrush nest along the tannin-stained (brownish water) streams that permeate the bottoms.

Sawmill Trail connects Bouton Lake and Boykin Springs. Therefore, it is possible to bird the forest that extends between these two special sites.

Birders will enjoy this drive and hike through lush East Texas thicket in the Angelina National Forest. The trail runs between two National Forest Service campsites – Boykin Springs and Bouton Lake – and features a rare, small waterfall on Boykin Creek. Birding is good along the Sawmill Hiking Trail to Boykin Springs, 5.5 miles away.

Birders should bring their own drinking water. Toilet facilities are available within a short distance of each camping site. A waste/dump station is available for RVs at nearby Caney Creek.

This is a "Pack it In - Pack It Out" area; please take your refuse home for proper disposal. No garbage facilities are available at this campground.

Bald Eagle

DIRECTIONS
From TX 63, continue northwest (toward Zavalla) to Angelina CR 348 (also FR 303). Travel south on CR 348 (FR 303) to Upland Island Wilderness and Bouton Lake.

CONTACT INFORMATION
111 Walnut Ridge Road, PO Box 507, Zavalla, TX 75980
Phone: 936-897-1068
This site is open for day use only.

EAST TEXAS LOOP
#7 Champion Woodland Trail

GPS ⊕ 30.951, -94.69

LOCATED ON FM 62, NORTH OF US 287

KEY BIRDS
Red-tailed hawk, golden eagle, bald eagle, and osprey

BEST SEASON
Spring, summer

AREA DESCRIPTION
Lowland hardwood forest, sometimes described as a dry woodland

This forest has some of the oldest longleaf pines within the state. Some of these old trees are estimated to be over 250 years old. This trail continues down and enters into a lowland hardwood forest. Birders should watch for birds with a preference for the woodlands.

Some of the species you are likely to observe are: eared grebe, double-crested cormorant, American bittern, great blue heron, cattle egret, yellow-crowned night-heron, white-faced ibis, wood stork, wood duck, mallard, gadwall, northern pintail, American wigeon, northern shoveler, blue-winged teal, green-winged teal, ring-necked duck, bufflehead, hooded merganser, ruddy duck, turkey vulture, red-shouldered hawk, red-tailed hawk, golden eagle, bald eagle, osprey, American kestrel, American coot, killdeer, black-necked stilt, greater yellowlegs, lesser yellowlegs, common snipe, mourning dove, Inca dove, rock dove, greater roadrunner, ruby-throated hummingbird, belted kingfisher, red-headed woodpecker, yellow-bellied sapsucker, pileated woodpecker, eastern wood-pewee, eastern kingbird, scissor-tailed flycatcher, loggerhead shrike, American crow, purple martin, barn swallow, tufted titmouse, eastern bluebird, American robin, gray-cheeked thrush, northern mockingbird, cedar waxwing, summer tanager, northern cardinal, blue grosbeak, indigo bunting, painted bunting, brown-headed cowbird, house finch, American goldfinch, and roseate spoonbill.

DIRECTIONS
From Zavalla, travel south on US 69 to FM 1745 in Colmesneil. Continue west on FM 1745 to US 287, then north on US 287 to FM 62 and Champion Woodland Trail.

Osprey

CONTACT INFORMATION

Angelina National Forest, 111 Walnut Ridge Road, Zavalla, TX 75980
Phone: 936-897-3406
E-mail: mailroom_r8_texas@fs.fed.us
Site open for day use only.

American Robin

EAST TEXAS LOOP
LPC Dogwood Trail

GPS 30.796, -94.372

NORTHEAST OF WOODVILLE OFF US 190

KEY BIRDS
American robin, titmouse, northern cardinal

BEST SEASON
Spring, summer

AREA DESCRIPTION
Dogwood, cypress, willow, beech, magnolia, and sweet bay are common, mixed among the evergreen pines

Large trees here support migrating as well as resident species. The Dogwood Trail offers another opportunity to enjoy the woodland birding that is available only in this area. Several of the bird species that you commonly see in this area will be exceedingly difficult to find between Beaumont and Brownsville.

The dogwoods bloom from mid- to late March.

DIRECTIONS
Drive south on US 287 to Woodville. From Woodville, travel east on US 190 to LPC Dogwood Trail.

CONTACT INFORMATION
No Contact information available.
Site open for day use only and there is no fee.

EAST TEXAS LOOP
Jasper State Fish Hatchery

GPS 30.949, -94.128

APPROXIMATELY TEN MILES NORTH OF JASPER OFF TEXAS HIGHWAY 63

KEY BIRDS
Eastern bluebird, assortment of water birds including cormorants

BEST SEASON
All seasons

AREA DESCRIPTION
Mostly open with trees and growing ponds for fish

The hatchery occupies 227 acres of land purchased by the state of Texas in 1930. It has 63 ponds covering approximately 65 surface acres. The original 33 ponds and three log buildings were built by the Civilian Conservation Corps and were completed in 1932. Additional construction was completed in 1947. Water for the hatchery flows by gravity flow from Indian Creek and into a 21-inch pipeline. A new incubation building built in 1993 houses incubation equipment, round tanks, troughs, and raceways used in the culture of game fish species.

Situated within Texas Pineywoods, the fish hatchery is located in a densely forested area with an assortment of aquatic habitats that are not found in other locations in the area.

The various ponds attract water birds, and the forests that border the hatchery can be quite good for woodland birding. Watch for eastern bluebirds perched on power lines and fence posts as you drive through this area.

Other species attracted to this area are: eared grebe, double-crested cormorant, American bittern, great blue heron, cattle egret, yellow-crowned night-heron, white-faced ibis, wood stork, wood duck, mallard, gadwall, northern pintail, American wigeon, northern shoveler, blue-winged teal, green-winged teal, ring-necked duck, bufflehead, hooded merganser, and ruddy duck.

DIRECTIONS
Drive east on US 190 to FM 1747, then travel north on FM1747 to CR 009 and the Jasper State Fish Hatchery.

CONTACT INFORMATION
Manager: Reese Sparrow, 289 CR 098, Jasper, TX 75951
Phone: 409-384-2221
E-mail: reese.sparrow@tpwd.state.tx.us
Site open for day use only.
It is normally open for visitors from 8:00am to 5:00pm weekdays.

Double-crested Cormorants

EAST TEXAS LOOP
Martin Dies State Park

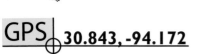

GPS 30.843, -94.172

LOCATED IN JASPER AND TYLER COUNTIES BETWEEN WOODVILLE AND JASPER ON STEINHAGEN RESERVOIR

KEY BIRDS
Red-headed woodpecker, other woodpeckers, brown creeper, heron and egret nesting colonies, anhinga

BEST SEASON
All seasons

AREA DESCRIPTION
Wooded areas around the lake with wetland areas

Martin Dies, Jr. State Park is a 705-acre recreational area in Jasper and Tyler Counties between Woodville and Jasper on the 15,000-acre B.A. Steinhagen Reservoir. Martin Dies SP is divided into three different units (the Hen House Ridge, Walnut Ridge, and Cherokee Units), placed both north and south of US 190.

Look for pileated and other woodpeckers throughout the year, and brown creepers in winter. In the summer, check the Cherokee Unit for yellow-throated warblers and indigo buntings.

If paddling is how you like to bird, you're in luck here. There are three paddling trails in the area that run from three miles to sixteen

Great Egret

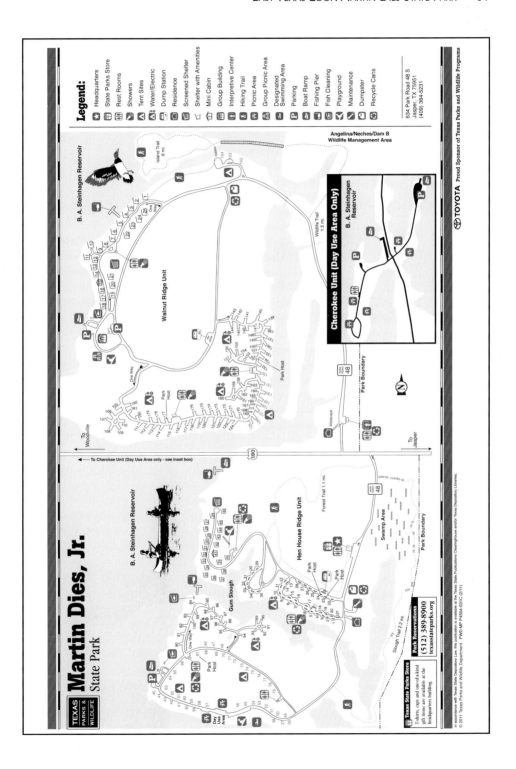

Martin Dies, Jr.
State Park

Legend:

- Headquarters
- State Parks Store
- Rest Rooms
- Showers
- Tent Sites
- Water/Electric
- Dump Station
- Residence
- Screened Shelter
- Shelter with Amenities
- Mini Cabin
- Group Building
- Interpretive Center
- Hiking Trail
- Picnic Area
- Group Picnic Area
- Designated Swimming Area
- Parking
- Boat Ramp
- Fishing Pier
- Fish Cleaning
- Playground
- Maintenance
- Dumpster
- Recycle Cans

634 Park Road 48 S
Jasper, TX 75951
(409) 384-5231

B. A. Steinhagen Reservoir

Island Trail
8 mi.

Angelina/Neches/Dam B
Wildlife Management Area

Walnut Ridge Unit

Wildlife Trail
1.5 mi.

Cherokee Unit (Day Use Area Only)

B. A. Steinhagen Reservoir

Park Host

One Way

To Woodville

To Cherokee Unit (Day Use Area only - see inset box)

Park Boundary

To Jasper

190

PARK ROAD 48

N

Hen House Ridge Unit

Gum Slough

B. A. Steinhagen Reservoir

Park Host

Forest Trail 1.1 mi.

Swamp Area

Park Boundary

Slough Trail 2.2 mi.

One Way

Park Host

Day Use Area

Texas State Parks Store
T-shirts, caps and one-of-a-kind
gift items are available at the
headquarters building.

Park Reservations
(512) 389-8900
texasstateparks.org

In accordance with Texas State Depository Law, this publication is available at the Texas State Publications Clearinghouse and/or Texas Depository Libraries.
© 2011 Texas Parks and Wildlife Department PWD MP P4504-031C (2/11)

TOYOTA Proud Sponsor of Texas Parks and Wildlife Programs

TEXAS PARKS & WILDLIFE

miles in length. They are the Walnut Slough Paddling Trail, Sandy Creek Paddling Trail, and Neches Paddling Trail and offer a variety of experiences on the park's backwater sloughs along Spring Creek, the wide open B.A. Steinhagen Reservoir, and the fast-moving Neches River, all filled with amazing bird watching opportunities.

There are several rookeries in the spring with several heron and egret nesting colonies in and around this reservoir. Anhingas are common in this location.

Accessible only by boat, Angelina-Neches Scientific Area and Dam B WMA are located north of the park.

DIRECTIONS
From Jasper, drive southwest on US 190 to PR 48 and the Martin Dies SP headquarters.

CONTACT INFORMATION
634 Park Road48 South, Jasper TX 75951
Phone: 409-384-5231,
Web: http://www.tpwd.state.tx.us/spdest/findadest/parks/martin_dies_jr/
The site is open daily with developed camping available. Normal state park entry and camping fees are charged. The park also has bicycle and canoe rentals.

West B.A. Steinhagen Reservoir

#11

GPS 30.85, -94.19

LOCATED OFF FM 92, TWO MILES SOUTH OF THE JUNCTION OF US 190 AND FM 92

KEY BIRDS
Yellow-throated warbler, indigo bunting, American redstart

BEST SEASON
All seasons

AREA DESCRIPTION
Pine and some hardwoods with lakeside habitat

American redstarts have nested in Magnolia Ridge Park near the Wolf Creek Trail parking area.

Local birders go to the area from Camper's Cove Park south to Town Bluff to find sparrows in the winter and migrant land birds in the spring.

Species to watch for: eared grebe, double-crested cormorant, American

Indigo Bunting

bittern, great blue heron, cattle egret, yellow-crowned night-heron, white-faced ibis, wood stork, wood duck, mallard, gadwall, northern pintail, American wigeon, northern shoveler, blue-winged teal, green-winged teal, ring-necked duck, bufflehead, hooded merganser, and ruddy duck.

DIRECTIONS

From Jasper, continue west on US 190 to West B.A. Steinhagen Lake. Continue west on US 190 to FM 92, then travel north on FM 92 to ACOE Magnolia Ridge Park.

CONTACT INFORMATION

Operated by US Army Corps of Engineers
Phone: 409-429-3491
The site is open daily with developed camping available. Entry and camping fees are charged.

EAST TEXAS LOOP

Big Thicket National Preserve

#12

GPS 30.473, -94.346

SEPARATE UNITS LOCATED NORTH OF BEAUMONT, TEXAS

KEY BIRDS
Pileated woodpecker, eastern wood-pewee, tropical kingbird

BEST SEASON
All seasons

AREA DESCRIPTION
Vast combinations of pine and cypress forest, hardwood forest, meadow, and black-water swamp

The original Big Thicket of Texas covered between one million and three million acres. Today the park protects nine land units and six water units, comprising approximately 100,000 acres that are not all connected to one another.

People have called the Big Thicket an American ark and the biological crossroads of North America. The preserve was established to protect the remnant of its complex biological diversity. What is extraordinary is not the rarity or abundance of its life forms, but how many species coexist here. Once vast, this combination of pine and cypress forest, hardwood forest, meadow, and black-water swamp is but a remnant.

Tropical Kingbird

Common snipe, mourning dove, Inca dove, rock dove, greater roadrunner, ruby-throated hummingbird, belted kingfisher, red-headed woodpecker, yellow-bellied sapsucker, pileated woodpecker, eastern wood-pewee, eastern kingbird, scissor-tailed flycatcher, loggerhead shrike, American crow, purple martin, barn swallow, tufted titmouse, eastern bluebird, American robin, gray-cheeked thrush, northern mockingbird, cedar waxwing are birds that find this habitat to their liking.

The BTNP is divided into a number of widely separated units. A complete list (as well as a detailed map) may be obtained at the visitor's center. BTNP locations preferred by birders include Cook's Lake, Hickory Creek Savannah, Kirby Nature Trail, Lance Rosier Unit, McQueen's Landing, Pitcher Plant Trail, Turkey Creek Trail, and Village Creek.

There are no fees for any park activity, but free permits are required for backpacking, overnight river use, and hunting. Visitors must get these permits in person at the preserve visitor center. The center does not issue the Interagency Senior Pass.

DIRECTIONS

From FM 92, continue south to Spurger and the intersection with FM 1013. The go west on FM 1013 to US 69/287, then south on US 69 to the BTNP.

Traveling from Warren, you may wish to visit Hickory Creek and the Sundew Trail. The Hickory Creek Savannah Unit is located west of US 69 on FM 2827. Continue south on US 69 to FM 420, then east on FM 420 to the visitors center.

CONTACT INFORMATION

Mail: 6044 FM 420, Kountze, TX 77625
Visitor Center and Information: 409-951-6700
Preserve Headquarters: 409-951-6800
There are no fees for any park activity. The free permits are required for backpacking, overnight river use, and hunting. Visitors must get these permits in person at the preserve's visitor center. They do not issue the Interagency Senior Pass. There is no fee to enter Big Thicket National Preserve.

EAST TEXAS LOOP

#13 Gore Store Road and Turkey Creek

GPS | **GORE STORE ROAD: 30.509, -94.399**
TURKEY CREEK TRAIL: 30.329, -94.372

GORE STORE ROAD IS LOCATED 3.5 MILES NORTH OF KOUNTZE OFF US 69 / TURKEY CREEK TRAIL IS LOCATED ON FIRETOWER ROAD

KEY BIRDS
Prairie and Swainson's warblers, yellow-breasted chat, eastern screech owl, yellow-billed cuckoo

BEST SEASON
Migrations, summer

AREA DESCRIPTION
Thick piney woods and creek side habitat

Threatened and endangered species have long been a real draw for birders to Gore Store Road and the vicinity. However, extensive timbering in the area has left the pine forests in a perpetual state of early succession. As a result, species such as red-cockaded woodpecker and Bachman's sparrow have become quite difficult to find in this area.

Watch for species preferring early succession growth and dense yaupon thickets, such as prairie and Swainson's warblers and yellow-billed cuckoo.

Situated on Village Creek, the sanctuary exhibits a unique intermingling of different forest and wetland communities. Of special importance are the longleaf pine communities that occur on the uplands.

The sanctuary is open to the public free of charge on a daily basis from sunrise to sunset. Six miles of nature trails offer hiking, photography, and nature study opportunities. A self-guiding interpretive trail guide is available for a 0.8-mile section of the trail system.

Eight miles of Village Creek flow through the sanctuary, providing an easy and enjoyable canoeing experience. This one-day float takes you through the more remote areas of the preserve's bottomland hardwood forest. Along the creek are beautiful white sandbars and enchanting backwater bald cypress sloughs. Slipping quietly along by canoe spotting birds can be thrilling. Keep your talking to a minimum.

Eastern Screech Owl

A few of the species to be spotted are: belted kingfisher, red-headed woodpecker, yellow-bellied sapsucker, pileated woodpecker, eastern wood-pewee, eastern kingbird, scissor-tailed flycatcher, loggerhead shrike, American crow, purple martin, barn swallow, tufted titmouse, eastern bluebird, American robin, gray-cheeked thrush, and northern mockingbird. Listen for the Bachman's sparrow.

DIRECTIONS
From Kountze, go north on US 69 approximately 3.5 miles to Gore Store Road and Turkey Creek. Travel east on Gore Store Road to Firetower Road (11.7 miles).

CONTACT INFORMATION
Texas Highway Department – Mostly private property and National Forest. Site open for day use only.

EAST TEXAS LOOP
Village Creek State Park

#14

GPS 30.252, -94.174

NEAR THE COMMUNITY OF LUMBERTON, 10 MILES NORTH OF BEAUMONT

KEY BIRDS
White-faced ibis, wood stork, wood duck, mallard

BEST SEASON
Migrations, summer

AREA DESCRIPTION
Young pine/hardwood forests and waterways

Located in Hardin County, this area comprises 1,090 heavily forested acres, although Hurricane Rita took out 30 to 80 percent of the trees in some areas of the park. Although the land was purchased in 1979, the state park was not opened until April, 1994. The park takes its name from the free-flowing Village Creek that forms the northern border of the park, and eventually flows into the Neches River.

Abundant rainfall in this area keeps the water flowing in Village Creek and helps sustain the beautiful swampy areas in the park. It is a very popular canoe float stream and gives access to the heart and soul of the Old Texas Big Thicket. The Big Thicket is considered the biological crossroads of North America, since more species of flora and fauna occur here than in any other area of similar size in North America. The park is also part of the 21-mile Village Creek Paddling Trail which provides a great way for birders to explore the area, including the cypress/tupelo swamps, baygalls, and backwater sloughs.

Some of the area birds are: northern mockingbird, cedar waxwing, summer tanager, northern cardinal, blue grosbeak, indigo bunting, painted bunting, brown-headed cowbird, house finch, American goldfinch, roseate spoonbill, white-faced ibis, wood stork, wood duck, mallard, gadwall, northern pintail, American wigeon, and northern shoveler. The young pine/hardwood forests within the park host a representative selection of eastern woodland birds.

DIRECTIONS

From Kountz, drive south on US 69 to FM 327. Drive east on FM 327 to FM 92, then continue south on FM 92 to US 96 and Village Creek State Park.

CONTACT INFORMATION

PO Box 8565, Lumberton TX 77657
Phone: 409-755-7322

White-faced Ibis

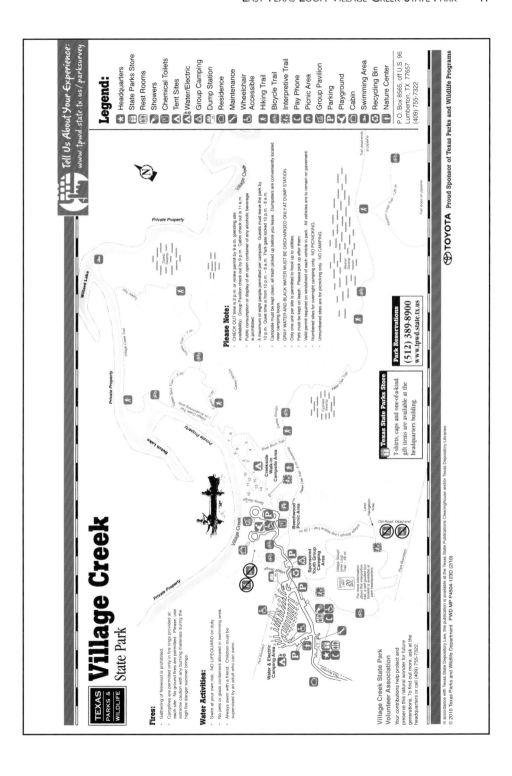

Village Creek State Park

TEXAS PARKS & WILDLIFE

Tell Us About Your Experience:
www.tpwd.state.tx.us/parksurvey

Legend:

- Headquarters
- State Parks Store
- Rest Rooms
- Showers
- Chemical Toilets
- Tent Sites
- Water/Electric
- Group Camping
- Dump Station
- Residence
- Maintenance
- Wheelchair Accessible
- Hiking Trail
- Bicycle Trail
- Interpretive Trail
- Pay Phone
- Picnic Area
- Group Pavilion
- Parking
- Playground
- Cabin
- Swimming Area
- Recycling Bin
- Nature Center

P.O. Box 8565, off U.S. 96
Lumberton, TX 77657
(409) 755-7322

Fires:
- Gathering of firewood is prohibited.
- Campfires are permitted only in fire rings provided at each site. No ground fires are permitted. Please, use extreme caution with any burning materials during the high fire danger summer temps.

Water Activities:
- Swim at your own risk. NO LIFEGUARD on duty.
- No pets or glass containers allowed in swimming area.
- Always swim with a friend. Children must be supervised by an adult who can swim.

Please Note:
- CHECK OUT time is 2 p.m. or renew permit by 9 a.m. (pending site availability). Group Pavilion check out by 9 p.m. Cabin check out is 11 a.m.
- Public consumption or display of an open container of any alcoholic beverage is prohibited.
- A maximum of eight people permitted per campsite. Guests must leave the park by 10 p.m. Quiet time is from 10 p.m. – 6 a.m. Park gate locked 10 p.m. – 8 a.m.
- Campsite must be kept clean; all trash picked up before you leave. Dumpsters are conveniently located near camping loops.
- GRAY WATER AND BLACK WATER MUST BE DISCHARGED ONLY AT DUMP STATION.
- Only one unit per site is permitted to hook up to utilities.
- Pets must be kept on leash. Please pick up after them.
- Valid permit required on windshield of each vehicle in park. All vehicles are to remain on pavement.
- Numbered sites for overnight camping only. NO PICNICKING.
- Unnumbered sites are for picnicking only. NO CAMPING.

Texas State Parks Store

T-shirts, caps and one-of-a-kind gift items are available at the headquarters building.

Park Reservations
(512) 389-8900
www.tpwd.state.tx.us

Village Creek State Park Volunteer Association
Your contributions help protect and preserve this natural wonder for future generations. To find out more, ask at the headquarters or call (409) 755-7322.

TOYOTA Proud Sponsor of Texas Parks and Wildlife Programs

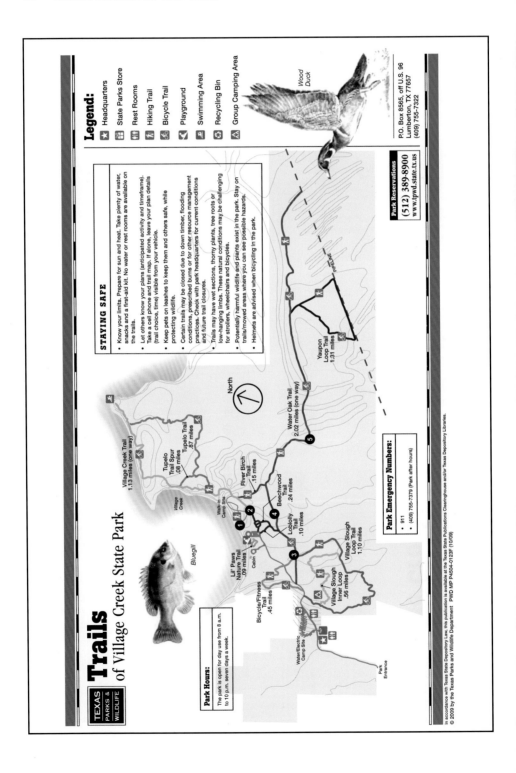

TEXAS PARKS & WILDLIFE

Trails
of Village Creek State Park

Park Hours:

The park is open for day use from 8 a.m. to 10 p.m. seven days a week.

Park Emergency Numbers:

- 911
- (409) 755-7379 (Park after hours)

STAYING SAFE

- Know your limits. Prepare for sun and heat. Take plenty of water, snacks and a first-aid kit. No water or rest rooms are available on the trails.
- Let others know your plans (anticipated activity and timeframe). Take a cell phone and trail map. If alone, leave your plan details (trail choice, time) visible from your vehicle.
- Keep pets on leashes to keep them and others safe, while protecting wildlife.
- Certain trails may be closed due to down timber, flooding conditions, prescribed burns or for other resource management practices. Check with park headquarters for current conditions and future trail closures.
- Trails may have wet sections, thorny plants, tree roots or low-hanging limbs. These natural conditions may be challenging for strollers, wheelchairs and bicycles.
- Potentially harmful wildlife and plants exist in the park. Stay on trails/mowed areas where you can see possible hazards.
- Helmets are advised when bicycling in the park.

North

Village Creek Trail 1.13 miles (one way)

Tupelo Trail Spur .08 miles

Tupelo Trail .87 miles

River Birch Trail .15 miles

Beechwood Trail .24 miles

Loblolly Trail .10 miles

Water Oak Trail 2.02 miles (one way)

Village Slough Loop Trail 1.10 miles

Village Slough Inner Loop .56 miles

Lil' Paws Nature Trail .09 miles

Bicycle/Fitness Trail .45 miles

Yaupon Loop Trail 1.31 miles

Bluegill

Wood Duck

Walk-in Camp Site

Village Creek

Cabin

Water/Electric Camp Site

Park Entrance

PIPELINE

Legend:

- ★ Headquarters
- 🏪 State Parks Store
- 🚻 Rest Rooms
- 👤 Hiking Trail
- 🚲 Bicycle Trail
- 🎡 Playground
- 🏊 Swimming Area
- ♻ Recycling Bin
- ⛺ Group Camping Area

P.O. Box 8565, off U.S. 96
Lumberton, TX 77657
(409) 755-7322

Park Reservations
(512) 389-8900
www.tpwd.state.tx.us

EAST TEXAS LOOP
Tyrrell Park and Cattail Marsh
#15

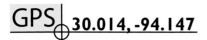

GPS 30.014, -94.147

5305 TYRRELL PARK ROAD
BEAUMONT, TEXAS

KEY BIRDS
Least grebe, double-crested cormorant, American bittern, great blue heron, cattle egret, yellow-crowned night-heron, white-faced ibis

BEST SEASON
All seasons

AREA DESCRIPTION
Marshy area made up of low expanses and shallow-water sloughs

As a multi-use facility, Tyrrell Park contains a nature center, botanical gardens, golf course, stables, a creative play area, basketball, a walking and jogging trail, as well as picnic areas and RV hookups.

Many eastern breeding birds are observed in this habitat. This is perhaps one of the best spots to observe fish crows. Since common crows are also present here, listen for the guttural "croaks" that are characteristic of the fish crow.

Cattail Marsh is the man-made wetland area between Tyrrell Park and Hillebrandt Bayou, and forms part of the final stages of the city of Beaumont's wastewater treatment facilities. It is located on Babe Zaharias Drive, at the entrance to Tyrrell Park. A one-hour tour of the wetland will lead you to the eight treatment cells with eight miles of levees on 900 acres. The water and plants attract many birds.

This 900-acre constructed wetland attracts an incredible diversity of water birds throughout the year. The water levels vary from compartment to compartment, so shorebirds and waterfowl are constantly shifting within this complex. Cars are not allowed on the levees, so be prepared to walk the levees. A good pair of hiking boots along with a supply of water and a spotting scope will come in handy.

Some of the species that may be seen are: American bittern, great blue heron, cattle egret, yellow-crowned night-heron, white-faced ibis, wood stork, wood duck, mallard, gadwall, northern pintail, American wigeon, northern shoveler, blue-winged teal, green-winged teal, ring-necked duck, bufflehead, hooded merganser, ruddy duck, turkey vulture, red-shouldered hawk, and red-tailed hawk. In all, more than 350 species reside in this area during all or part of the year.

DIRECTIONS
From Beaumont, take US Highway 69/96 North. Take Mitchell Road exit onto Mitchell Road (just before the US Highway 69/96 split). Go approximately .4 miles on the access road and turn east (right) onto Mitchell Road. Then turn immediately north (left) onto FM 3513 (Village Creek Parkway). Go approximately 2 miles and turn east (right) on Alma Drive. Cross the railroad tracks (veer to the left) and go .5 mile to park entrance. Stop at the park headquarters to pay entry and get directions to the access site.

CONTACT INFORMATION
Site open for day use only.
From October through March, the marsh is open to the public from 6:00am to 6:00pm, and from 6:00am to 9:00pm the rest of the year.

Least Grebe

EAST TEXAS LOOP
Clairborne West Park

#16

GPS 30.136, -93.925

LOCATED 12 MILES WEST OF ORANGE, TEXAS ON I-10

KEY BIRDS
Ringed kingfisher and great kiskadee

BEST SEASON
Spring, summer

AREA DESCRIPTION
Extreme variety of landscape, see below

Major North American biological influences bump up against each other here: southeastern swamps, Appalachians, eastern forests, central plains, and southwest deserts. Bogs sit near arid sandhills.

Claiborne West Park is a living memorial to Claiborne West, who played an important role in making Texas independent from Mexico. The park area comprises 453 acres of land and is a wildlife and bird sanctuary as well as featuring a fishing pond, picnic sites, and nature trails. It also allows primitive camping.

For those who wish to continue directly to the upper coast, Claiborne West Park offers an opportunity to see an interesting selection of Big Thicket woodland birds. Check this park in migration for landbirds that have over-flown the coast and settled into the interior forests.

You will find species such as the eastern

Great Kiskadee

bluebird, American robin, gray-cheeked thrush, northern mockingbird, cedar waxwing, summer tanager, northern cardinal, blue grosbeak, indigo bunting, painted bunting, brown-headed cowbird, house finch.

Directions
From the intersection of I-10 and TX 87 in Orange, Texas (where the Big Thicket Loop begins), continue west on I-10 to FM 1442 (Exit 869). After exiting, remain on the north service road and continue west to the entrance to Claiborne West Park.

Contact Information
Orange County Parks Board
Phone: 409-745-2255

EAST TEXAS LOOP

#17 Lower Neches WMA and Bailey's Fish Camp

GPS 30.057, -93.732

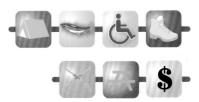

NEAR BRIDGE CITY IN ORANGE COUNTY

KEY BIRDS
Herons, egrets, spoonbills, waterfowl, and shorebirds

BEST SEASON
All seasons, but try winter and early spring for waterfowl

AREA DESCRIPTION
Briny coastal marshland

Covering 7,998 acres located near Bridge City in Orange County, the WMA is divided into three main units: the Nelda Stark Unit, the Old River Unit, and the Adams Bayou Unit.

The TPWD observation platform is located approximately 1.5 miles from TX 73/87, and overlooks a broad expanse of coastal marsh. This platform dates back to the 1920s when a boat ferry was established to transport people across the Neches River to Port Arthur.

The rivers and bayous of this area are attractive to migratory birds, both game and non-game, in the Central Flyway. There are special hunts that are scheduled in this area for both game birds and alligators.

DIRECTIONS
Old River Unit: From Port Arthur travel northeast on SH 87/73 about 10 miles to Bridge City. Turn right on Lake Street and drive for about 2 miles to the unit headquarters/ sign-in station, parking lot, and viewing stand on the east side of Lake Street.
Nelda Stark Unit: From Bridge City take FM 1442 west 5 miles to Bessie Heights Road. Turn left (south) to the unit headquarters, just over 1 mile on the left.

CONTACT INFORMATION

Jim Sutherlin - 10 Parks & Wildlife Drive, Port Arthur, TX 77640
Phone: 409-736-2551
Web site: http://www.tpwd.state.tx.us/huntwild/hunt/wma/find_a_wma/list/?id=58
Site open for day use only. Fee charged. Open year round. The wildlife viewing platform is handicap accessible, but there are no restroom facilities or drinking water.

Little Blue Heron

EAST TEXAS LOOP
Pleasure Island

#18

GPS 29.902, -93.897

PORT ARTHUR, TEXAS

KEY BIRDS
Loons, concentrations of waterfowl, gulls, and terns

BEST SEASON
Winter

AREA DESCRIPTION
Pleasure Island is surrounded by the Sabine Neches Waterway and Sabine Lake and has hills, bluffs, and vistas of Sabine Lake

Pleasure Island is an 18.5-mile-long man-made body of land. It is across the Sabine Neches Intracoastal Waterway from Port Arthur with Sabine Lake on its southeast side.

The land is made up of deposits dredged by the U.S. Corps of Engineers while they were constructing the Port Arthur Canal, which was completed in 1899. The rest of the land came from dredging for this part of the Intracoastal Waterway that the corps completed in 1908. In the early part of the 20th century, it was truly a "pleasure island" with dance halls, a roller coaster, and a golf course, but storms, erosion, and fires eventually destroyed all the buildings. A resurgence of building began again in the 1980s.

Watch for loons on the Sabine Lake side of the levee roads, while grebes and waterfowl abound in the winter. Shorebirds may be present in impressive numbers during low tides when the mud flats are exposed. Both the north and south ends of Pleasure Island are productive, so wander the levee roads and scope the concentrations of ducks, gulls, and terns.

Some other species seen at this location are: common loon, canvasback, bufflehead, common goldeneye, red-breasted merganser, mottled duck, northern shoveler, pintail, blue- and green-winged teal, gadwall, ruddy duck, wigeon, fulvous whistling duck, white pelican, white-tailed kite, brown pelican, spotted sandpiper, chickadee, American pipit, Caspian tern, Forster's tern, tricolored heron, black tern, little blue heron, least tern, black-crowned night-heron, gull, red-winged blackbird, grackle, white ibis, cattle egret, roseate spoonbill, snowy egret, yellow-crowned night-heron, great egret, black skimmer, anhinga, purple martin, black-necked stilt, and neotropic cormorant.

Waterfowl

DIRECTIONS
From Bridge City, take TX 73/87 southwest to Groves. Remain on TX 73 when the two roads divide in Groves, and continue southwest to the intersection with TX 82. Travel south on TX 82 across the Gulf Intracoastal Waterway (GIWW). Once across the MLK Bridge, exit on T.B. Ellison Parkway for Pleasure Island.

CONTACT INFORMATION
Jimmy Dike, Director, 520 Pleasure Pier Blvd., Port Arthur, TX 77640
Phone: 409-982-4675
E-mail: jdike@pleasureislandtx.com
Site open for day use only.

EAST TEXAS LOOP
Sabine Pass

GPS 29.733, -93.894

SOUTH OF PORT ARTHUR BETWEEN SABINE LAKE AND THE GULF OF MEXICO

KEY BIRDS
Waterfowl, gulls, and terns

BEST SEASON
All seasons

AREA DESCRIPTION
Ocean-side environment and marine habitat

Sabine Pass is the natural outlet of Sabine Lake into the Gulf of Mexico. It borders Jefferson County, Texas and Cameron Parish, Louisiana. It lies on the west bank of Sabine Pass, near the Louisiana border.

Birders should drive slowly through the area and look for cormorants, waterfowl, gulls, and terns as you drive along the south end of Sabine Lake.

Before entering the town of Sabine Pass, you will cross the Sabine Pass Marshes. This wetland is host to roseate spoonbills, clapper rails, least bitterns, common yellowthroats, seaside sparrows, and white, white-faced, and glossy ibis.

The boat-tailed grackle is also a resident of this marsh. Be on the lookout for a few boat-tailed grackles that sport eye colors that are more yellow than usual.

DIRECTIONS
In Port Arthur, take TX 82 to TX 87 and continue south on TX 87 to Sabine Pass.

CONTACT INFORMATION
No contact information available.
Site open for day use only.

Various Gulls

EAST TEXAS LOOP
#20 Sabine Pass Battleground SHP and Texas Point

GPS ⊕ 29.73, -93.875

ON DICK DOWLING ROAD, 1.5 MILES SOUTH OF SABINE PASS AND 15 MILES SOUTH OF PORT ARTHUR VIA STATE HIGHWAY 87

KEY BIRDS
Vireos, warblers, tanagers, buntings, grosbeaks, and orioles

BEST SEASON
All seasons, but especially the spring and fall migrations

AREA DESCRIPTION
Grassy areas with marsh habitat and small trees and shrubs

The location of a significant Civil War battlefield, Sabine Pass Battleground State Historic Site honors a small band of heroic Confederate soldiers led by Lt. Richard Dowling. In less than an hour, his small band of men destroyed two Union gunboats and captured the other two along with almost 350 prisoners.

Considered a minor birding site on the Texas Coast, it does offer a variety of migrant birds in the spring and again in the fall.

You can continue east to Texas Point and Pilot Station but this road is poorly maintained, so be prepared

Baltimore Oriole

for a rough ride. However, orchard orioles, painted buntings, and white-tailed kites breed in the area.

Migrant landbirds such as buntings, grosbeaks, orioles, vireos, tanagers, and warblers migrate through this area, especially after a cold front moves through in the spring. In winter, both seaside and Nelson's sharp-tailed sparrows are found in large numbers in the cordgrass marshes here.

Directions
Traveling from Sabine Pass, continue east on FM 3322 to the Sabine Pass Battleground State Historical Park.
Directions to Texas Point: Continue east on FM 3322 to South 1st. Turn south on South 1st and continue to the dead-end at the Pilot Station and Texas Point, about 3.5 miles.

Contact Information
6100 Dick Dowling Rd., Port Arthur, TX 77640
Phone: 512-463-7948.
Open Daily, 8:00am to – 5:00pm. Closed: Thanksgiving, Christmas Eve, Christmas Day, New Year's Eve, and New Year's Day. Small fees are charged for camping.

EAST TEXAS LOOP
#21 Sabine Woods

GPS ⊕ 29.698, -93.95

UPPER TEXAS COAST SOUTH OF BEAUMONT, TEXAS

KEY BIRDS
Hundreds of hummingbirds and migrant land birds

BEST SEASON
Spring and fall migrations

AREA DESCRIPTION
Stand of live oaks

The Texas Ornithological Society currently owns and manages "Sabine Woods" bird sanctuary. This isolated stand of live oaks is among the most productive stopover sites along the entire Texas Coast for neotropical migrants, especial during spring migration. Besides the live oaks, the land supports large mulberry trees and some areas of thick underbrush. In the early fall, birds will find hundreds of hummingbirds (mostly ruby-throated) that swarm the lantana thickets.

For those birders who may have visited here before, some enhancements have been made. Gate, fencing, and a parking area with entrance gate have been constructed.

Rufous Hummingbird

DIRECTIONS
Drive west on TX 87 to Texas Ornithological Society (TOS) Sabine Woods (located 4.2 miles from Sabine Pass on the north side of TX 87).

CONTACT INFORMATION
Phone: 281-440-6364 or 281-787-3888
Site open for day use only.

EAST TEXAS LOOP
Sea Rim State Park

#22

GPS⊕ 29.665, -95.019

SOUTH OF PORT ARTHUR, TEXAS

KEY BIRDS
Rails, cave swallows, marsh and water birds

BEST SEASON
All seasons

AREA DESCRIPTION
4,141 acres; gulf willows, salt cedars, and red mulberries along with grassy areas and low, thick brush

Sea Rim State Park — 4,141 acres of marshland with 5.2 miles of Gulf of Mexico beach shoreline — is located in Jefferson County, south of Port Arthur. Hurricane Rita did extensive damage to this park, but a master plan is in place to restore the park.

Enter the Marshlands Unit (north of TX 87) and continue to the boathouse at the end of the entrance road. Cave swallows (as well as barn and cliff swallows) have nested under the eaves of this boathouse for the past several years.

The boardwalk east of the headquarters (the Gambusia Trail) offers an excellent spot from which to view a variety of marsh and water birds, especially rails.

A boardwalk is being constructed through this woodland with funds provided by the GTCBT project. The beach may be accessed at a number of points as you continue west on TX 87, and be sure to check the gull and tern flocks.

The gulf willows, salt cedars, and red mulberries along the southern edge of TX 87 are remarkably attractive to migrant landbirds.

DIRECTIONS
Drive west on TX 87 to Sea Rim SP. Return to TX 87, and continue west for approximately 0.5 mile to the Sea Rim State Park headquarters and Beach Unit. Leaving the headquarters, continue west on TX 87.

Contact Information
Phone: 409-971-2559
Only a few facilities currently exist at the park, such as portable toilets, trash receptacles, and self-pay check-in stations. Come prepared to be self-sufficient. This site is open daily with a daily entrance fee of $3 per person. The primitive overnight fee is $10 per night plus the entrance fee. Limit eight people per site.

Clapper Rail

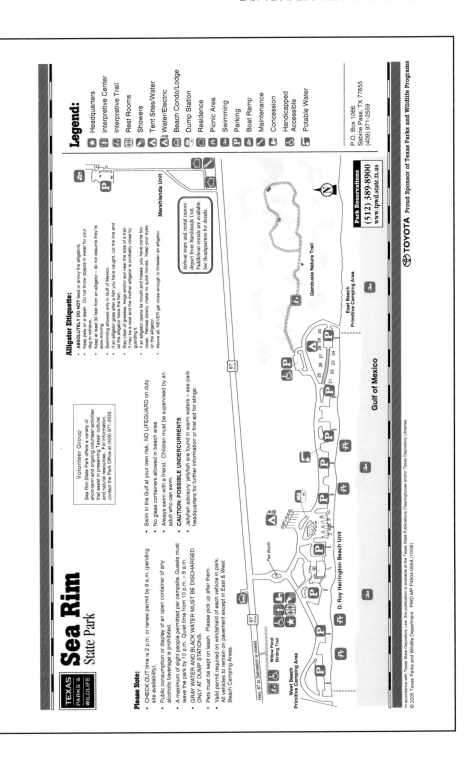

Sea Rim State Park

TEXAS PARKS & WILDLIFE

Please Note:

- CHECK OUT time is 2 p.m. or renew permit by 9 a.m. (pending site availability).
- Public consumption or display of an open container of any alcoholic beverage is prohibited.
- A maximum of eight people permitted per campsite. Guests must leave the park by 10 p.m. Quiet time from 10 p.m. – 6 a.m.
- GRAY WATER AND BLACK WATER MUST BE DISCHARGED ONLY AT DUMP STATIONS.
- Pets must be kept on leash. Please pick up after them.
- Valid permit required on windshield of each vehicle in park. All vehicles to remain on pavement except in East & West Beach Camping Areas.

Volunteer Group

Sea Rim State Park offers a variety of short-term and ongoing volunteer activities that assist in preserving Texas' cultural and natural resources. For information, contact the Park Office at (409) 971-2559.

- Swim in the Gulf at your own risk. NO LIFEGUARD on duty.
- No glass containers allowed in beach area.
- Always swim with a friend. Children must be supervised by an adult who can swim.
- **CAUTION: POSSIBLE UNDERCURRENTS**
- Jellyfish advisory: jellyfish are found in warm waters – see park headquarters for further information or first aid for stings.

Alligator Etiquette:

- **ABSOLUTELY DO NOT** feed or annoy the alligators.
- Keep pets on a leash. Do not throw objects in water for your dog to retrieve.
- Keep at least 30 feet from an alligator – do not assume they're slow-moving.
- Swimming allowed only in Gulf of Mexico.
- If an alligator goes after a fish you have caught, cut the line and let the alligator have the fish.
- Stay clear of grasses, twigs and/or soil near the side of a trail. It may be a nest and the mother alligator is probably close by guarding it.
- If an alligator opens its mouth and hisses, you have come too close. Retreat slowly; make no quick moves. Keep your eyes on the alligator.
- Above all, NEVER get close enough to threaten an alligator.

Airboat tours and rental canoes depart from Marshlands Unit. Paddleboat rentals are available. See Headquarters for details.

Park Reservations
(512) 389-8900
www.tpwd.state.tx.us

Legend:

- Headquarters
- Interpretive Center
- Interpretive Trail
- Rest Rooms
- Showers
- Tent Sites/Water
- Water/Electric
- Beach Condo/Lodge
- Dump Station
- Residence
- Picnic Area
- Swimming
- Parking
- Boat Ramp
- Maintenance
- Concession
- Handicapped Accessible
- Potable Water

P.O. Box 1066
Sabine Pass, TX 77655
(409) 971-2559

TOYOTA Proud Sponsor of Texas Parks and Wildlife Programs

Marshlands Unit

Gambusia Nature Trail

Gulf of Mexico

East Beach Primitive Camping Area

West Beach Primitive Camping Area

Willow Pond Birding Trail

Hwy. 87 to Galveston is closed.

Fee Booth

D. Roy Harrington Beach Unit

EAST TEXAS LOOP

#23 J.D. Murphree WMA

GPS 29.888, -94.034

SOUTHWEST OF PORT ARTHUR, TEXAS

KEY BIRDS
Least bittern, brown pelican, piping plover

BEST SEASON
All seasons

AREA DESCRIPTION
Running from brackish to fresh water, this site can best be described as a diverse coastal wetlands example

The J. D. Murphree WMA is a 24,250-acre tract of fresh, intermediate, and brackish water within the prairie-marsh zone along the upper coast of Texas.

Access to this WMA is restricted, although a nature trail has been developed near the headquarters. The nature trail offers some great marshland and at times salt marsh birding, and late spring and summer are particularly interesting. Least bitterns are abundant in these marshes.

Boat access to the area may be arranged. To arrange for a boat ride into the WMA, contact the following:

Texas Marshland Tours
Capt. Jerry Norris
3262 Bell St.
Port Arthur, TX 77640
409-736-3023

DIRECTIONS
From Port Arthur, take TX 73 west to J.D. Murphree WMA.

CONTACT INFORMATION
Jim Sutherlin, #10 Parks & Wildlife Dr., Port Arthur, TX 77640
Phone: 409-736-2551
The headquarters is on the south side of Highway 73 at the intersection of Jade Avenue in Port Arthur. Site open for day use only.

Brown Pelican

EAST TEXAS LOOP
Taylor Bayou

#24

GPS 29.825, -93.961

EAST OF WINNIE, TEXAS

KEY BIRDS
Prothonotary, Swainson's, Kentucky, and hooded warblers, reddish egret, tri-colored heron, anhinga, yellow-billed cuckoo

BEST SEASON
Spring, summer

AREA DESCRIPTION
A riverine system with two major forks, north and south

It is very important to note that all property bordering Taylor Bayou is private. Please, do not trespass. Bird only along the main rights-of-way.

Taylor Bayou is host to many of the eastern woodland birds that inhabit the Pineywoods. The woodlands that border the stream represent an isolated slice of the Big Thicket that has inched toward the coast. Many of the eastern woodland birds that inhabit the Pineywoods are present along the bayou.

The summer brings sightings of swallow-tailed kites, and northern parulas breed in the area as well as Kentucky, prothonotary, Swainson's, yellow-throated, and hooded warblers.

As you drive to the bayou, watch for the rice fields along TX 73. They hold thousands of shorebirds in spring, so look for those fields that have been recently flooded.

DIRECTIONS
Drive west on TX 73 to Jap Road. Go north on Jap Road to the South Fork of Taylor Bayou. Go north on Jap Road to the North Fork of Taylor Bayou, and then continue north on Jap Road to Patterson Road. Travel west on Patterson Road to Craigen Road, and then go west on Craigen Road back to the North Fork of Taylor Bayou. Continue north on Craigen Road to TX 124, and then go south on TX 124 to TX 73. Travel west on TX 73 to Winnie.

CONTACT INFORMATION
No contact information available and the site is for day use only.

Tri-colored Heron

EAST TEXAS LOOP
#25 Lake Charlotte

GPS 29.868, -94.724

NORTHERN TIP OF TRINITY BAY, EAST OF HOUSTON, TEXAS

KEY BIRDS
Bald eagle, ring-billed gull, mottled duck, great egret, roseate spoonbill, double-crested cormorant, coot, snow goose, snowy egret, osprey

BEST SEASON
All seasons

AREA DESCRIPTION
Cypress swamps bordering Lake Charlotte

Lake Charlotte is named for Charlotte Barthe Labadie, the mother of historical Texas figure Nicholas Descomps Labadie. By the time of the Texas revolution, Lake Charlotte was a resort area with two-masted scow schooners plying the waters from the Trinity River through Lake Pass and into the lake.

The recreational facilities at Lake Charlotte have yet to be constructed. Therefore, access to this site is presently restricted. However, permission to visit Lake Charlotte may be obtained. The cypress swamp bordering Lake Charlotte is one of the most extraordinary remaining on the upper Texas Coast. Bald eagles have nested in this area for several years.

Snowy Egret

Some other species may include black-crowned night-herons, Forster's terns, royal terns, ring-billed gulls, mottled ducks, great egrets, roseate spoonbills, double-crested cormorants, coots, snow geese, snowy egrets, osprey, and even eagles are possible. Usually we see lots of white ibis in the swamp. Sometimes there are hundreds of feeding egrets and herons and quite a few roseate spoonbills when the water is low.

DIRECTIONS

Using the town of Winnie as an initial point of reference, from Winnie, continue west on I-10 to FM 563, and then travel north on FM 563 to Lake Charlotte Road. Turn west on Lake Charlotte Road for about 1.3 miles to Lake Charlotte.

CONTACT INFORMATION

Please contact the Chambers County Commissioner's Pct. 3 office at 281-576-2243 for permits and fee information, or call the ACOE Wallisville office at 409-389-2285. This site is access restricted.

EAST TEXAS LOOP
Liberty

#26

GPS 30.056, -94.796

NORTHEAST OF HOUSTON, TEXAS ON US 90

KEY BIRDS
Red-bellied, downy, and pileated woodpeckers, blue jay, Carolina wren, eastern bluebird, several species of kite

BEST SEASON
All seasons

AREA DESCRIPTION
Riverside and marshy habitats

Liberty is situated on the banks of the Trinity River, one of the great Texas rivers that bisect the state on the way to the Gulf. Although not a major birding destination it can serve as a comfortable base from which to bird, since the town has a number of attractive traditional hotels and charming bed-and-breakfasts. There are also several parks and sanctuaries in the area.

To bird Liberty properly, drive west on US 90 going from its intersection with FM 563 to Main Street or Loop 227. Go north (veering east) on Main Street to Cook Road, and then go north on Cook Road to the Liberty Municipal Park.

Return to Main Street, and go south to Monta. Travel west on Monta to Bowie. From Bowie, you may continue west to the Liberty Flood Control Levee along the Trinity River, or veer south to the Liberty City Cemetery.

In addition, check out the Trinity River historic bridge on US 90 as well as the Liberty ferry landing on the river at Lamar Street. The U.S. Fish and Wildlife Service is currently establishing a national wildlife reserve on the Trinity River. It is not currently open to the public, but birding access will be provided in the future. You can check with their regional office in Liberty.

DIRECTIONS
From Lake Charlotte, return to FM 563, and then continue north on FM 563 to US 90 and Liberty.

CONTACT INFORMATION
Liberty County Convention and Visitors Bureau
Phone: 912-368-3471

Downy Woodpecker

EAST TEXAS LOOP
#27 TNCT Roy E. Larsen Sandyland Sanctuary

GPS 30.361, -94.247

NORTH OF BEAUMONT, TEXAS

KEY BIRDS
Bachman's sparrow, red-headed woodpecker, yellow-bellied sapsucker, pileated woodpecker, eastern wood-pewee

BEST SEASON
Spring and summer

AREA DESCRIPTION
Dry sandy soils, desert plants, along with widely scattered longleaf pines and drought-resistant oaks

The Roy E. Larsen Sandyland Sanctuary consists of 5,654-acres and is owned and managed by The Nature Conservancy of Texas. It was established in order to preserve one of the most unique and ecologically varied natural areas of the Big Thicket region of Texas.

Open to the public from sunrise to sunset, the sanctuary visits are free of charge. There is ample opportunity for birding, hiking, and photography on the six miles of nature trails.

A self-guiding interpretive trail guide is available for a 0.8-mile section of the trail system. This location is designated as a site on the Great Texas Coastal Birding Trail.

The sanctuary also offers birders eight miles of Village Creek flow, by providing an enjoyable canoeing and birding experience. This one-day float takes you through some of the more remote areas of the preserve.

DIRECTIONS
For detailed directions, call The Nature Conservancy of Texas' Roy E. Larsen Sandyland Sanctuary at: 409-781-5071.

CONTACT INFORMATION
Phone: 409-385-0445
Guided tours for groups may be arranged by contacting the Pineywoods office in advance at 409-385-1455.
Site open for day use only and no fees are charged.

Song Sparrow

Beaumont Loop

Arriving in Texas from the east, one of the first places you will find on Interstate 10 is the city of Beaumont surrounded by the stream, lakes, and the pine trees and hardwoods of east Texas.

Beaumont, the city, is located on Interstate 10 creating a "main road" for some interesting birding adventures. Smaller towns such as Silsbee and Dayton, located on old Highway 90 are great attractions for "off the beaten trail" bird watchers.

The largest city in Texas, Houston offers birders several Audubon groups catering to the areas birds and the people who love to find them and add them to their life lists. The habitats west of Houston can be flat, with many potholes and water impoundments off Interstate 10 and Highway 290. This is one of the areas in Texas where it is a wise suggestion NOT to hurry through watching only through your windshield.

If north is your direction of choice, venture east and west from Interstate 45 and explore the many small areas along the route. The large expanse of Lake Conroe is west of the city of Conroe, on Texas Highway 105. Routes around the lake and through the wooded areas are mostly well marked and can be very productive in spotting various bird species.

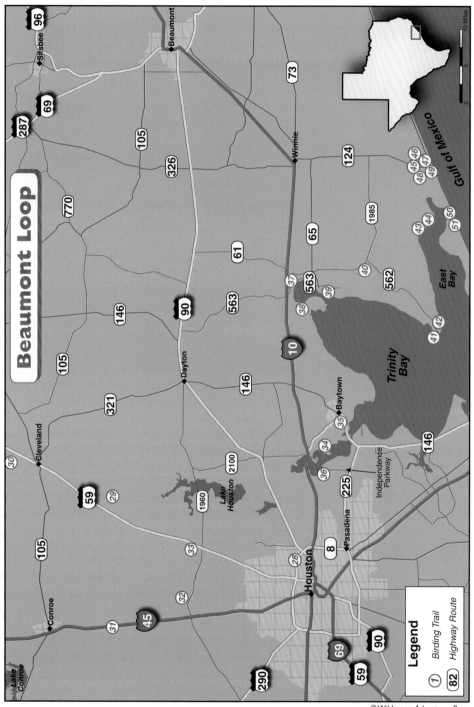

Beaumont Loop

Lake Conroe

Conroe

105

31

45

290

32

33

28

Houston

8

69

90

59

59

90

Legend

1 Birding Trail

82 Highway Route

©Wilderness Adventures Press

30

29

59

321

105

146

105

770

326

Silsbee

96

69

287

Beaumont

73

Winnie

124

61

90

563

146

Dayton

146

2100

2100

1960

Lake Houston

36

34

35

Baytown

225

Pasadena

Independence Parkway

146

10

37

563

38

39

65

40

562

1985

43 44

45 46
47
48 49 50
51

41 42

Trinity Bay

East Bay

Gulf of Mexico

0   5   10 Miles

Beaumont Loop Locations

28. Sheldon State Park
29. Lake Houston Wilderness Park
30. Big Creek Scenic Area
31. W.G. Jones State Forest
32. Mercer Arboretum and Botanical Gardens
33. Jesse H. Jones Nature Center
34. Baytown Nature Center
35. Eddie V. Gray Goose Creek Wetlands Education Center
36. San Jacinto Battleground/Monument SHP
37. White Memorial Park
38. Wallisville Reservoir
39. Fort Anahuac Park
40. Double Bayou Park
41. Smith Point & James H. Robbins Memorial Park
42. Candy Abshier WMA
43. UTC Anahuac NWR – Main entrance
44. Anahuac NWR – East Bay Bayou
45. TXDOT High Island Roadside Park
46. HAS Smith Oaks Bird Sanctuary
47. HAS Eubanks Woods Bird Sanctuary
48. HAS SE Gast Red Bay Sanctuary
49. HAS Boy Scout Woods Bird Sanctuary
50. Rollover Pass
51. UTC Yacht Basin Road

BEAUMONT LOOP
Sheldon State Park
and WMA

#28

GPS 29.852, -95.175

NORTHEAST SIDE OF HOUSTON, TEXAS

KEY BIRDS
Anhinga, osprey, waterfowl, Le Conte's sparrow

BEST SEASON
Migrations and winter

AREA DESCRIPTION
East Texas pines and hardwood with lakeside and marsh habitats

The park is described as a 2,800-acre outdoor education and recreation facility located in northeast Harris County. Formerly in the "country", Sheldon Lake has survived a tremendous influx of urbanization over the past 50 years as Houston has grown. Sheldon Lake is now a green and blue "oasis" for wildlife and people on the edge of the largest city in Texas. The park vegetation consists of a variety of grasses, woody plants, and trees such as oak, pine, cypress, sycamore, and others typical of the Houston area.

You will find an exceptional area to bird for ospreys and anhingas on your way to the park. Take time to visit Buckhorn Lake, which is located just north of Garrett Road just after the turn-off of Sheldon Road.

Along with migrations, winter is the best time to visit the park and wildlife management area. Flocks of waterfowl can be observed on the ponds and lakes in the area. More than twenty species of ducks and geese, along with other waterfowl are present. Also during the winter months you will find bald eagles and osprey in the area. A wide variety of sparrows, including Le Conte's, are found in the weedy fields of the park.

Spring – March through June – brings the sightings of egret and heron rookeries on the barrier islands along Pineland/Fauna Roads.

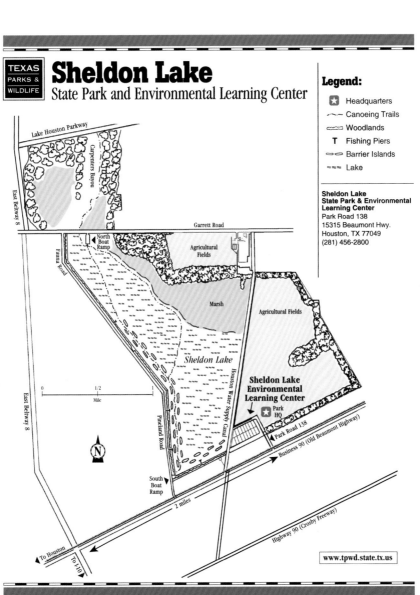

Sheldon Lake
State Park and Environmental Learning Center

TEXAS PARKS & WILDLIFE

Legend:

⭐ Headquarters
᠆ᩔ᠆ Canoeing Trails
ᆼᆼ Woodlands
T Fishing Piers
ᆼᆼ Barrier Islands
═══ Lake

**Sheldon Lake
State Park & Environmental
Learning Center**
Park Road 138
15315 Beaumont Hwy.
Houston, TX 77049
(281) 456-2800

Lake Houston Parkway

Carpenters Bayou

East Beltway 8

Garrett Road

North Boat Ramp

Fauna Road

Agricultural Fields

Marsh

Agricultural Fields

Sheldon Lake

Houston Water Supply Canal

Sheldon Lake
Environmental
Learning Center

⭐ Park HQ

0   1/2   1
Mile

East Beltway 8

Pineland Road

South Boat Ramp

Park Road 138

Business 90 (Old Beaumont Highway)

Highway 90 (Crosby Freeway)

2 miles

To Houston

To I 10

N

www.tpwd.state.tx.us

Sheldon Lake
Environmental Learning Center

TEXAS PARKS & WILDLIFE

Please Note:

• You are responsible for knowing and obeying park rules and regulations.

• For your safety, read a copy of "Alligator Etiquette" available at the park headquarters.

• **DO NOT FEED OR ANNOY ALLIGATORS!**

• Please stay on gravel trail.

Sheldon Lake Environmental Learning Center is open 8 a.m. to 5 p.m., Tuesday through Sunday

Trail Information

	Trail	Distance	Walking Time
	Pond Loop Trail	.5 mile loop	30-60 minutes
	Bridge	.1 mile from Plaza	5 minutes
	Bent Pine Trail	.2 mile loop	10 minutes
	Swamp Rabbit Trail	.4 miles one way	15 minutes
	Kinglet Trail	.1 miles one way	5 minutes
	Armadillo Trail	.1 miles one way	5 minutes

Outdoor Access Route

Grade is between 8% and 12.5%.

The trails at Sheldon Lake Environmental Learning Center meet ADA Accessible Trail guidelines.

User Groups

Grade
Average 2%
Maximum 12.5% for 45 feet

Cross-Slope
Average 2%
Maximum 2% for 30 feet

Width
Minimum 3 feet

Surface
Crushed Granite/Concrete Sidewalk

Legend:

⭐ Headquarters
🏪 State Parks Store
🚻 Accessible Rest Rooms
🅿 Parking
🏠 Park Residence
🏫 Learning Station
❓ Information
🏕 Picnic Area
⛺ Picnic Shelter

Park Road 138
15315 Beaumont Hwy.
Houston, TX 77049
(281) 456-2800

Sheldon Lake
Environmental Learning Center

Carpenter's Bayou

Garrett Road

Houston West Canal

PR 138

Beltway 8

Business Highway 90

Sheldon Lake Environmental Learning Center

Sheldon Lake

Pleasant Road

Boat Ramp & Parking

N

Trail Pavilion

Swamp Rabbit Trail

Armadillo Trail

Kinglet Trail

Pond Crossing

Bridge

Floating Deck

Pond Loop Trail

Bent Pine Trail

Bent Pine Tree

Aquatic Lab 1

Aquatic Lab 2

Picnic Shelter

Geothermal Wells

Pond Center

Heron Plaza

Wind Turbine

Solar PV Array

Pond Center

Acorn Annex

Office

Solar Water Heater

Heron Plaza

Picnic Area

Welcome Garden

Pond Loop Trail

Hiking Shed

Fishing Shed

Fishing Deck

In accordance with Texas State Depository Law, this publication is available at the Texas State Publications Clearinghouse and/or Texas Depository Libraries.

© 2006 Texas Parks and Wildlife Department   PWD MP P4504=13BL (9/06)

DIRECTIONS
From Sheldon, drive west on US 90 to Sheldon Road. Go north on Sheldon Road to Beaumont Highway. Turn right on Beaumont and go to Park Road 138. Turn right on Park Road 138 over the railroad tracks to the park entrance.

CONTACT INFORMATION
15315 Beaumont Highway or Business 90 at Park Road 138,
Houston, TX 77049
Phone: 281-456-2800
Site open for day use only. Fee charged.

Anhinga

BEAUMONT LOOP
Lake Houston Wilderness Park

#29

GPS 30.147, -95.168

25840 FM 1485
NEW CANEY, TEXAS

KEY BIRDS
Pileated woodpecker, eastern wood-pewee, eastern kingbird, scissor-tailed flycatcher

BEST SEASON
All seasons

AREA DESCRIPTION
Forested and park-like setting

This location is no longer in the Texas State Park System. The entrance used to be on Baptist Encampment Road, but the new entrance was opened in May, 2012 as part of a multi-million dollar upgrade.

With nearly 5,000 acres of forest, 12 miles of hiking and biking trails, 8 miles of equestrian trails, and camping facilities, the park offers a variety of activities for birders to experience.

The park is situated on the northern edge of Lake Houston, in the San Jacinto River bottomlands. The hiking trails are surrounded by pines and cypresses, trees which attract several species of waterbirds along the shores. Birds abound, including many of the typical eastern woodland birds and, other than an occasional passing jet from Intercontinental Airport, there is nothing there to remind you that civilization is close by.

Birders should watch for belted kingfisher, red-headed woodpecker, yellow-bellied sapsucker, pileated woodpecker, eastern wood-pewee, eastern kingbird, scissor-tailed flycatcher, loggerhead shrike, American crow, purple martin, barn swallow, tufted titmouse, and eastern bluebird.

DIRECTIONS
From northeast Houston, travel north on US 59 to New Caney. Go east on FM 1485 to the park entrance on the south side of the road.

CONTACT INFORMATION
Houston Parks and Recreation Department
Phone: 281-354-6881 – Main Office, 832-394-8805 – Permits Office
Site open daily. Developed camping available. Fee charged.

Scissor-tailed Flycatcher

BEAUMONT LOOP
#30 Big Creek Scenic Area

GPS 30.51, -95.092

LOCATED SIX MILES WEST OF SHEPHERD, TEXAS IN EAST-CENTRAL SAN JACINTO COUNTY

KEY BIRDS
Louisiana waterthrush, worm-eating warbler, red-cockaded woodpecker

BEST SEASON
Migrations and all seasons, with late summer ideal

AREA DESCRIPTION
1,460 acres; Meandering creeks, lush pine-hardwood forest, and varied flora and fauna

The site is maintained by the Texas Forestry Association and features a 3.5-mile hiking trail in four loops that partially follows Big Creek. A specially designated area within the Sam Houston National Forest, Big Creek takes in 1,460 acres.

Big Creek rises near Cold Springs in central San Jacinto County and flows southeasterly into northern Liberty County, where it joins the Trinity River. The creek is narrow with a sandy bottom, follows a run, riffle, pool sequence and contains abundant woody debris.

For a chance to see many of the typical birds of the eastern Texas Pineywoods/Big Thicket region, you could hardly do better than to take a short (or longer) hike along the trails at this beautiful spot located just a few minutes off U.S. Highway 59.

An interpretive trail through the Big Creek Scenic Area and the Lone Star Hiking Trail provide access to the creek and provide an opportunity to see many resident birds as well as migrating birds during the spring and fall.

Bird species often found include Louisiana waterthrushes and worm-eating warblers, as well as the endangered red-cockaded woodpecker. The Louisiana waterthrushes have been known to nest along Big Creek and have been found along the nature trails in summer. The Sam Houston National Forest has developed an interpretive site in a red-cockaded woodpecker group approximately 0.2 mile south of the intersection of FM 2025 and FM 2666.

DIRECTIONS

From Houston, drive north on US 59 to Cleveland and FM 2025, and continue north on FM 2025 to FM 2666. Travel east on FM 2666 to FR 221, north on FR 221 to FR 217, and then east on FR 217 to Big Creek Scenic Area.

CONTACT INFORMATION

NFS Headquarters and information: 394 FM 1375 West, New Waverly, Texas 77358
Phone: 936-344-6205

BEAUMONT LOOP
W.G. Jones State Forest

GPS 30.223, -95.488

SOUTHWEST OF CONROE, TEXAS

KEY BIRDS
Red-cockaded woodpecker

BEST SEASON
All seasons

AREA DESCRIPTION
1,722 acres; Managed pine and hardwood forests with maintained waterways

Consisting of 1,722 acres, the W.G. Jones State Forest practices scientific forest management that protects and perpetuates native flora and fauna. The W.G. Jones State Forest is a working forest owned and administered by the Texas Forest Service.

In 1997, the Texas Forest Service reported that they had observed 18 different groups of red-cockaded woodpeckers in the forest. An information packet containing a bird checklist and a detailed map of the woodpecker clusters may be obtained from the Conroe District Office. The forest service discourages distractions in the area of these groups. Please do not play tapes or knock on the painted cavity trees.

Birders should also watch for the eastern wood-pewee, eastern kingbird, scissor-tailed flycatcher, loggerhead shrike, American crow, purple martin, barn swallow, tufted titmouse, eastern bluebird, American robin, gray-cheeked thrush, and northern mockingbird.

Texas State Forests are Game Sanctuaries, and no firearms or hunting are allowed. Additional information about maps, permits, and restrooms is available at the Conroe District Office on F.M. 1488, 1.5 miles west of Interstate 45.

DIRECTIONS
From Cleveland, go west on TX 105 to Loop 336 near Conroe. Go south on Loop 336 to I-45, continue south on I-45 to FM 1488. Travel west on FM 1488 to W.G. Jones State Forest.

CONTACT INFORMATION

Conroe District Office is open from 8:00am to 5:00pm, Monday through Friday. Call the office at 936-273-2261. This area is open for day use only.

Northern Mockingbird

BEAUMONT LOOP
#32 Mercer Arboretum and Botanical Gardens

GPS 30.039, -95.38

22306 ALDINE WESTFIELD ROAD
HUMBLE, TEXAS 77338-1071

KEY BIRDS
American crow, northern cardinal, purple martin, barn swallow, tufted titmouse, eastern bluebird

BEST SEASON
All seasons

AREA DESCRIPTION
A botanic gardens located along Cypress Creek

Over 300 acres, this beautiful tract of natural land along Cypress Creek attracts nature lovers and birders from Texas and other states. It should be mentioned that this site is primarily an urban nature center and botanical garden, including a large picnic area with 58 picnic tables, barbeque pavilion, boardwalk, hickory bog, and cypress swamp.

Some of these species are the ruby-throated hummingbird, belted kingfisher, red-headed woodpecker, yellow-bellied sapsucker, pileated woodpecker, eastern wood-pewee, eastern kingbird, scissor-tailed flycatcher, loggerhead shrike, American crow, purple martin, barn swallow, tufted titmouse, eastern bluebird, American robin, gray-cheeked thrush, northern mockingbird, cedar waxwing, summer tanager, blue grosbeak, indigo bunting, painted bunting, brown-headed cowbird, house finch, and American goldfinch.

DIRECTIONS
If coming from Conroe and the W.G. Jones SF, return to I-45, and continue south to FM 1960. Go east on FM 1960 to Aldine-Westfield Road, then north on Aldine-Westfield to Mercer Arboretum and Botanical Gardens.

CONTACT INFORMATION
Phone: 281-443-8731
E-mail: mercerarboretum@hcp4.net
Site open for day use only.

Northern Cardinal

BEAUMONT LOOP
Jesse H. Jones Nature Center
#33

GPS 30.006, -95.28

HUMBLE, TEXAS 77338

KEY BIRDS
Osprey, green kingfisher, Louisiana waterthrush, indigo bunting, barred owl, common yellowthroat

BEST SEASON
All seasons

AREA DESCRIPTION
Loblolly pines dominate, along with black hickory, common persimmon, post oak, southern magnolia, southern red oak, sweet gum, water oak, and white oak

Like Mercer Arboretum, Jesse H. Jones Nature Center is in the urban environment close to Houston and the George Bush International Airport, making it a handy retreat for locals as well as visitors.

There are over six miles of paved, wheel-chair accessible trails within the 300-acre wooded park. There are also two trails that have wildlife viewing blinds: the Jones-Bender Trail that overlooks the pond, and the Cypress Overlook Trail which is near the turtle pond.

Year-round residents here are the Carolina chickadee and northern cardinal. Lucky birders might see a bald eagle, osprey, green kingfisher, Louisiana waterthrush, indigo bunting, barred owl, common yellowthroat, northern parula, white ibis, or roseate spoonbill to name a few.

DIRECTIONS
From the Mercer Arboretum, return to FM 1960, and continue east on FM 1960 to Kenswick. Go north on Kenswick to Jesse H. Jones Nature Center.

CONTACT INFORMATION
Phone: 281-446-8588
E-mail: jjp@hcp4.net
Open daily from 8:00am to 4:30pm, except Thanksgiving, Christmas Eve, Christmas, and New Year's Day. Site open for day use only.

Osprey

BEAUMONT LOOP
#34 Baytown Nature Center

GPS 29.755, -95.036

6213 BAYWAY DRIVE
BAYTOWN, TEXAS 77520

KEY BIRDS
Pelicans, gulls, terns, and bay ducks

BEST SEASON
All seasons

AREA DESCRIPTION
450 acres, wetland marsh, woodlands, tall grasses, and weedy areas with the habitat of surrounding bays

The Baytown Nature Center is a 450-acre area made up of two peninsulas surrounded by three bays in the city of Baytown.

The site includes an area that was a former housing division that was abandoned due to land subsidence. In 1994, the Brownwood Marsh Restoration Project was approved and work started that year to create a superb nature center comprising both uplands and wetlands. Work continues on the site, but birders can now enjoy over five miles of marked nature trails of varying lengths that are available in the natural areas of the nature center.

Waterfowl, raptors, sparrows, woodpeckers, and songbirds make their home at the nature center as well as pelicans, gulls, and terns. Many of the large wading birds and some of the woodland birds are present all year long.

DIRECTIONS
From the intersection of TX 146 and I-10, go west on I-10 to Crosby-Lynchburg Road and Spur 330. Go east on Spur 330 to Bayway Drive, south on Bayway Drive to Shreck, and then west on Shreck to Baytown Nature Center.

CONTACT INFORMATION

Baytown Nature Center Phone: 281-424-9198

Christina Butcher, Naturalist Phone: 832-262-8698

Gates open 30 minutes before sunrise and close 30 minutes after sunset. There is an entrance fee of $3 per person. Yearly passes may also be purchased for a fee of $25 per person or $50 per family.

This site is open for day use only.

Green-winged Teal

BEAUMONT LOOP
#35 Eddie V. Gray Goose Creek Wetlands Education Center

GPS 29.733, -94.985

1724 MARKET STREET
BAYTOWN, TX 77520

KEY BIRDS
Black-crowned night-heron, eared grebe, great blue heron

BEST SEASON
All seasons

AREA DESCRIPTION
Mainly a city habitat with adjoining wetlands

The Wetlands Center, located on the banks of Goose Creek, opened on January 26, 1998. The Goose Creek Wetland Center staff is available to direct birders to local areas of interest. Look for black-crowned night-heron, eared grebe, double-crested cormorant, American bittern, great blue heron, cattle egret, yellow-crowned night-heron, white-faced ibis, and various other shorebirds in the wetlands behind the center.

DIRECTIONS
In Baytown, return to Bayway Drive and continue south to Market Street and the Goose Creek Wetland Center.

CONTACT INFORMATION
Phone: 281-420-7128
Web Site: http://www.baytown.org/content/eddie-v-gray-wetlands-center
This site is open for day use only.

Black-crowned Night-heron

BEAUMONT LOOP
San Jacinto Battleground/ Monument SHP

GPS 29.75, -95.089

1 MONUMENT CIRCLE
LA PORTE, TX 77571

KEY BIRDS
Hooded merganser and greater scaup

BEST SEASON
Migrations, winter

AREA DESCRIPTION
Grassy park areas with trees in a well-manicured park area on the banks of the Houston Ship Channel

The busy season in this park can be any day where the Texas coastal weather permits outside activities, although summer will always be the most active. Birders visiting during the busy season should plan their visits either early or later in the day to avoid people traffic resulting in shy or absent birds.

The south end of the park is known by local birders as a place to find wood storks in late summer and fall. During the winter, greater scaup and hooded mergansers are often sighted.

Other species common to this area are great blue heron, cattle egret, yellow-crowned night-heron, white-faced ibis, wood stork, mallard, gadwall, northern pintail, American wigeon, northern shoveler, blue-winged teal, green-winged teal, ring-necked duck, bufflehead, hooded merganser, and ruddy duck.

DIRECTIONS
Drive east on TX 225 to TX 134 (Battleground Road), and then travel north on TX 134 to PR 1836 and the San Jacinto Battleground/Monument SHP.

CONTACT INFORMATION

Phone: 281-479-2421

Activities are available seven days a week. Admission prices apply.

This site is open for day use only.

Hooded Merganser

BEAUMONT LOOP
White Memorial Park

#37

GPS 29.838, -94.655

ON TURTLE BAYOU, JUST SOUTH OF I-10 ON TX 61

KEY BIRDS
Pileated, golden-fronted, red-bellied, red-headed, downy, and hairy woodpeckers

BEST SEASON
Migrations, summer

AREA DESCRIPTION
A sheltered and enclosed area, almost dwarfed by the rich stands of pine, sweetgum, magnolia, and grand old cypress trees

White Memorial Park, located on Turtle Bayou, hosts an impressive selection of eastern woodland birds. Older trees still remaining after two destructive hurricanes continue to attract woodpeckers, though park custodians have removed several of the snags.

Swainson's, pine, and hooded warblers nest here, and Turtle Bayou

Golden-fronted Woodpecker

in the summer attracts prothonotary warblers. It is also possible to find a few hairy woodpeckers and brown-headed nuthatches at times.

Be careful parking along this road, traffic is light but fast moving, you are close to Houston, so don't stand in the road and be sure and park completely off the roadway.

Some other species that may be found in this location are pileated, red-bellied, red-headed, and downy woodpeckers, great crested and Acadian flycatchers, Carolina chickadee, tufted titmouse, Carolina wren, summer tanager, and Louisiana waterthrush.

Directions

Drive east from Houston on I-10 to TX 61 (Exit 813). Then drive south on TX 61 a short distance to White Memorial Park.

Contact Information

Address: 225 White Memorial Park Drive

Precinct 2, Commissioner's Office, Phone: 409-267-2409

Limit three nights maximum stay at no charge. There are no hookups and RVs must be fully self-contained. Campers must obtain a camping permit to stay. This site is open daily.

BEAUMONT LOOP
Wallisville Reservoir

#38

GPS 29.802, -94.726

LOCATED JUST OFF I-10, OFF THE SERVICE ROAD WEST NEAR THE TRINITY RIVER

KEY BIRDS
Anhinga, white ibis, little blue heron

BEST SEASON
All seasons

AREA DESCRIPTION
Water areas with marshlands and low wetlands, and some heavily wooded areas

The Wallisville Reservoir levee is four miles in length, and is accessible only by foot.

Visiting the rookery in the spring, drive west on the service road to the I-10 E access ramp, across the Trinity River, to Exit 806 (approximately one mile). Loop back west on the service road to the Trinity River and the Trinity River Mouth Waterbird Rookery (immediately to the south). The rookery may be viewed from the service road. Look for anhingas, white ibis, little blue herons, and roseate spoonbills in this area.

DIRECTIONS
From White Memorial Park, drive west on I-10, to the Trinity River. Cross the Trinity River bridge, and exit immediately. Turn back east toward the river on the service road, and continue under the bridge to the Wallisville Reservoir West Levee. Continue east on I-10 to Levee Road (approximately 1.1 miles) and the Wallisville Reservoir East Levee. The East Levee is being developed as a public access point for the reservoir.

Another interesting location in this area is the Horseshoe Ponds Trail. Continue east from Exit 807 at Wallisville, cross under the freeway, and then return west on the north service road for approximately 0.5 mile.

CONTACT INFORMATION
To obtain permission to visit this area, contact the ACOE Wallisville office at 409-389-2285.
Open for day use only.

White Ibis

BEAUMONT LOOP
Fort Anahuac Park

#39

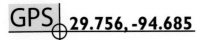

GPS 29.756, -94.685

1704 S. MAIN ST.
ANAHUAC, TEXAS 77514

KEY BIRDS
Double-crested cormorant, American bittern, great blue heron

BEST SEASON
Migrations

AREA DESCRIPTION
City park and lakeside habitats with some large trees

The park is located in Chambers County on Trinity Bay. Some traces remain of Fort Anahuac, a combination Mexican fort and customhouse on Galveston Bay near the mouth of the Trinity River. Besides some relaxed birding, the park offers picnicking, camping, rest rooms, and a boat ramp.

Birders should watch for eared grebe, double-crested cormorant, American bittern, great blue heron, cattle egret, yellow-crowned night-heron, white-faced ibis, wood stork, wood duck, mallard, gadwall, northern pintail, American wigeon.

The trees in this city park, bordering Lake Anahuac, should be checked during migrations for landbirds.

DIRECTIONS
In Anahuac, drive east on TX 61 to South Main, then go south on South Main to Fort Anahuac Park.

CONTACT INFORMATION
Precinct 2 Commissioner's Office – Phone: 409-267-2409
Site open daily. Developed camping available. Fee charged.

Great Blue Heron

BEAUMONT LOOP
Double Bayou Park

#40

GPS 29.679, -94.63

2814 EAGLE FERRY RD.
ANAHUAC, TEXAS 77514

KEY BIRDS
White-faced ibis, wood duck

BEST SEASON
Migrations

AREA DESCRIPTION
30 acres; East Texas wood lots with open grasslands and waterfront habitat with some paddling areas

As the name implies, Double Bayou has two bayou forks that come together near its mouth on Galveston Bay, by the town of Oak Island. Located just off Eagle Ferry Road, the park has about 30 acres. This is a small park but does have some camping, water, and restrooms. Although this is a small park, it can be worth a quick stop on your way to High Island.

Watch for these birds on your drive: yellow-crowned night-heron, white-faced ibis, wood stork, wood duck, mallard, gadwall, northern pintail, American wigeon, northern shoveler, blue-winged teal, and green-winged teal.

Both the East Fork and the West Fork afford nice birding opportunities. Using a canoe or kayak (no outboard motors allowed), will take you through pastures and cattle ranches, giving way to pine and oak forests in the upper reaches.

DIRECTIONS
Drive south on TX 61 to Eagle Ferry Road, and go east on Eagle Ferry Road to Double Bayou Park.

CONTACT INFORMATION
Precinct 2 Commissioner's Office - Phone: 409-267-2409
This site is open daily. Some developed camping available for a fee. No fees or rates have been posted; call for information.

Wood Duck

BEAUMONT LOOP

Smith Point and James H. Robbins Memorial Park

#41

GPS 29.543, -94.783

LOCATED ON **FM 562** AT ITS SOUTHERN END OF ROAD ON **GALVESTON BAY** AND **TRINITY BAY**

KEY BIRDS
Magnificent frigatebird, both species of pelican, white-faced ibis

BEST SEASON
All seasons

AREA DESCRIPTION
Coastal marshlands with stands of live oak and low brush and grass

Smith Point is one of the most isolated and undeveloped coastal peninsulas left along the Texas Coast. The marshes and open grasslands along FM 562 are productive throughout the year.

The Gulf Coast Bird Observatory, the Houston Audubon Society, and HawkWatch International, are responsible for the two-tiered birding tower. The observation platform in Robbins Park provides birders an excellent view of Trinity Bay and the surrounding area. In the summer and fall, scan the areas and the skies above for magnificent frigatebirds, several species of gulls and terns, along with both species of pelican.

This area is a prime spot for viewing raptors during the migrations. The location extends into Galveston Bay, adding to the great birding. Migrating raptors, passerines, and other birds will concentrate on Smith Point when the weather permits.

During the hawk migrations there is a staff of paid counters on the tower, normally from August 15 until November 15.

Other species may include swallowtail kite, American kestrel, merlin, peregrine falcon, and broad-winged hawk. The oak mottes attract flycatchers, gnatcatchers, warblers, buntings, and orioles. One of the most unusual birds seen here is a groove-billed ani.

The isolated stands of oak mottes along Hawkins Camp Road attract migrant landbirds in spring and fall. The Spoonbill RV Park, situated on Trinity Bay off Hawkins Camp Road, caters to birders. This is private property so, if you are not staying at the park, ask permission before entering.

White-faced Ibis

Directions
From Double Bayou Park, continue east on Eagle Ferry Road to FM 562. Go south on FM 562 to its intersection with FM 1985, then veer west to continue on FM 562 to Smith Point Road in Smith Point. Drive west on Smith Point Road to Hawkins Camp Road, then north on Hawkins Camp to James H. Robbins Memorial Park.

Contact Information
Phone: 409-267-4190
Site open for day use only.
Spoonbill RV Park — Phone: 409-355-2357
Website: www.spoonbillrvpark.com

BEAUMONT LOOP
#42 Candy Abshier WMA

GPS ⊕ **29.528, -94.759**

Near Smith Point

Key Birds
Mississippi kite, broad-winged hawk, Swainson's hawk, and falcons

Best Season
Migrations, especially fall and winter

Area Description
207 acres; Coastal prairie habitat with significant important coastal woodlot or oak mottes

Candy Cain Abshier Wildlife Management Area consists of 207 acres on Galveston Bay and Trinity Bay. Chambers County near Smith Point is one of a few public access points. An oak motte covers about 60 acres while the rest of the habitat is coastal prairie vegetation. Watch the oaks for several of perching species.

The live oak and freshwater ponds make this a prime target for migrating birds coming and going to South America.

Bird watchers should make a point to make use of the organized hawk watches along the coast. Birders should see Mississippi kites, Swainson's hawks, broad-winged hawks, and falcons. The Gulf Coast Bird Observatory, the Houston Ornithology Group Hawk, and HawkWatch International sponsors these events.

Texas Parks and Wildlife, along with the Gulf Coast Bird Watchers, built a hawk watchtower and observation platform overlooking the water. These two features are the focus of the birding center. An annual hawk watch begins each year around August 15 and continues until November 15.

Smith Point and Candy Abshier WMA attract red-tailed hawks, and other birds of prey make their stopping point here on their migrations. The spring migration sees a great expansion in the bird population, including more than just the birds of prey. While the fall brings many birds to the area to congregate before the winter migration, the birds aren't quite as numerous as in the spring.

The oaks in Candy Abshier WMA attract migrant landbirds, and Henslow's sparrows have wintered in the grassy fields near the observation platform.

DIRECTIONS

From Hawkins Camp Road drive to Smith Point Road, then return west to the Candy Abshier WMA; look for a sign marking the entrance road.

CONTACT INFORMATION

Jim Sutherlin, 10 Parks & Wildlife Drive, Port Arthur, TX 77640
Phone: 409-736-2551
For hawk watch information and dates call 713-789-GCBO(4226)
Site open for day use only.

Immature Red-tailed Hawk

BEAUMONT LOOP

#43 UTC Anahuac NWR – Main Entrance

GPS ⊕ **29.566, -94.533**

EAST OF ANAHUAC, TEXAS

KEY BIRDS
Empidonax flycatcher, common moorhen, purple gallinule, yellow rail

BEST SEASON
All seasons

AREA DESCRIPTION
Marshes, combined with the coastal prairies

The 34,000-acre Anahuac NWR is one of the major waterfowl areas along the Texas Coast. Greater white-fronted and snow goose flocks including the Ross's variety are found in the marshes and feeding in both wet and dry fields most of the winter. This area consists of both agricultural and coastal prairie marshes that provide feeding and roosting areas for migrating waterfowl.

After entering the refuge, drive west to the first levee, toward Shoveler Pond. The willows just to the north of the levee are good places to watch for spring and fall migrants. During late August birders should carefully glass the trees, watching for several species of flycatchers.

Drive around Shoveler Pond and watch for least bitterns in summer and American

Common Moorhen

bitterns during the winter and during spring and fall migrations. Summertime birders will see marsh wrens that will occupy the cattail marshes. Glass the open waters of the pond for canvasbacks and redheads.

Birders will find nesting masked ducks as well as common moorhen and purple gallinule breeding pairs in the marshes bordering the road. Birders should be aware that American alligators are in this area.

Entering through the main entrance road and continuing south toward Trinity Bay, birders may spot short-eared owls patrolling the prairies in the winter and spring. Sprague's pipits will spend the winter in the low habitat along the road.

All of the species of rail can be sighted here. These are the clapper, king, Virginia, and sora rail. As for yellow rails, birders will need to take some slow walks and hikes into the yellow rail prairie.

DIRECTIONS
Return east on Smith Point Road/FM 562 to the intersection of FM 562 and FM 1985. Continue east on FM 1985 to Anahuac NWR (Main Entrance).

CONTACT INFORMATION
P.O. Box 278, 4017 FM 563, Anahuac, TX 77514
Phone: 409-267-3337 for information
This site is open for day use only.

BEAUMONT LOOP
#44 Anahuac NWR – East Bay Bayou Tract

GPS⊕ **29.567, -94.533**

EAST OF ANAHUAC, TEXAS

KEY BIRDS
Snow goose, buff-breasted sandpiper, and white-rumped sandpiper

BEST SEASON
Migrations, winter

AREA DESCRIPTION
Vast expanses of coastal marsh and prairie bordering Galveston Bay

This refuge was established in 1963, and the 34,000-acre sanctuary is an important link to the chain of National Wildlife Refuges along the Texas Gulf Coast.

Between October and March, birders are likely to see as many as 27 species of ducks, including green-winged teal, gadwall, shoveler, and northern pintail. Massive flocks of snow geese — sometimes in excess of 80,000 — will be seen feeding in the rice fields and moist soil units.

During spring and fall migrations, warblers and other songbirds can be seen or heard on walks in the small wooded areas. Roseate spoonbills, great and snowy egrets, white-faced ibis, and mottled ducks are seen on the refuge year round.

Refuge personnel, assisted by the Friends of Anahuac Refuge, have developed a 1.5-mile nature trail along the east side of East Bay Bayou. The woods along the bayou offer another excellent opportunity to watch for land birds during the migration.

The refuge maintains a series of wet fields to attract shorebirds and is located near the entrance to this tract along FM 1985. Birders will enjoy spotting white-rumped sandpipers, buff-breasted sandpipers, and Hudsonian godwits.

A spring morning spent birding in this area may provide sightings of freshwater shorebirds, and an afternoon of birding the Bolivar Flats for saltwater species may add between 30 and 35 different shorebird species and additional life-list entries for traveling birders.

Snow Geese

DIRECTIONS
From the Anahuac NWR Main Entrance, drive farther east on FM 1985 to TX 124 and the East Bay Bayou Tract. From the intersection of FM 1985 and TX 124, go south on TX 124 to High Island and the Bolivar Loop.

CONTACT INFORMATION
P.O. Box 278 Anahuac, TX 77514
Phone: 409-267-3337
E-mail: fw2_rw_anahuac@fws.gov
Site open for day use only.

#45 TXDOT High Island Roadside Park

GPS ⊕ 29.568, -94.398

TX 124 ON THE TEXAS GULF COAST

KEY BIRDS
Tanagers, orioles, and buntings

BEST SEASON
Fall and spring migrations

AREA DESCRIPTION
Roadside park habitat surrounded by coastal prairie

Located on TX 124, the roadside park offers birders a nature trail and an information kiosk. Funding from the Great Texas Birding Trail was used to build the nature trail, educational kiosk, and the popular hummingbird gardens. Maps are available at the kiosk for more birding sites.

Dotted throughout the coastal prairies are many high areas, or salt domes, and many of these will have live oak and sugar hackberry trees. Long overlooked by birders, its oaks and picnic tables offer a great location for sitting and glassing the roosting birds. It is often passed in the rush to visit Houston Audubon Society's High Island Sanctuaries.

This area does receive many inches of rain that brings in vireos, buntings, thrushes, grosbeaks, warblers, tanagers, and orioles. In the spring, the rain attracts several species of wading birds.

The information kiosk includes a map of the various Houston Audubon Society (HAS) High Island sanctuaries. Orient yourself with the directions to the other sanctuaries by using this park as a reference point. But don't just grab the map; take time to bird this area.

DIRECTIONS
From Anahuac NWR, go south on TX 124 to the roadside park.

CONTACT INFORMATION
No contact information given.
Site open for day use only.

Scarlet Tanager

BEAUMONT LOOP
#46 UTC HAS Smith Oaks Bird Sanctuary

GPS 29.572, -94.391

JUST OFF ON WINNIE STREET IN HIGH ISLAND, TEXAS

KEY BIRDS
Vireos, warblers, tanagers, orioles

BEST SEASON
Migrations

AREA DESCRIPTION
Oak mottes with live oaks over 100 years old, ponds, wetlands, and coastal prairie

Spring migration in 177-acre Smith Oaks is a "must see" for birders with its major migration viewing locations. Birders may spot vireos, orioles, warblers, and tanagers stopping over and resting after their long flight crossing the Gulf of Mexico.

Birders are asked to purchase an annual or day pass before entering. A day pass is $7, or you can purchase a patch for $25 that gives you entry to all High Island Sanctuaries for a year. These funds are used to maintain the Houston Audubon Society's 2,000-acre sanctuary system.

The sanctuary also maintains a viewing platform on Clay Bottom Pond. There is a rookery located very close to the platform.

Be sure to check the heron rookery in Clay Bottom Pond on the north side of Smith Oaks for close looks at egrets, herons, and spoonbills. From the platform, birders can see virtually all of the showy waders, including the neotropical cormorant, as well as the great, snowy, and cattle egrets, little, blue, and tri-colored herons, black-crowned night-heron, roseate spoonbill, and even a few anhingas.

Bring insect repellent and wear a long-sleeved shirt to help avoid the mosquitoes.

DIRECTIONS
Leaving the Roadside Park, go north on TX 124 to Weeks Avenue. Turn south on Weeks Avenue to Winnie Street (look for the Smith Oaks Bird Sanctuary sign). Go east on Winnie Street to Smith Oaks Bird Sanctuary.

Contact Information

The gate is open from dawn to dusk from March 15 through May 15, and on weekends in September and October, and also by advanced arrangement. There is a fee per car to enter this park. For more information contact the Houston Audubon Society - 440 Wilchester Blvd., Houston, TX 77079

Phone: 713-932-1639 or 713-461-2911

Web site: www.houstonaudubon.org

Email: info@houstonaudubon.org

Office Hours: 9:00am to 5:00pm, Mon.-Fri.

Black-whiskered Vireo

BEAUMONT LOOP
#47 UTC HAS Eubanks Woods Bird Sanctuary

GPS 29.567, -94.391

ON HIGH ISLAND, JUST OFF OLD MEXICO ROAD

KEY BIRDS
Barn owl, buff-bellied hummingbird, ruby-throated hummingbird, northern waterthrush, Louisiana waterthrush, Kentucky warbler

BEST SEASON
Migrations

AREA DESCRIPTION
An area of woods and wetlands mixing and merging birding sites

The Houston Audubon Society's (HAS) Eubanks Woods Bird Sanctuary consists of 9.5-acres of woods and wetlands named in honor of Ted Eubanks. It is open to the public sunrise to sunset year round.

Birders should slowly use the boardwalk for the best birding. The boardwalk will allow you to reach the trees after the many wet fronts and rains have passed. The oaks are young, and some migrants may be spotted nearly at eye level. This is a good location for photographers and digiscopers when the birds will stay on their perch longer.

Some of the species found here are: black-billed cuckoo, screech owl, great horned owl, barred owl, common nighthawk, chuck-will's-widow, chimney swift, buff-bellied hummingbird, ruby-throated hummingbird, northern waterthrush, Louisiana waterthrush, Kentucky warbler, mourning warbler, common yellowthroat, hooded warbler, Wilson's warbler, Canada warbler, yellow-breasted chat, eastern towhee, chipping sparrow, field sparrow, savannah sparrow, Nelson's sparrow, and seaside sparrow.

DIRECTIONS
From the Roadside Park, travel north on TX 124 to Weeks Avenue (which may also be reached by returning west from Smith Oaks Bird Sanctuary on Winnie Street). Go south on Weeks Avenue to Old Mexico Road, then east on Old Mexico Road to Eubanks Woods Bird Sanctuary.

Contact Information

For more information contact the Houston Audubon Society - 440 Wilchester Blvd., Houston, TX 77079
Phone: 713-932-1639 or 713-461-2911
Web site: www.houstonaudubon.org
Email: info@houstonaudubon.org
Office Hours: 9:00am to 5:00pm, Mon.-Fri.
Site open for day use only.

Barn Owl

BEAUMONT LOOP
UTC HAS S.E. Gast Red Bay Sanctuary

#48

GPS 29.561, -94.398

WESTERN EDGE OF HIGH ISLAND

KEY BIRDS
Indigo bunting, Canada warbler, scarlet tanager

BEST SEASON
Migrations

AREA DESCRIPTION
A mixture of coastal woodlands, prairies, and island habitats

At 8.8 acres, this is the smallest of the HAS island sanctuaries. It is located on the western edge of High Island on one of the many salt domes in the area. The area offers a combination of woodland birding and a chance to bird the surrounding coastal prairie.

In the numbers of "fall-outs" that will be stopping throughout the spring migration, multiple subspecies of warblers have been spotted here from one location.

Species that may be seen here are: buff-bellied hummingbird, ruby-throated hummingbird, northern and Louisiana waterthrush, Kentucky warbler, mourning warbler, common yellowthroat, hooded warbler, black-billed cuckoo, barn owl, screech owl, great horned owl, barred owl, gray catbird, common nighthawk and the rose-breasted grosbeak.

Take your time approaching the small pond near the main entrance. Be quiet and use the benches to spot migrating birds.

DIRECTIONS
Starting at the Roadside Park, go south on TX 124 to 7th Street. Turn west on 7th Street to S.E. Gast Red Bay Sanctuary.

CONTACT INFORMATION

For more information contact the Houston Audubon Society - 440 Wilchester Blvd., Houston, TX 77079
Phone: 713-932-1639 or 713-461-2911
Web site: www.houstonaudubon.org
Email: info@houstonaudubon.org
Office Hours: 9:00am to 5:00pm, Mon.-Fri.
Site open for day use only. Fee charged.

Canada Warbler

BEAUMONT LOOP
#49 HAS Boy Scout Woods Bird Sanctuary

GPS⊕ 29.561, -94.391

ON 5TH STREET IN HIGH ISLAND

KEY BIRDS
Brown-eyed grackle, gulls, common yellowthroat, hooded warbler

BEST SEASON
Migrations

AREA DESCRIPTION
High Island habitat with some freshwater ponds, salt marshes, and bays

Houston Audubon Society staffs an information booth and shop here on the sanctuary during certain times of the year. There are entrance fees, day passes, and annual permits are available at the information booth. Pick up a sighting sheet in the information booth and see what has been seen in the area. Migrants may be spotted in the trees.

The fall migration is usually from late August through October, while during the spring migration this sanctuary is packed with local and visiting birders. If you enjoy being with only a few birders, choose the fall migration for your visit. Purkey's Pond is an excellent choice of spots here.

Consisting of 60 acres, this sanctuary also has a covered picnic shelter overlooking Bessie's Pond.

Species that can be found in the sanctuary are: black-billed cuckoo, chuck-will's-widow, screech owl, barn owl, great horned owl, barred owl, northern waterthrush, common nighthawk, chimney swift, buff-bellied hummingbird, ruby-throated hummingbird, Louisiana waterthrush, Kentucky warbler, mourning warbler, common yellowthroat, hooded warbler, Wilson's warbler, Canada warbler, savannah sparrow, yellow-breasted chat, eastern towhee, chipping sparrow, field sparrow, Nelson's sparrow, and seaside sparrow.

Birding just off TX 124 can be very productive. Drive some of the roads and lanes just off the highway and follow them to where the lanes end. This is all private property, so do not cross the fences or block driveways.

After exploring the sanctuary, continue south on TX 124 from High Island to the coast and TX 87. TX 87 is still passable for a short distance east of High Island, and several

Ringbilled Gull

species of gulls are often seen along this beach. Watch the pond just to the east of High Island for ducks. This road has been washed out toward Port Arthur and should not be attempted in any vehicle when signs are up.

DIRECTIONS
From the Roadside Park, travel south on TX 124 to 5th Street (also reached from the Gast Sanctuary by returning to TX 124). Turn east on 5th Street and proceed to Boy Scout Woods Bird Sanctuary.

CONTACT INFORMATION
For more information contact the Houston Audubon Society - 440 Wilchester Blvd., Houston, TX 77079
Phone: 713-932-1639 or 713-461-2911
Web site: www.houstonaudubon.org
Email: info@houstonaudubon.org
Office Hours: 9:00am to 5:00pm, Mon.-Fri.
Site open for day use only. Fee charged.

BEAUMONT LOOP
Rollover Pass

#50

GPS 29.508, -94.5

BOLIVAR PENINSULA ON TX 87, RUNNING PARALLEL TO THE BEACH

KEY BIRDS
Scaup, mergansers, and occasionally scoters and oldsquaw

BEST SEASON
All seasons

AREA DESCRIPTION
Tidal marshes and saltwater edges with a small bridge crossing the "fish cut" known as the pass

Rollover Pass is a man-made channel across Bolivar Peninsula; and this "fish cut" has caused the formation of an extensive tidal flat on the bay (north) side of the peninsula.

Thousands of shorebirds, gulls, and terns are to be found here. The best viewing times are at low tide. These low tide periods are good times to glass the many spoil islands in East Bay. Of special interest are the water bird rookeries found there.

Waterfowl, such as lessor and greater scaup and mergansers, are seen here throughout the fall and winter. If you are very lucky, you may see one of the scoters and oldsquaws that may be visiting the coastline.

The canal at Rollover Pass allows you to drive to the bay and bird the coastal flats. Birders should park as close as possible, then if the tide is right, walk slowly and glass the water's edge for feeding and at times roosting shorebirds, such as several subspecies of terns and gulls.

Yacht Basin Road will take you to a small cut. Glass these flats carefully in winter for flocks of migrating shore and wading birds. Birding Park Road may also be quite productive. Visitors from out of Texas may add several species to their life lists.

While birding the Texas Coast from April to September, watch for bobolink and black terns flying along the water's edge.

Lesser Scaup

DIRECTIONS
From the intersection of TX 124 and TX 87, continue southwest on TX 87 to Rollover Pass.

CONTACT INFORMATION
Site open for day use only.

BEAUMONT LOOP
UTC Yacht Basin Road

#51

GPS 29.506, -94.507

LOCATED ON THE HIGH GROUND ON BOLIVAR FLATS

KEY BIRDS
Clapper rail, willet, and seaside sparrow

BEST SEASON
All seasons

AREA DESCRIPTION
Saltwater marsh habitat and some tall grass prairie

As you drive southwest along TX 87 toward Bolivar Flats, there are several roads that cut back toward the Gulf Intracoastal Waterway (GIWW) that are worth checking. Make a note and keep in mind that most of this property is private, especially along Crystal Beach, Tuna Drive, and Bob's Road. Remember that the land bordering these roads is private. Bird only from the shoulder, and please do not trespass.

Whimbrels and long-billed curlews are often seen on these flats and during the migration, Le Conte's sparrows, clapper and king rails are sighted along with migrating bobolinks. Bird the mud and sand flats and also watch for the willet and the marbled godwit.

DIRECTIONS
Drive southwest on TX 87 to Yacht Basin Road (0.5 mile west of Rollover Pass). Yacht Basin dead-ends at the Gulf Intracoastal Waterway, but this short drive crosses an interesting coastal marsh.

CONTACT INFORMATION
Contact the Texas DOT for road information and closings.
Phone: 1-800-452-9292 /
Website: www.txdot.gov
Site is open for day use only.

Willet

 BIRDING TRAILS: TEXAS GULF COAST

Galveston Loop

The northern Texas Coastline is a great example of the concentration of birds living or migrating through the northern coast. The Galveston FeatherFest & Nature PhotoFest is held in the spring of the year.

The island offers 32 miles of beaches for the visiting birders. During a past festival over 235 species of resident, seasonal, and migrating birds were seen and recorded.

Before crossing the ferry (no fees charged) to the island proper, take some time on the Bolívar Peninsula seeking the lone groups of birds along the water and in the marsh grasses. Watch for several species of turn, gulls, and both the white and brown pelican on the ferry crossing.

The birding locations along Galveston Bay north of the towns of San Leon and Baycliff will be well worth the time spent with your binoculars and spotting scope. After leaving Seabrook the NASA Parkway will take you back to Interstate 45 and your drive north.

On this loop there are numerous birding locations that will keep you birding for days. There are plenty of hotels and eating places located all over the area.

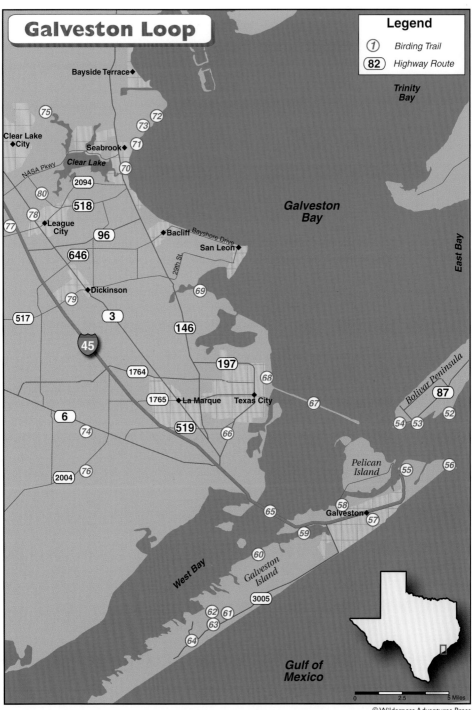

Galveston Loop

Legend
- ① Birding Trail
- 82 Highway Route

Trinity Bay

Bayside Terrace◆

75

72
73
71

Clear Lake
◆City

Seabrook◆

70

Clear Lake

NASA Pkwy

2094

Galveston
Bay

80

518

78

77

◆League
City

96

646

Baycliff◆ Bayshore Drive

San Leon◆

East Bay

79

Dickinson◆

29th St

69

517

3

146

45

197

68

1764

Bolivar Peninsula

87

1765

◆La Marque

Texas City◆

67

54 53 52

6

519

66

74

76

Pelican
Island

55

56

2004

65

58

Galveston◆

57

59

60

West Bay

Galveston
Island

3005

62 61

63

64

Gulf of
Mexico

0   2.5   5 Miles

© Wilderness Adventures Press

Galveston Loop Locations

52. HAS Bolivar Flats Shorebird Sanctuary
53. UTC Fort Travis Seashore Park
54. Frenchtown Road
55. The Corps Woods at Galveston
56. Big Reef and Apffel Park
57. Galveston's Kempner Park
58. Harborside Wetlands of Galveston
59. Offatts Bayou
60. 8-Mile Road and Sportman's Road
61. Settegast Road
62. Lafitte's Cove
63. Lafitte's Grove
64. Galveston Island State Park
65. John M. O'Quinn I-45 Estuarial Corridor
66. AMOCO Settling Ponds and Swan Lake
67. Texas City Dike
68. Bay Street Park
69. TNCT Galveston Bay Preserve
70. McHale Park
71. Hester Garden Park
72. Pine Gully Park
73. Robinson Park
74. Armand Bayou Nature Centre
75. Bay Area Park
76. Lake Nassau Park
77. Challenger 7 Memorial Park
78. Walter Hall County Park
79. Paul Hopkins Community Park
80. Dr. Ned and Fay Dudney Nature Center

GALVESTON LOOP
#52 UTC HAS Bolivar Flats Shorebird Sanctuary

GPS 29.382, -94.724

BASE OF THE NORTH JETTY ON BOLIVAR PENINSULA

KEY BIRDS
Peregrine falcon, American avocet, gulls, terns, and shorebirds

BEST SEASON
All seasons

AREA DESCRIPTION
1,146 acres; Coastal saltwater flats, beach, and jetty habitats

Agreements in the late 1980s between the General Land Office and Galveston County made it possible for the Houston Audubon Society to complete the sanctuary and close the beach to motor vehicles.

Bolivar Flats is just off the end of the North Jetty near the entrance to Galveston Bay and covers 1,146 acres. Birders may see oceangoing ships passing in the distance. Bolivar Flats has been, and still is, created by sediments that are carried southwestward along the coast. The result is an extensive tidal flat attracting large numbers of gulls, terns, and shorebirds. Low tide is probably the best time to bird this area, but high tide also brings a lot of roosting birds.

According to the HAS, several thousand American avocets spend the winter on the flats and have been joined by over 100 piping plovers.

Birders are encouraged to watch for Nelson's sharp-tailed sparrows that will spend the winter in the wild cordgrass. This is a must-visit location.

Drive southwest on TX 87 to the North Jetty, about 1.9 miles from Rettilon Road. A walk along the jetty at low tide will offer good looks at many of the birds feeding on Bolivar Flats.

DIRECTIONS

Continue southwest on TX 87 to Loop 108/Rettilon Road. Go south on Rettilon Road to the beach, then turn west and parallel the shoreline to Bolivar Flats Shorebird Sanctuary.

CONTACT INFORMATION

For more information contact the Houston Audubon Society - 440 Wilchester Blvd., Houston, TX 77079
Phone: 713-932-1639 or 713-461-2911
Web site: www.houstonaudubon.org
Email: info@houstonaudubon.org
Site open for day use only.

American Avocets

GALVESTON LOOP
UTC Fort Travis Seashore Park

#53

GPS ⊕ 29.364, -94.758

WESTERN END OF BOLIVAR PENINSULA CLOSE TO THE FERRY LANDING

KEY BIRDS
Groove-billed anis, Nashville and yellow warblers

BEST SEASON
During spring and fall migrations

AREA DESCRIPTION
Rocky shoreline and picnic areas with benches and wide grassy areas attracting both birds as well as birders

The first fortifications were built on this site in the early 19th century, but the namesake fort was built in 1899 and named for William B. Travis of Alamo fame. Some of the old concrete bunkers still remain on this 70-acre site.

Birders should watch the thick shrubs around the park entrance for groove-billed anis that have been consistently seen in this area. The trees and shrubs at this location may hold migrants that you may have otherwise missed along this part of the coast.

Remember that each woodlot along the coast is unique as to its exact mix of trees and shrubs. Migrants will occur along the upper coast in low densities.

Groove-billed Ani

For example, Cape May and black-throated blue warblers are just as likely to appear in one of the minor sites as in the woods at High Island.

In addition, species such as Nashville and yellow warblers prefer scrubbier habitat, and are not frequently seen in the more mature mottes. Here is where some serious birding is required if some of these species are to be seen.

DIRECTIONS
Drive southwest on TX 87 to Fort Travis Seashore Park.

CONTACT INFORMATION
Address: 900 SH 87 or P.O. Box B., Port Bolivar, 77650
Phone: 409-684-1333, Reservations: 409-934-8100
Web Site: info.parks.seniors@co.galveston.tx.us
Site open daily. Developed camping available and some fees are charged. Call for more information and fee schedule.

GALVESTON LOOP
#54 Frenchtown Road

GPS 29.364, -94.775

THE ROAD TO THE BOLIVAR FERRY IN PORT BOLIVAR

KEY BIRDS
American oystercatcher and wading birds

BEST SEASON
All seasons

AREA DESCRIPTION
Saltwater wetlands and coastal flats with some areas of brackish water

Take TX 87 southwest to Frenchtown Road and when you see the ferry-landing, take the road north and continue toward Port Bolivar. This part of the Texas Coast can add several species to a birder's life-time list. During low tides, watch for American oystercatchers and several species of terns and gulls. Look for the stand of wild bamboo and the species terns and gulls that are attracted to bamboo.

American Oystercatcher

DIRECTIONS
Drive southwest on TX 87 to the Bolivar ferry landing, and cross to Galveston. The ferry to Galveston is a free ride. Watch for birds during the crossing.

CONTACT INFORMATION
None available

GALVESTON LOOP
The Corps Woods at Galveston

#55

GPS 29.329, -94.769

LOCATED NEAR THE COAST GUARD STATION IN GALVESTON, TEXAS

KEY BIRDS
Shore birds, migrating species in the spring and fall

BEST SEASON
Migrations

AREA DESCRIPTION
A woodlot surrounded on three sides by Galveston Bay

Centrally located for both long-time as well as first-time birders, this location is where birders may see and watch a variety of species. It is considered one of the best birding locations for in the U.S.

Surrounded on three sides by water, shore birds are most common throughout the year while rare species are spotted during fall and spring migration. Water and shore birds from other coasts also travel to the island during migration.

While you are in the area, take the Bolivar Ferry from Galveston to Port Bolivar. Get out of your car and watch for brown pelicans and the magnificent frigatebirds. Also watch the gulls and terns feed in the ferry's wake. Enjoy your time on board during the 15-minute ferry ride that passes between Galveston Bay and the Gulf of Mexico.

This woodlot is being improved as a birding destination with Birding Trail funds From TPW, including a nature trail, parking area, and observation platform.

DIRECTIONS
After exiting the ferry on the Galveston side of the bay, continue south on TX 87 to TX 168 (0.6 mile). Go north on TX 168 to the Corps Woods at Galveston.

Wilson's Plover

CONTACT INFORMATION

Address: 900 SH 87 or P.O. Box B., Port Bolivar, 77650
Phone: 409-684-1333, Reservations: 409-934-8100 or toll-free at 1-888-GAL-ISLE (1-888-425-4753)
Web Site: info.parks.seniors@co.galveston.tx.us
Call for more information and fee schedule. Site is open daily.

GALVESTON LOOP
Big Reef and Apffel Park

#56

GPS ⊕ 29.332, -94.733

EAST END OF GALVESTON ISLAND

KEY BIRDS
Seabirds, herons, egrets, roseate spoonbill, white and white-faced ibises, sandpipers

BEST SEASON
All seasons

AREA DESCRIPTION
Saltwater beaches and wetlands, depending on the tidal flows

Birders will find access to both Big Reef and Apffel Park from Boddeker Drive.

Water and shore birds are common on the island throughout the year, while rare species are spotted during fall and spring migration. Water and shore birds from other coasts also travel to the island during their migrations.

The area named Big Reef is an extensive sand spit isolated by the entrance to Galveston Bay. The reef may be reached by crossing a small bridge located on the east side of the entrance road.

Thousands of shorebirds, gulls, and terns roost on this bar. Continue east on the entrance road to Apffel Park and watch the water near the South Jetty for seabirds.

Birders in this area should watch for herons, egrets, roseate spoonbills, white and white-faced ibises, sandpipers, plovers, rails, gulls, and terns. Some waterfowl are located here during most seasons. Birders should also especially watch for the magnificent frigatebirds as they fly along the coast looking for something to eat or, make that, steal.

DIRECTIONS
Return to TX 87 or Ferry Road, and continue south to Seawall Blvd. Travel northeast on Seawall Blvd. to the dead-end at the east end of Galveston Island. Turn east to reach Big Reef and Appfel Park, also known as East Galveston Beach.

Roseate Spoonbill

CONTACT INFORMATION
For more information on Galveston Island birding, contact the Galveston Island Convention & Visitors Bureau
Phone: 1-888-GAL-ISLE
Web Site: www.galveston.com
There is a fee charged for parking at some locations.

GALVESTON LOOP
Galveston's Kempner Park

#57

GPS 29.293, -94.795

2704 AVENUE O
GALVESTON, TX 77550

KEY BIRDS
American robin, white-winged dove, landbirds, and Inca dove

BEST SEASON
All seasons and during migrations

AREA DESCRIPTION
Grassy park areas with tall oak trees

Depending on spring weather conditions, this park has become an important location for some migrant land birds. Several species have been spotted in the trees roosting or flying overhead. In their movement north, white-winged doves are common in the nearby housing developments. Birders have reported American robins nesting in these trees in this location. This writer was amazed to learn the native underbrush was cleared in hopes of attracting more birds.

DIRECTIONS
From Apffel Park, continue southwest on Seawall Blvd. to Broadway. Drive west on Broadway to 27th Street, then south on 27th Street to Avenue O. Turn west on Avenue O to reach Kempner Park.

CONTACT INFORMATION
For more information on Galveston Island birding, contact the Galveston Island Convention & Visitors Bureau
Phone: 1-888-GAL-ISLE
Web Site: www.galveston.com
This site is open for day use only.

Inca Dove

GALVESTON LOOP
#58 Harborside Wetlands of Galveston

GPS⊕ 29.297, -94.826

JUST OFF 51ST STREET IN GALVESTON, TEXAS

KEY BIRDS
Great blue heron, yellow-crowned night-heron, cattle egret, wood stork, white-faced ibis, wood duck, mallard, gadwall, northern pintail, American wigeon, northern shoveler, blue-winged teal, green-winged teal, ring-necked duck

BEST SEASON
All seasons

AREA DESCRIPTION
Very marshy, with quite a few wet areas

The city of Galveston is transforming this marsh into a birding destination, and the site will have parking facilities and a nature trail when completed. At the time of this writing, the site was still under construction.

This area has a small colony of Eurasian collared doves that can be seen, although spending some time glassing the trees may be needed to find the doves. It is feared that this invasive species will harm the populations of mourning dove and other native species of dove. This species likes populated and wooded areas to establish their colonies.

Cattle Egret

DIRECTIONS

From Kempner Park, go north on 29th Street to Broadway. Go west on Broadway to 51st Street, then north on 51st Street to Harborside Wetlands of Galveston.

CONTACT INFORMATION

For more information on Galveston Island birding, contact the Galveston Island Convention & Visitors Bureau
Phone: 1-888-GAL-ISLE
Web Site: www.galveston.com
This site is open for day use only.

Common Merganser

GALVESTON LOOP
Offatts Bayou

#59

GPS 29.28, -94.857

ADJACENT TO MOODY GARDENS AND OFF 61ST STREET IN GALVESTON, TEXAS

KEY BIRDS
Common and pacific loons (rare), eared grebe, red-breasted merganser

BEST SEASON
Winter, spring

AREA DESCRIPTION
Bayou habitat with low brush and grass

Drive down 61st Street until it crosses the east end of Offatts Bayou. This is where birders may spot diving ducks and grebes. This is also the area where reports state that Pacific loons have been spotted.

This area is under a planned development for bird watchers. Many have said this location is the best place in Texas to see loons. Offatts Bayou may be viewed from the parking areas on the west side of 61st Street.

A birder's favorite attraction is the Galveston Moody Gardens area. This is a top viewing area offering terrace gardens and picnic tables along the bayou. While at Moody Gardens, sneak a peek at their tropical rainforest pyramid. The Colonel Paddlewheeler, docked at Moody Gardens, also offers a tour through Offatts Bayou.

Loons, grebes, and diving ducks often can be seen in this bayou during the fall and winter. Watch for eared grebes and red-breasted mergansers from late winter and into late spring.

DIRECTIONS
On Broadway, drive west to 61st Street (Spur 342). Go south on 61st Street to Offatts Bayou. Drive until you see water on both sides of the road.

CONTACT INFORMATION
Site open for day use only.

GALVESTON LOOP
#60 UTC 8-Mile Road and Sportmen's Road

GPS 29.264, -94.898

STEWART ROAD, AT THE END OF 8-MILE ROAD IN GALVESTON, TEXAS

KEY BIRDS
Common loon, common goldeneye, American oystercatcher

BEST SEASON
All seasons

AREA DESCRIPTION
Bayou habitat with low brush and grass

Park in the lot at Moody Gardens for another view of Offatts Bayou. This is the place to watch for grebes and some loons. The ponds provide safe roosting for waterfowl and shorebirds.

There are fields lining 8-Mile Road. American golden plovers and upland sandpipers may be seen here in the spring. After birding this area, drive west on Sportsmen's Road, driving to where the road ends. "Rail Road" is the nickname given to this road by local birders. Watch for clapper and sora rails along the road here in the winter.

The marshes along Sportsmen's Road extend to the edge of the pavement, and waterbirds (white ibis, roseate spoonbill, clapper rail) may wander to within a few feet of your vehicle. Check West Galveston Bay for common loons, common goldeneyes, and American oystercatchers on the shell reefs.

Other species to be found in this area are the American avocet, greater and lesser yellowlegs, solitary sandpiper, willet, long-billed curlew, marbled godwit, ruddy turnstone, semipalmated, western, least, white-rumped, and pictorial sandpipers. Also watch for all the herons and egrets, including the tri-colored heron and great egret and others. In the winter, birders should be on the alert for Nelson's sharp-tailed sparrow.

North Deer Island can be viewed from the end of 8-Mile Road. The area is jointly owned and operated by the National Audubon Society and Houston Audubon Society. This is also the location of a major colonial waterbird rookery on the northern Texas Coast.

Barrow's Goldeneye

DIRECTIONS
Continue south on 61st Street to Stewart Road; travel west on Stewart Road to 81st Street. Moody Gardens (butterfly gardens, IMAX theatre) may be reached off of 81st Street. Continue west on Stewart Road to 8-Mile Road. Drive north on 8-Mile Road to its end at West Galveston Bay and Sportsmen's Road.

CONTACT INFORMATION
Houston Audubon Society - 440 Wilchester Blvd. Houston, TX 77079
Phone: 713-932-1639, Galveston County call 409-772-3126
Email: info@houstonaudubon.org
Web Site: http://www.houstonaudubon.org
Office Hours: 9:00am to 5:00pm, Mon.-Fri.
Site open for day use only

GALVESTON LOOP

#61 Settegast (Nottingham Ranch) Road

GPS 29.219, -94.924

LOCATED OFF STEWART ROAD, GALVESTON, TEXAS

KEY BIRDS
Plovers, whimbrel, curlew, sandhill crane

BEST SEASON
Migrations

AREA DESCRIPTION
Grassy roadside habitats with tall trees along the road

Look carefully at anything you see here for, on Nottingham Road, you never know just what might turn up! Look for plovers, whimbrel, curlew in the fields, and sandhill cranes in winter. This is for road birding, so be careful of traffic.

Between 10-Mile and 11-Mile Roads, watch for American bittern and purple gallinule around and in the small pond at the beginning of the road. This particular road attracts more western vagrants than any given spot within the area, such as curve-billed thrasher, common ground-dove, western meadowlark, yellow-headed blackbird, bronzed cowbird, pyrrhuloxia, black-headed grosbeak, and lark sparrow.

Trees along the road are good for warblers, orioles, and tanagers in migration. Gull-billed terns are often seen over wet areas to the south. White-tailed kites nest in tall trees at the end of the road, across the lagoon.

The grassy fields along Settegast Road will attract and hold American golden-plovers, whimbrels, long-billed curlews, and upland sandpipers during spring migration.

DIRECTIONS
Drive west on Stewart Road to Settegast Road (also known as Nottingham Ranch Road).

CONTACT INFORMATION
There is no contact information for this site.
Site open for day use only.

Sandhill Cranes

GALVESTON LOOP
Lafitte's Cove
#62

GPS 29.216, -94.935

Located on Eckert Drive after driving through a private subdivision in Galveston, Texas

Key Birds
Sora rail, bitterns, night-herons

Best Season
Migrations

Area Description
Marshy areas and ponds

When it comes to attracting migrant landbirds this is the location. Taking into consideration the weather conditions, this location can be better bird viewing than High Island.

The marshes here are good places to watch for night-herons, sora rails, and bitterns. Birders can spend time watching migrants, such as several species of warblers, perched and around ponds and in the trees and bushes.

Directions
Drive west on Stewart Road to Lafitte's Cove. To enter Lafitte's Cove, turn off of Stewart Road onto Eckert Drive at the entrance to the Lafitte's Cove subdivision and drive 0.2 mile to the parking area at the beginning of the nature trail.

Contact Information
No contact information available at this time, but birders may try the web site: http://www.galveston.com/birding/
Site open for day use only.

Black-crowned Night-herons

GALVESTON LOOP
Lafitte's Grove

#63

GPS 29.21, -94.94

JUST WEST OF THE ENTRANCE TO LAFITTE'S COVE, GALVESTON, TEXAS

KEY BIRDS
Warblers, sora rails, bitterns, night-herons

BEST SEASON
Migrations

AREA DESCRIPTION
A 20-acre oak motte with ponds and wetlands

Lafitte's Cove is an excellent place to find migrating songbirds in spring and fall. Reports of at least 137 species were recorded in this location during the spring migration of 1997.

A fort and settlement were established here in 1817 by the pirate, Jean Lafitte, and he used this location for his headquarters in order to continue robbing passing ships.

The Karankawa Indians and Lafitte's men fought the Battle of the Three Trees on February of 1821. Lafitte abandoned and burned the improvements in 1821 after he was ordered by the United States government.

Black-crowned Night-heron

The oaks here are also attractive to migrant landbirds. Be aware that fall migrants often linger along the immediate coast throughout the Christmas season. These small oak mottes bordering ponds should be checked throughout the fall and early winter months.

DIRECTIONS

Return to Stewart Road and drive west to Lafitte's Grove (about 0.1 mile west of the entrance to Lafitte's Cove). Park on the pavement near the historical marker.

CONTACT INFORMATION

No contact information available at this time, but birders may try the web site: http://www.galveston.com/birding/
Site open for day use only.

GALVESTON LOOP
Galveston Island State Park

#64

GPS 29.188, -94.956

14901 FM 3005
GALVESTON, TX 77554

KEY BIRDS
Ibis, herons, egrets, gulls, terns, white-tailed kite, northern harrier

BEST SEASON
All seasons

AREA DESCRIPTION
Salt marsh habitat

Extending from the bay to the beach and covering a little over 2,013 acres, the park offers the most birding on its bay section. There is also a better chance of not being crowded.

Upon entering the park off of FM 3005, check the willow groves that border the park road. Turn west at your first opportunity, and park near the observation tower.

This nature trail is worth walking, and the trees across the road should be checked for migrants. The marshes that border the bay abound with ibis, herons, egrets, gulls, and terns.

Black rails have been known to nest in this location. Many times, birders have heard them during the night. As the sun sets, watch for barn owls leaving their nests and starting to hunt in the open grassy areas.

Reddish Egret

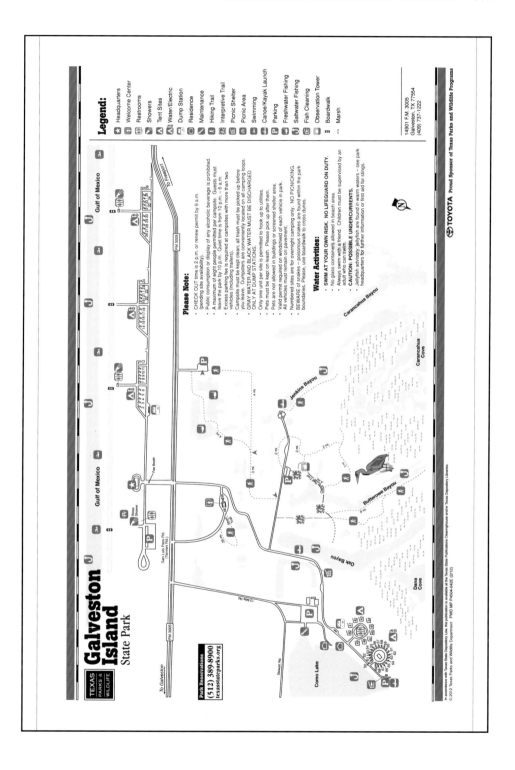

Galveston Island State Park

Park Reservations
(512) 389-8900
texasstateparks.org

Legend:

- Headquarters
- Welcome Center
- Restrooms
- Showers
- Tent Sites
- Water/Electric
- Dump Station
- Residence
- Maintenance
- Hiking Trail
- Interpretive Trail
- Picnic Shelter
- Picnic Area
- Swimming
- Canoe/Kayak Launch
- Parking
- Freshwater Fishing
- Saltwater Fishing
- Fish Cleaning
- Observation Tower
- Boardwalk
- Marsh

14901 FM 3005
Galveston, TX 77554
(409) 737-1222

Please Note:

- CHECK OUT time is 2 p.m. or renew permit by 9 a.m. (pending site availability).
- Public consumption or display of any alcoholic beverage is prohibited.
- A maximum of eight people permitted per campsite. Guests must leave the park by 10 p.m. Quiet time is from 10 p.m. – 6 a.m.
- Excess parking fee is required at campsites with more than two vehicles (including trailers).
- Campsite must be kept clean; all trash must be picked up before you leave. Dumpsters are conveniently located on all camping loops.
- GRAY WATER AND BLACK WATER MUST BE DISCHARGED ONLY AT DUMP STATIONS.
- Only one unit per site is permitted to hook up to utilities.
- Pets must be kept on leash. Please pick up after them.
- Pets are not allowed in buildings or screened shelter area.
- Valid permit required on windshield of each vehicle in park. All vehicles must remain on pavement.
- Numbered sites are for overnight camping only. NO PICNICKING.
- BEWARE of snakes – poisonous snakes are found within the park boundaries. Please, use boardwalk to cross dunes.

Water Activities:

- **SWIM AT YOUR OWN RISK. NO LIFEGUARD ON DUTY.**
  - No glass containers allowed in beach area.
  - Always swim with a friend. Children must be supervised by an adult who can swim.
- **CAUTION: POSSIBLE UNDERCURRENTS.**
  - Jellyfish advisory: jellyfish are found in warm waters – see park headquarters for further information or first aid for stings.

TOYOTA Proud Sponsor of Texas Parks and Wildlife Programs

Gulf of Mexico

To Galveston

San Luis Pass Rd.
(Termini Rd.)

Fee Booth

FM 3005

To Freeport

Como Lake

Dana Cove

Oak Bayou

Butterowe Bayou

Jenkins Bayou

Carancahua Cove

Carancahua Bayou

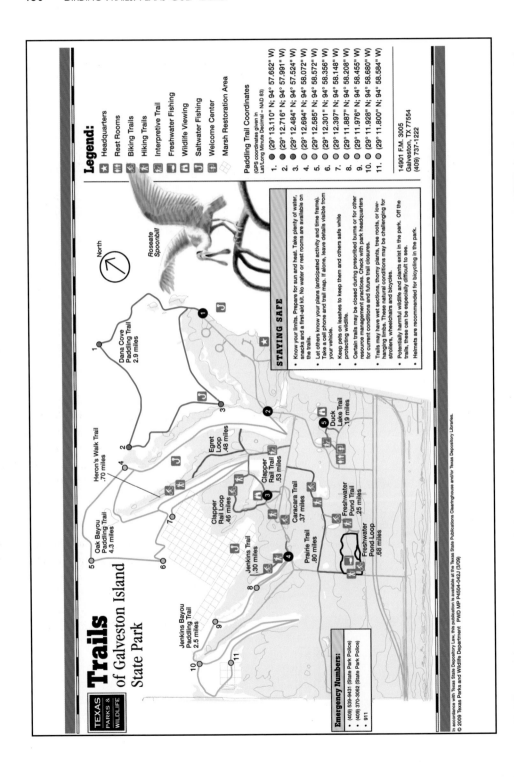

Trails of Galveston Island State Park

TEXAS PARKS & WILDLIFE

North

Roseate Spoonbill

Dana Cove Paddling Trail 2.9 miles

Heron's Walk Trail .70 miles

Oak Bayou Paddling Trail 4.3 miles

Jenkins Bayou Paddling Trail 2.5 miles

Jenkins Trail .30 miles

Prairie Trail .80 miles

Clapper Rail Loop .46 miles

Egret Loop .48 miles

Clapper Rail Trail .53 miles

Caracara Trail .37 miles

Freshwater Pond Trail .25 miles

Freshwater Pond Loop .68 miles

Duck Lake Trail .19 miles

Legend:

- Headquarters
- Rest Rooms
- Biking Trails
- Hiking Trails
- Interpretive Trail
- Freshwater Fishing
- Wildlife Viewing
- Saltwater Fishing
- Welcome Center
- Marsh Restoration Area

Paddling Trail Coordinates
(GPS coordinates given in Lat/Long Minute Decimal – NAD 83)

1. (29° 13.110" N; 94° 57.652" W)
2. (29° 12.716" N; 94° 57.991" W)
3. (29° 12.484" N; 94° 57.524" W)
4. (29° 12.694" N; 94° 58.072" W)
5. (29° 12.585" N; 94° 58.572" W)
6. (29° 12.301" N; 94° 58.356" W)
7. (29° 12.397" N; 94° 58.148" W)
8. (29° 11.887" N; 94° 58.208" W)
9. (29° 11.976" N; 94° 58.455" W)
10. (29° 11.928" N; 94° 58.680" W)
11. (29° 11.800" N; 94° 58.584" W)

14901 F.M. 3005
Galveston, TX 77554
(409) 737-1222

STAYING SAFE

- Know your limits. Prepare for sun and heat. Take plenty of water, snacks and a first-aid kit. No water or rest rooms are available on the trails.
- Let others know your plans (anticipated activity and time frame). Take a cell phone and trail map. If alone, leave details visible from your vehicle.
- Keep pets on leashes to keep them and others safe while protecting wildlife.
- Certain trails may be closed during prescribed burns or for other resource management practices. Check with park headquarters for current conditions and future trail closures.
- Trails may have wet sections, thorny plants, tree roots, or low-hanging limbs. These natural conditions may be challenging for strollers, wheelchairs and bicycles.
- Potentially harmful wildlife and plants exist in the park. Off the trails, these can be especially difficult to see.
- Helmets are recommended for bicycling in the park.

Emergency Numbers:

- (409) 539-9431 (State Park Police)
- (409) 370-3062 (State Park Police)
- 911

DIRECTIONS
Drive west on Stewart Road to its merger with 13-Mile Road and the intersection with FM 3005. Continue west on FM 3005 to PR 66 and Galveston Island State Park.

CONTACT INFORMATION
Phone: 409-737-1222
Web Site: www.tpwd.state.tx.us/galveston
This site is open daily with some developed camping available. Fees are charged.

GALVESTON LOOP
John M. O'Quinn
I-45 Estuarial Corridor

GPS 29.296, -94.886

BOTH SIDES OF I-45 BETWEEN TEXAS CITY AND GALVESTON

KEY BIRDS
Spoonbills, herons, egrets, and rails

BEST SEASON
All Seasons

AREA DESCRIPTION
Wetland habitat skirting a major Interstate Highway

The corridor consists of almost 900 acres of the I-45 Estuary wetland habitat for migratory and resident waterfowl and wading species. As you drive along I-45, the wetlands you are passing are known as the Interstate-45 Estuary. Traveled by millions each year that are only interested in their destination, this area is an area of interest for birdwatchers and outdoor nature lovers. This part of Texas is the focus of the Texas Mid-Coast Initiative of the Gulf Coast Joint Venture.

The North American Waterfowl Management Plan has selected this area as internationally significant migration and wintering for the mid-continent waterfowl resource. This site is also a sensitive acreage in the Galveston Bay National Estuary Program.

Interstate frontage will be permanently protected and will work to fully restore over 1,000 acres of the I-45 Estuary wetland habitat for threatened and endangered species, migratory waterfowl, and other wetland-dependent species.

The marshes that extend from Galveston Bay (Virginia Point) north to TX 146 are part of an estuarial corridor being developed by Scenic Galveston.

"Funds from the 1997 Great Texas Birding Classic were used to assist with this acquisition. In the near future, most of the structures will be removed, and this entire area will be returned to its original wetland state. An observation station is planned near the intersection of I-45 and TX 146, and the marshes themselves can be birded from the service road that borders both sides of I-45," stated the Galveston Bay Information Center.

Herons, egrets, spoonbills, and rails may be seen feeding within a few feet of the highway.

DIRECTIONS
Drive southwest on FM 3005 across San Luis Pass. To continue to Houston and the loops of that region, travel north from Galveston Island on I-45 to TX 146. Exit on TX 146 for Texas City and the John M. O'Quinn I-45 Estuarial Corridor.

CONTACT INFORMATION
No contact information available, but using caution while stopping to bird watch is advised. Site open for day use only.

Barn Swallow

GALVESTON LOOP
#66 AMOCO Settling Ponds and Swan Lake

GPS ⊕ 29.354, -94.924

APPROXIMATELY 1.3 MILES FROM THE INTERSECTION OF TX 146 AND LOOP 197 IN TEXAS CITY, TEXAS

KEY BIRDS
Bufflehead, canvasback, redhead, and other waterfowl species

BEST SEASON
All Seasons

AREA DESCRIPTION
Roadside areas and wetlands

These settling ponds are located to the west of Loop 197 and can be birded from the shoulders of the road, if special care and road safety is observed. These ponds attract several species of waterfowl in the winter including canvasback, bufflehead, and redhead (diving ducks).

It must be mentioned that some of the area locals are not in favor of this project. Your birding visits as comments will be valuable.

DIRECTIONS
Go north on TX 146 to Loop 197, and then continue north on Loop 197 to the Amoco Settling Ponds and Swan Lake (approximately 1.3 miles from the inter-section of TX 146 and Loop 197).

CONTACT INFORMATION
No contact information available but using caution while stopping to bird watch is advised.
Site open for day use only.

Redhead

GALVESTON LOOP
Texas City Dike

#67

GPS⊕ **29.38, -94.854**

BAY STREET AND 8TH AVENUE
TEXAS CITY, TEXAS

KEY BIRDS
Brown pelican, loons, gulls, grebes, diving ducks, common goldeneye, red-breasted merganser

BEST SEASON
Winter

AREA DESCRIPTION
A narrow five-mile spit of land with a road down the middle; bay on one side, Texas City Channel on the other

The drive to the end of the Texas City Dike is five miles and always worthwhile in the winter according to birders. In my younger days, there was no time of the year when the Texas Dike trip was not worthwhile.

Common and Pacific loons are regulars, while the red-throated loon is only an occasional visitor. Birders may also spot diving ducks, grebes, gulls, as well as the common

Brown Pelican

goldeneye and the red-breasted merganser. Especially watch for Bonaparte's gull and the black-legged kittiwake that may be seen during the drive to the end of the dike and back.

The makings of a good birding trip is to drive slowly along the dike, allowing faster traffic to pass and keeping a careful watch for perching birds and birds resting on the water. This is a popular fishing area, so please afford the courtesy to the anglers as you would expect for yourself.

DIRECTIONS
Drive north on Loop 197 to 2nd Avenue in Texas City, and then go east on 2nd Avenue to Bay Street. Travel north on Bay Street to 8th Avenue and the Texas City Dike.

CONTACT INFORMATION
City Hall: 1801 9th Ave. N.
Phone: 409-948-3111
Site open for day use only.

GALVESTON LOOP
#68 Bay Street Park

GPS ⊕ **29.398, -94.893**

1100 BAY STREET NORTH
TEXAS CITY, TX

KEY BIRDS
Several species of hummingbirds regularly during the winter, large flocks of ruddy ducks

BEST SEASON
Migrations, winter

AREA DESCRIPTION
A park with a fresh water lagoon, many trees, and managed trails

The park is composed of about 50 acres of land and 50 acres of fresh-water lagoon. During the winter month's birders should watch for Sprague's pipits in the grass and on the shoulders of this levee.

There is an observation tower located a half mile north on Skyline Drive. Birders watching from this platform can see the lake and, as often happens during cooler months, the water especially during drought years, will attract several species of ducks including flocks of the small ruddy ducks.

Broad-tailed Hummingbird

There is a hummingbird garden that was planted using Birding Trail funds. The mature plants attract migrant hummingbirds and are a great place to spend some time with binoculars. This garden should be a regular stop for area birders and visitors during the winter and late spring. There are also a series of nature trails that wind through the park. There are several improved nature trails that should not be overlooked by birders.

Directions
Exiting the Texas City Dike, drive north on Skyline Drive. At the northern end of Skyline Drive, turn west and continue to Bay Street and Bay Street Park (Bay Street will eventually circle back to the south, and the park will be located to the east).

Contact Information:
Site open for day use only.

GALVESTON LOOP
TNCT Galveston Bay Preserve

GPS 29.462, -94.949

On TX 146 near Texas City, Texas

Key Birds
Attwater prairie chicken

Best Season
All Seasons

Area Description
Coastal prairie habitat

In spite of this location being highly restricted, it consists of a large percentage of the rare coastal prairie habitat needed for the survival of the Attwater's prairie chicken. It would be well worth trying to gain entrance because this 2,263-acre preserve is one of the three remaining sites that support this wild endangered bird.

Directions
From Bay Street Park, drive south on Bay Street to 9th Avenue, then turn west on 9th Avenue (FM 1764) and continue to TX 146. Go north on TX 146 to TNCT Galveston Bay Preserve.

Contact Information
TNCT – Coastal Texas Stewardship Office, P.O. Box 163, Collegeport, Texas 77428-0163
Phone: 512-972-2559
Email: txfo@tnc.org
Site access is very restricted. Please call ahead.

Attwater's Prairie Chicken

#70 McHale Park

GPS ⊕ 29.553, -95.022

400 TODVILLE ROAD & WATERFRONT
SEABROOK, TX 77586

KEY BIRDS
Pelicans, grebes, seagulls, herons, egrets

BEST SEASON
All Seasons

AREA DESCRIPTION
Waterfront habitat with large trees and grassy park areas

McHale Park is a lovely spot from which to view the western shoreline of Galveston Bay. Rafts of American white pelicans fish in their group fashion: driving the fish before them, then all dipping their bills into the water to feed. A migrating species, these large white birds are some of the national winter visitors. When birding the adjacent marshes, birders will see wading birds such as several species of egrets and herons.

There is a raised, shaded wooden observation deck overlooking Galveston Bay. Seagulls, grebes, and pelicans, with other wading birds give visiting birders a chance to spot species not found in the northern states.

Ships and barges create wakes that attract gulls that dive to the water hoping to catch something for lunch. Honking big pleasure craft zoom by, following the shrimping fleet and oil tankers and barges full of cars that are going towards the ship channel.

DIRECTIONS
Proceed north on TX 146 to the Kemah/Seabrook Bridge, and then immediately exit after crossing. Circle back south on Waterfront Drive, across Todville, and into McHale Park.

CONTACT INFORMATION
Web Site: www.seabrooktourism.com/parks.html
Site open for day use only.

Laughing Gull

GALVESTON LOOP
Hester Garden Park
#71

GPS 29.572, -95.011

3029 TODVILLE ROAD
SEABROOK, TX 77586

KEY BIRDS
Wading birds, gulls, and migrating land birds in the spring and fall

BEST SEASON
Migrations and winter

AREA DESCRIPTION
A variety of trees and shrubs in the wooded area, plus partial wetland, pond, and trails

This 8.65-acre park is a former commercial nursery and considered by many local birders to be an undiscovered gem. Until after World War II, most Houston birders traveled to this region of Galveston Bay to look for migrant land birds.

Hester Garden Park consists of an impressive variety of trees and shrubs. Check these woods in late fall and

Western Tanager

winter, since many of these plants are evergreen and are therefore attractive to lingering insectivores.

A few species seen here are yellowlegs, lesser yellowlegs, common snipe, mourning dove, Inca dove, rock dove, greater roadrunner, ruby-throated hummingbird, and belted kingfisher.

DIRECTIONS
As you leave McHale Park turn north on Todville Road. Stay on Todville Road to Hester Garden Park.

CONTACT INFORMATION
Web Site: http://www.seabrooktourism.com/parks.html
Phone: 281-474-3286
Site open for day use only.

GALVESTON LOOP
Pine Gully Park

#72

GPS 29.592, -94.993

605 PINE GULLY ROAD
SEABROOK, TX

KEY BIRDS
Shore and seabirds

BEST SEASON
Migrations and winter

AREA DESCRIPTION
52 acres; Wooded areas with brush and grassy park areas with a good length of Galveston Bay frontage

Pine Gully Park daily gate admission is free for Seabrook residents and $20.00 per vehicle for non-residents, including non-resident senior citizens.

This 52.27-acre park is an old Karawankawa Indian campsite where the much-hated and dreaded tribe would hunt and fish. The 1,000-foot fishing pier on Galveston Bay is a great place to view shore and seabirds. The park also has wetlands, a wooded area, nature trails, restrooms, picnic tables, and barbeque grills.

Magnificient Frigatebird

This multi-use facility offers another view of Galveston Bay, and the trees within the park are worth inspecting for migrant landbirds. The wetland has been restored within this park, and should be checked for waterbirds.

DIRECTIONS
Continue north on Todville Road to Pine Gully Drive, and then go east on Pine Gully Drive to Pine Gully Park.

CONTACT INFORMATION
Phone: 866-611-4688 or 281-474-2425
Web Site: http://www.seabrooktx.gov/Facilities.aspx?Page=detail&RID=12
Site open for day use only. Summer hours are 7:00am to 8:30pm. The rest of the year, the park is open 7:00am to 6:30pm.

Blue-winged Teal

GALVESTON LOOP
Robinson Park

#73

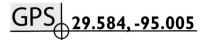

GPS 29.584, -95.005

702 RED BLUFF ROAD
SEABROOK, TX 77586

KEY BIRDS
White-faced ibis, wood duck, wood stork, blue-winged teal, green-winged teal, mallard, northern pintail, gadwall, American wigeon, northern shoveler, ring-necked duck, bufflehead, hooded merganser

BEST SEASON
Migrations

AREA DESCRIPTION
Wooded area with wetlands, hiking trails, footbridge, gazebo, benches, and parking

Robinson Park contains approximately 20 acres of old oaks and a trail that connects these woodlands with Pine Gully Park. The park is one more woodlot to stop and view the birds as you are traveling this edge of Galveston Bay.

Some of the attractive features here are a gazebo and benches, as well as hiking trails, a footbridge, and parking.

DIRECTIONS
Drive south on Todville to Red Bluff. Robinson Park is located near the intersection of Todville and Red Bluff.

CONTACT INFORMATION
Phone: 866-611-4688
Web Site: http://visitbayareahouston.com/index.cfm
Site open for day use only.

GALVESTON LOOP
Armand Bayou Nature Center

GPS ⊕ **29.354, -95.052**

8500 BAY AREA BOULEVARD PASADENA, TX 77507

KEY BIRDS
Waterfowl, sedge wren, and Le Conte's sparrow

BEST SEASON
Winter, spring migrations, and nesting season

AREA DESCRIPTION
Wetlands, oak and hackberry woodlands, and tall-grass prairie

Located between NASA and the Bayport Industrial District, Armand Bayou Nature Center (ABNC) is a working preserve offering birders wetlands prairie, forest, and marsh habitats. Areas surrounding and along Armand Bayou attract many species of birds.

Here one of the main goals is education, where birders can learn about the plant and animal inhabitants. Other activities are bird-watching and hiking on the center's trails.

The ABNC is a 2,500-acre wildlife preserve encompassing three distinct ecosystems: wetlands (estuarine bayou), woodlands (hardwood riparian forest), and tall-grass prairie. The 1900-acre nature center proper is one of the largest urban nature preserves.

Visiting birders who are in the area all winter should consider volunteering at the center for whatever free time they might have. They can enjoy being in nature, meeting like-minded people, greeting visitors, or working with the naturalist instructors and cultural docents as they guide school field trips or outreach programs.

A system of nature trails honeycombs the property. ABNC staff and volunteers have spent countless hours restoring several hundred acres of coastal prairie, and grassland species such as sedge wren and Le Conte's sparrow are not difficult to find here. ABNC staff is available to answer questions about when and where to bird in the Clear Lake area.

Other species found along Armand Bayou are: red-bellied and pileated woodpeckers, blue jay, Carolina wren, black vulture, osprey, as well as many species of waterfowl, egrets, herons, gulls, and terns.

Northern Spoonbill

The center operates a pontoon boat that offers an unusual wildlife adventure. Birders may make reservations to bird Armand Bayou from the deck of the "Bayou Ranger", an electric pontoon boat. Another option is to take a guided canoe tour.

DIRECTIONS
From the intersection of Todville and Red Bluff Roads, go west on Red Bluff Road to Old 146, then north on Old 146 a short distance back to Red Bluff Road. Continue northwest on Red Bluff Road to Bay Area Blvd., then west on Bay Area Blvd. to Armand Bayou Nature Center (ABNC).

CONTACT INFORMATION
Phone: 281-474-2551
Email: abnc@ghgcorp.com
Web Site: www.ghgcorp.com/abnc/
Site open for day use only. Fees charged: 3 years & under = Free / 4 - 12 = $2.00 / 13 - 59 years = $4.00 / 60 years & above = $2.00

GALVESTON LOOP
#75 Bay Area Park

GPS 29.595, -95.086

7500 E. BAY AREA BOULEVARD
HOUSTON, TX 77058

KEY BIRDS
Osprey

BEST SEASON
All seasons

AREA DESCRIPTION
City park habitat

Located on Armand Bayou in Harris County, the park is situated near the water and offers an unobstructed view of the bayou. One of conveniences of the park is the parking area. Birders should watch for osprey during migrations and during the winter. The fish hawks will be here year round and will nest on platforms and trees in the spring.

DIRECTIONS
Drive west on Bay Area Blvd. to Bay Area Park.

CONTACT INFORMATION
City of Houston / P.O. Box 1562 / Houston, TX 77251
Physical Address: City of Houston / 901 Bagby / Houston, TX 77002
City Hall Annex Address: 900 Bagby / Houston, TX 77002
City Switchboard: 713-837-0311
Site open for day use only.

Osprey

GALVESTON LOOP
Lake Nassau Park

#76

GPS 29.32, -95.052

SOUTHERN-MOST END OF UPPER BAY ROAD, NASSAU BAY, TEXAS

KEY BIRDS
Wading birds and seasonal migrations

BEST SEASON
All seasons

AREA DESCRIPTION
City park habitat

The Lyndon B. Johnson Space Center and Space Center Houston are both located along NASA Road One. Go south on Upper Bay Road to Nassau Bay Park. Although not a major birding destination, this city park offers a respite amenity for birders in a very good birding area.

A paved bicycle and pedestrian path connects Lake Nassau Park and Lake Nassau Pocket Park. The Pocket Park has picnic tables and a dock for birders and other wildlife watchers.

DIRECTIONS
Continue driving west on Bay Area Blvd. to Middlebrook Drive, then east on Middlebrook Drive to Space Center Blvd. Go south on Space Center Blvd. to NASA Road One, then west on NASA Road One to Upper Bay Road.

CONTACT INFORMATION
Nassau Bay Parks, 18100 Upper Bay Road, Suite 200, Nassau Bay, TX 77058
Phone: 281-333-4211
Site open for day use only.

Green Heron

GALVESTON LOOP

#77 UTC Challenger 7 Memorial Park

GPS 29.511, -95.136

2301 W. NASA BLVD. WEBSTER, TX 77598

KEY BIRDS
Eastern bluebird, white-tailed hawk

BEST SEASON
All seasons

AREA DESCRIPTION
326 acres, of which about 100 are bird sanctuary; City park habitat

On January 28, 1986, the Space Shuttle Challenger during Mission 51-L exploded at 11:39 a.m., 73 seconds after liftoff and all aboard the shuttle were killed in the explosion. That year the park was named in honor of the seven NASA astronauts who lost their lives in the explosion.

The crew members were Francis R. Scobee, Shuttle Commander; Michael J. Smith, Pilot; Ellison S. Onizuka, Judith A. Resnik, and Ronald E. McNair, Mission Specialists; Gregory B. Jarvis, Payload Specialist. Also on board was Christa McAuliff, a schoolteacher and the first civilian chosen to fly the shuttle.

An extensive nature trail and boardwalk has been developed in this park along Clear Creek. Many of the eastern woodland birds can be spotted here. During the spring white-tailed hawks have been known to nest in this area.

The park has three elevated observation platforms that are connected to the boardwalk. The platforms allow birders to view the wetlands along Clear Creek. The creek is a natural tributary flowing along Harris County's southern boundary and emptying into Clear Lake.

There are approximately 100 acres of the 326-acre Challenger 7 Memorial Park that have been sanctioned by the Audubon Society and designated a bird sanctuary. The nature trails allow you to access the bird sanctuary and other undeveloped areas of the park.

Eastern Bluebird

DIRECTIONS
Return to NASA Road One, and continue west to I-45 (you will cross TX 3 before you reach I-45). At I-45, NASA Road One becomes Wilson Road; continue west on Wilson Road to West NASA Blvd. Go south on West NASA Blvd. to Challenger 7 Memorial Park.

CONTACT INFORMATION
Phone: 713-440-1587
Audubon Web Address: (http://www.audubon.org/)
Site open for day use only.

GALVESTON LOOP
Walter Hall County Park

#78

GPS 29.518, -95.101

807 HWY 3 NORTH
LEAGUE CITY, TX 77573

KEY BIRDS
Purple gallinule, red-headed woodpecker, white pelican, and the once-endangered brown pelican

BEST SEASON
Migrations, winter

AREA DESCRIPTION
Open park habitats with large trees and a lake

This multi-use facility has been developed for a variety of outdoor activities, but birding opportunities do exist along Clear Creek. Since this is multi-use, along with the birders, there will be other people enjoying the lake and park property especially in the summer.

Birders should watch the moss-covered trees for birds like the yellow-rumped, pine, and orange-crowned warblers.

DIRECTIONS
Return to the intersection of TX 3 and NASA Road One, and go south on TX 3 for two miles to Walter Hall County Park

CONTACT INFORMATION
Phone: 281-316-2777
Email: info.parks.seniors@co.galveston.tx.us
Web Site: http://www.galvestonparks-seniors.org/locations/ls_overview.asp
Site open for day use only.

Purple Gallinule

GALVESTON LOOP
Paul Hopkins Community Park

GPS 29.453, -95.069

EAST OF I-45 ON FM 517 IN DICKINSON, TEXAS

KEY BIRDS
Red-shouldered hawk

BEST SEASON
Migrations and winter

AREA DESCRIPTION
Park habitat with heavy pine cover with water areas

This pocket park has a nature trail along the bayou, and migrant landbirds often pass along this waterway in spring. The water is very nice for canoeing. Watch the trees for a good number of eastern woodland birds, including the red-shouldered hawk. This species has been known to nest in this woodland.

Once you hit Dickinson Bayou go to your right, which will take you upstream. The bayou is big enough here to resemble a river and still has many pockets of beautiful woods along the banks. This section is definitely still like other parts of East Texas with all of the loblolly pine.

Several homes with bulkheads dot the banks of the bayou; these don't in anyway corrupt the view or the birding. Cross under I-45 and watch how the bayou becomes smaller and the pines decrease as you continue upstream. Development along the banks gets smaller as well.

Canoeing birders will find it easy to put in almost anywhere on Magnolia Bayou, close to the bridge, or at the launch site in the park. Don't forget your optics, and paddle stealthily through the bayou.

The bayou can be paddled past Hwy 646 and even to and above Cemetery Road, if desired, before returning to the park.

DIRECTIONS
Drive south on TX 3 to FM 517, then west on FM 517 to Paul Hopkins Community Park.

CONTACT INFORMATION
Bayou Preservation Association, 3201 Allen Parkway, Suite 200, Houston, Texas 77219-1563
Phone: 713-529-6443
Email: bpa@hic.net
Web Site: http://www.bayoupreservation.org/
Site open for day use only.

Harris's Hawk

GALVESTON LOOP

Dr. Ned and Fay Dudney Nature Center

GPS 29.529, -95.089

1220 S. EGRET BAY BLVD. LEAGUE CITY, TX 77058

KEY BIRDS
Sandhill crane, great blue heron, ibises, egrets, great white heron, owls

BEST SEASON
All seasons and winter migrations

AREA DESCRIPTION
Park-like setting with quality wetlands

Located on the South Shore of Clear Creek off Highway 270, the park consists of 148 acres. Once known as the Davis tract, this is one of the last remaining large underdeveloped properties with quality wetlands. The first phase of the park includes a 1.3-mile concrete and fly ash observation trail complete with bird blinds and restrooms. Phase 2 will provide a nature educational center, bird rehabilitation center, along with more trails.

The nature center is an excellent habitat for migrant birds, such as sandhill crane, great blue heron, ibis, egrets, great white heron, owls, and various songbirds that use the area to nest and feed. Ducks, pelicans, shorebirds, and wading birds can also be found along the isolated pond along Clear Creek.

This location is best birding on foot with your optics and cameras. Slow walking and stopping from time to time to glass the area for different species can be very fruitful. Keeping the talking to a minimum is best.

DIRECTIONS
From Harper's Church Road, return to Highway 270 and drive the short distance to Egret Bay North Road. Turn there and drive to the center.

CONTACT INFORMATION
Phone: 281-554-1181
Hours: 7:00am to 7:00pm

Great White Heron

BIRDING TRAILS: TEXAS GULF COAST

Houston Loop

Houston, the town where I was born and spent the majority of my youth, ranks high on my list of birding areas. One of the main features of this loop is the miles upon miles of lowland and wetlands that attract birds from Texas State Hwy 6 to the town of Katy. Migrating birds are numerous, as well as natives like the Attwater's prairie chicken on their refuge.

Houston proper is nearly as good, but has a larger variety of local birds and many perching species as they migrate through the area, with some spending either the summer or winter in the area. The many large parks and grassy areas also provide birding possibilities. Look for the green and bird away.

The eleven numbered locations on this loop are only the beginning. Take your time traveling from one to the other and enjoy the Texas scenery and the "by chance" birds you will encounter.

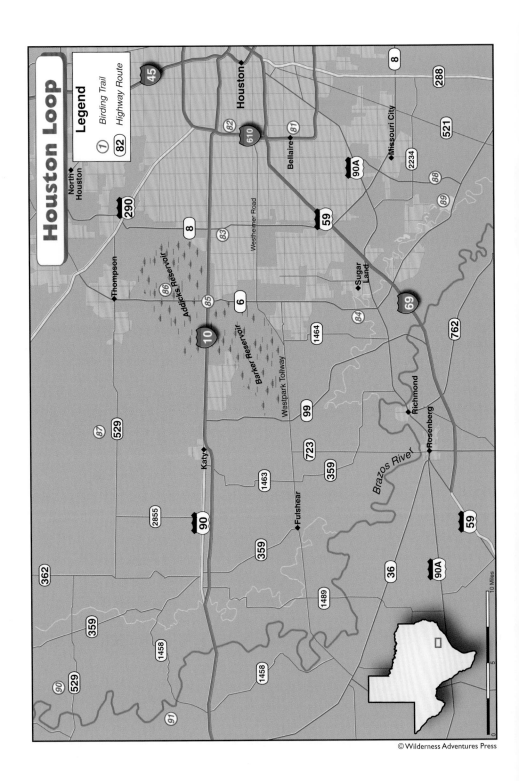

Houston Loop

Legend
1 Birding Trail
82 Highway Route

North Houston

Thompson

Addicks Reservoir

Barker Reservoir

Katy

Westpark Tollway

Fulshear

Houston

Westheimer Road

Bellaire

90A

Sugar Land

Missouri City

Richmond

Rosenberg

Brazos River

10 Miles

© Wilderness Adventures Press

Houston Loop Locations

81. Russ Pittman Park (Nature Discovery Center)
82. Houston Arboretum and Memorial Park
83. HAS Edith L. Moore Bird Sanctuary
84. Joseph S. and Lucie H. Cullinan Park
85. Barker and Addicks Reservoirs
86. Bear Creek Park
87. Longenbaugh Waterfowl Pond
88. Warren Lake
89. KPC Nelson Farm Preserve
90. UTC Harper's Church Road
91. Stephen F. Austin State Park

HOUSTON LOOP
Russ Pittman Park (Nature Discovery Center)

#81

GPS 29.7, -95.451

7112 NEWCASTLE
BELLAIRE, TX 77401

KEY BIRDS
Warblers, vireos, orioles, swifts, hummingbirds

BEST SEASON
Migrations and winter

AREA DESCRIPTION
Mixture of prairie grasses, tall pecans, native understory, and wide lawns

The park has counted over 80 species of warblers, vireos, orioles and swifts - giving birders a great opportunity to watch and photograph them. This four-acre urban oasis attracts migrant landbirds during migration, and the hummingbird feeders maintained by the nature center staff are magnets for wintering hummingbirds. Buff-bellied, ruby-throated, black-chinned, broad-tailed and rufous are among the species that have been seen here during the winter months.

Large trees and plentiful vegetation, along with food and water features offer birders a very active place to watch birds. The park and center attract local birders from all parts of the Houston area.

In spite of the small site, the bushes, trees, and brush piles provide cover for the birds. Bird

Yellow Warbler

feeders — both seed and nectar — birdhouses, birdbaths, and misters provide food and water, adding to this already great bird habitat.

Birders are often rewarded with sights of birds not typically seen in their own backyards. Some birds seen in the park, such as the calliope hummingbird and Allen's hummingbird, are considered rare in the Houston area.

DIRECTIONS
Drive southwest on Fannin to Holcombe, then west on Holcombe (which becomes Bellaire) to Newcastle. Go south on Newcastle to Evergreen. Russ Pittman Park is located at the intersection of Newcastle and Evergreen. The Nature Discovery Center itself is housed in the historic Henshaw House at the north end of the park.

CONTACT INFORMATION
Nature Discovery Center Phone: 713-667-6550
Park hours are from 6:00am to 9:30pm daily.

HOUSTON LOOP
Houston Arboretum and Memorial Park

GPS 29.768, -95.45

4105 WOODWAY DRIVE
HOUSTON, TX 77024

KEY BIRDS
American woodcock, Kentucky and hooded warblers, several species of hummingbird

BEST SEASON
All seasons

AREA DESCRIPTION
1,466 acres; Mixed pine/oak woodlands

Opened in 1924, the Memorial Park covers approximately 1,466 acres and is one of the largest urban parks in the United States. The Houston Arboretum and Nature Center is located in Memorial Park and consists of 155 acres. A large portion of the park is in its natural condition, especially the area from south of Memorial Drive to Buffalo Bayou, which is the park's southern boundary. Birding is best in the picnic areas, the arboretum, and along the bayou. There are extensive loblolly pine groves in the park.

Trails from the arboretum center lead to Buffalo Bayou, where mixed pine/oak woodlands still support a diverse population of eastern woodland bird species. The park provides a place for nature in an area surrounded by urban sprawl.

The best birding is during migration fallouts, when Northerners with rain force the birds to land. Some of these are American woodcocks, pine warblers, as well as Swainson's, Kentucky, and hooded warblers. Birders should pay special attention for Mississippi kites feeding on dragonflies as they skim the treetops over the bayou during late August and early September.

Other species found in the park are ruby-throated hummingbird, wood thrush and, in some years, the red-eyed vireo and northern flicker.

Rufous Hummingbird

DIRECTIONS
Drive west on Evergreen Street to Loop 610, and then go north on Loop 610 to the Woodway exit. Drive east on Woodway to the Houston Arboretum and Memorial Park.

CONTACT INFORMATION
Houston Parks and Recreation phone: 713-837-0311
Web Site: http://www.houstonaudubon.org
Web Site: http://www.houstontx.gov/parks/index.html
Site is open for day use only.

HOUSTON LOOP
#83 HAS Edith L. Moore Bird Sanctuary

GPS ⊕ **29.769, -95.569**

440 WILCHESTER BLVD.
HOUSTON, TX 77079

KEY BIRDS
Owls, woodpeckers, northern mockingbird, cedar waxwing, summer tanager, northern cardinal

BEST SEASON
All seasons

AREA DESCRIPTION
Mixed oaks and pines

Edith Moore was a brave and intelligent nature-loving person. She was an early member of the National Audubon Society and was the earliest known member living in the Houston area. The Houston Audubon Society was incorporated in 1969 and she became a member and supporter, remaining a member for the rest of her life. When Houston expanded its limits and surrounded her log cabin along Rummel Creek, she hung onto her way of life.

This urban nature center contains the Houston Audubon Society (HAS) administrative offices, and provides information about their many sanctuaries including High Island and the Bolivar Flats, which may be obtained here. Although situated within a suburban neighborhood, the 17.5 acres of mixed oaks and pines still attract an interesting selection of woodland birds.

A few of the species found here are belted kingfisher, red-headed woodpecker, ruby-throated hummingbird, yellow-bellied sapsucker, pileated woodpecker, eastern kingbird, eastern wood-pewee, and scissor-tailed flycatcher.

DIRECTIONS
Drive west on Woodway to Loop 610, and go north on the Loop 610 service road to Memorial Drive. Proceed west on Memorial Drive to Wilchester, then south (only 0.1 mile) to the entrance to Edith L. Moore Nature Sanctuary.

CONTACT INFORMATION
Phone: 713-932-1639
Email: gmueller@hern.org
Open to the public 365 days a year, the site is open for day use only. The automatic gate currently opens at 7:00am and closes at 7:00pm (9:00pm in summer)

Cedar Waxwings

HOUSTON LOOP

#84 Joseph S. and Lucie H. Cullinan Park

GPS 29.635, -95.661

WEST OF ADDICKS-HOWELL ROAD AT OYSTER CREEK IN SUGAR LAND, TEXAS

KEY BIRDS
Wood duck, chimney swift, eastern wood-pewee, western kingbird

BEST SEASON
All seasons

AREA DESCRIPTION
Open areas with grass, some trees, and streamside habitat

Joseph S. and Lucie H. Cullinan Park at Oyster Creek is located in far southwest Houston, and has been a well-used natural green area and an asset to the City of Houston since it was dedicated as a park in 1989. The Houston Parks Board purchased the park with funds from the Nina J. Cullinan Estate and The Brown Foundation in partnership with the City of Houston. It consists of 750 acres in a rapidly growing area.

Enter the park and proceed to the parking area near the boardwalk. The observation platform at the end of the boardwalk offers an excellent view of the surrounding lake.

A few of the species you may encounter are white ibis, great and little blue herons, great egret, green heron, snowy egret, American coot, pie-billed grebe, common moorhen, whistling duck, ring-necked duck, redhead, scaup, wigeon, gadwall, blue and green-winged teal, northern shoveler, and wood duck.

DIRECTIONS
Go west on Memorial Drive to the intersection with TX 6. The next two sites are south of this intersection. Go south on TX 6 to the Joseph S. and Lucie H. Cullinan Park that is located on the west side of TX 6 before you reach US 90 in Sugar Land.

CONTACT INFORMATION
Located at Oyster Creek and Addicks-Howell Road, Sugar Land, TX 77498
Web Site: cullinanparkconservancy.org
Site open for day use only.

Tropical Kingbird

HOUSTON LOOP

#85 Barker and Addicks Reservoirs

GPS 29.785, -95.645

NORTH AND SOUTH SIDES OF INTERSTATE 10, 17 MILES FROM DOWNTOWN HOUSTON, TEXAS

KEY BIRDS
Woodpeckers, quail, doves

BEST SEASON
All seasons

AREA DESCRIPTION
Three major wildlife environments: open land, woodland, and wetland

Addicks and Barker Reservoirs is a flood damage reduction project in the Galveston District. Addicks and Barker Reservoirs prevent downstream flooding of Buffalo Bayou in the City of Houston. Covering 26,000 acres, these two dam areas have been holding birds in this location since the late 1950s.

Today the many acres of grasslands provide homes and

Ladderbacked Woodpecker

feeding areas for many species of birds and animals. This remains an undeveloped area in spite of the surrounding development.

Bird watchers can watch quail, doves, woodpeckers, and a large variety of songbirds on almost any day of the year in the open land habitat. It is not unusual to see a large variety of ducks. Wetlands within the reservoir are being restored, and a variety of waterbirds may be seen here such as herons, egrets, waterfowl, and several species of shorebirds.

Directions

Return north on TX 6 to Briarforest, then park in the lot on the west side of TX 6 for Barker Reservoir. Barker Reservoir may be entered by walking along the road that crosses the levee.

Contact Information

Phone: 281-497-0740
Web Site: http://www.swg.usace.army.mil/Addicks/
Site open for day use only.

HOUSTON LOOP
Bear Creek Park

#86

GPS ⊕ **29.828, -95.637**

3535 WAR MEMORIAL DRIVE
HOUSTON, TX 77084

KEY BIRDS
Swainson's, Kentucky, Canada, yellow-rumped, and hooded warblers, golden-crowned kinglet

BEST SEASON
All seasons

AREA DESCRIPTION
Mature pine and oak woodlands all along Bear Creek and open park grasslands habitat

SPECIAL ATTENTION: To all Bear Creek Pioneers Park birders and visitors, Bear Creek Park is subject to flooding at any time. Please be aware this park is part of a federally-owned reservoir and it is the priority of the U.S. Army Corps of Engineers to impound water when needed.

The birding habitat of Bear Creek Pioneers Park is comprised of the duck and goose ponds, plus trees and edge brush that encircle the park. The mature pine/oak woodlands along Bear Creek are home to a number of eastern woodland birds at their western limit on the trail.

Birds that may be encountered in the park are pine, Swainson's, Kentucky, and hooded warblers, and golden-crowned kinglet. The rusty blackbird is occasionally seen along with flocks of common grackles.

Hooded Warbler

DIRECTIONS
Return north on TX 6 to I-10. Continue north on TX 6 to Clay Road. Go east on Clay Road to War Memorial Drive.

CONTACT INFORMATION
Parks Administration Office: 281-496-2177
Phone: 281-531-1592
Email: pct3parks@hctx.net
Site open for day use only.

HOUSTON LOOP
Longenbaugh Waterfowl Pond

#87

GPS 29.889, -95.807

ON LONGENBAUGH ROAD IN THE KATY PRAIRIES

KEY BIRDS
Bald eagle, waterfowl, American golden-plover, Hudsonian godwit

BEST SEASON
Winter and migrations

AREA DESCRIPTION
Prairie habitat - however most of the native grassland has been converted to agricultural uses

This area, west of Houston, once consisted of little but endless stretches of prairie. Virtually all of the native grassland has been converted to agricultural uses, particularly rice growing.

Rice fields are artificial wetlands, and they provide important habitat for waterbirds. The Katy Prairie is one of the country's premier wintering waterfowl regions. As a youngster, it was a visit I made quite often to hunt as well as to observe birds and wildlife.

Bald eagles follow the waterfowl to this area, and it is not unusual to see several while birding on a winter's day. Plowed rice fields, particularly those that have been recently flooded, are irresistible to migrant shorebirds such as American golden-plover, Hudsonian godwit, two species of yellowlegs, pectoral sandpiper, and buff-breasted sandpiper. Birders should be on the lookout for both species of whistling duck in these same fields in summer.

Although waterfowl hunting is common in this area, the Longenbaugh Waterfowl Pond has been established by hunting guides as a refuge for ducks and geese. The numbers of dabblers here in winter can be mind-boggling, and bald eagles and northern harriers are frequently seen scavenging for dead ducks and geese on the levees.

To experience the Katy Prairie, you must wander the back roads. Please remember that these lands are private.

DO NOT TRESPASS UNDER ANY CIRCUMSTANCES.

Bald Eagle

DIRECTIONS

Return to Clay Road, and proceed west on Clay Road to Katy-Hockley Cutoff. Drive north on Katy-Hockley Cutoff to Longenbaugh Road and the Longenbaugh Waterfowl Pond.

CONTACT INFORMATION

Main Office, 3015 Richmond Avenue, Suite 230 Houston, TX 77098-3114
Phone: 713-523-6135
Email: info@katyprairie.org
Web Site: www.katyprairie.org
Site open for day use only.

HOUSTON LOOP
Warren Lake

#88

GPS ⊕ 29.551, -95.503

Located just off Warren Ranch Road between Jack Road and Betka Road, or three miles south of US 290 at Hockley, Texas

Key Birds
Geese

Best Season
Winter

Area Description
The area around the lake is open, allowing roosting geese to feel safe from predators

Warren Lake has become a major goose roosting site. Early mornings as well as late afternoons are the best times to see the geese as they leave and return to their roosting sites on the lake. Birders are advised to watch for the smaller white goose – Ross' goose – that will roost and feed with their larger cousins, the snow geese.

This lake offers the largest number and variety of wintering waterbirds in the state. Birders should watch this lake carefully from the road for resting waterfowl and wading birds. Other species may be double-crested cormorant, American white pelican, roseate spoonbill, osprey, bald eagle, and both varieties of whistling duck.

Canada Geese

DIRECTIONS

Continue north on Katy-Hockley Cutoff to Jack Road. Go west on Jack Road to Warren Ranch Road, then north on Warren Ranch Road to Warren Lake.

CONTACT INFORMATION

Katy Prairie Conservancy, 3015 Richmond Avenue, Suite 230, Houston, Texas 77098-3114
Phone: 713-523-6135
Web Site: www.katyprairie.org
Email: info@katyprairie.org
Site open for day use only.

HOUSTON LOOP
KPC Nelson Farm Preserve

#89

GPS 29.551, -95.523

On Sharp Road near Cypress Creek in Waller and Harris Counties

Key Birds
Various rails, waterfowl, moorhens, coots

Best Season
Winter

Area Description
1,675 acres; Remnant prairie with potholes, lakes, and wetlands

This 1,675-acre preserve is owned and operated by the Katy Prairie Conservancy, a nonprofit land trust. The conservancy recently acquired this property and is working to restore the wetlands that once was a common feature in this region. The production of rice is an important way the KPC uses to enhance wildlife habitat and to generate revenues used for the maintenance of the preserve and the wildlife. The prairie is also full of little bluestem, brownseed paspalum, and Indiangrass.

Moorhens, stilts, coots, and various rails also call these shallow ponds or depressions home.

The organization has constructed a blind along Sharp Road that allows birders to view one of these wetland enhancement projects. The isolated stand of pines adjacent to the Nelson Farm Preserve, known among local birders as Barn Owl Woods, may hold a number of interesting winter species such as red-breasted nuthatch and golden-crowned kinglet. Great horned and barn owls also reside in these pines.

Directions
Go back to Katy-Hockley Cutoff to Sharp Road, and then go west on Sharp Road to the Katy Prairie Conservancy (KPC) Nelson Farm Preserve.

American Coot

CONTACT INFORMATION

Katy Prairie Conservancy, 3015 Richmond Avenue, Suite 230, Houston, Texas 77098-314
Web Site: www.katyprairie.org
Email: info@katyprairie.org
Phone: 713-523-6135
Site open for day use only.

HOUSTON LOOP
#90 UTC Harper's Church Road

GPS  29.936, -96.09

WEST OF NELSON FARM PRESERVE

KEY BIRDS
Eastern phoebe, ash-throated flycatcher, yellow-rumped warbler, bay-breasted warbler, blue-headed vireo

BEST SEASON
Winter

AREA DESCRIPTION
Roadside trees, tall and low brush with grassland habitats

Driving to this location you will drive into and through the very productive pastures and fields. Continuing west toward the Brazos River, the bottomland forests here can provide some of the best woodland birding in the area.

Wintering passerines, such as Harris' and fox sparrows and rufous-sided towhee can be spotted. In addition, watch for the ash-throated flycatcher and bay-breasted warbler.

Birders may see eastern Bewick's wrens and Harris' sparrows in the thickets, and eastern bluebirds on the power lines and fence posts. There will also be a variety of woodland birds such as the eastern phoebe, blue-headed vireo, yellow-rumped warbler or "butter-butt" in the pecan forests near the river.

Yellow-rumped Warbler

Watch the increasing huisache thickets as you near Monaville. This type of habitat welcomes the ladder-backed woodpecker, ash-throated flycatcher, and eastern and Bewick's wrens during the winter.

Directions
Continue west on Sharp Road (which becomes a gravel road in Waller County) to Pattison Road, then south on Pattison Road to Morrison Road. Proceed east on Morrison Road to FM 2855, then south on FM 2855 to FM 529. Finally, go west on FM 529 (be patient as FM 529 is briefly diverted to FM 362) to Stefka, then north on Stefka to Harper's Church Road.

Contact Information
No contact information available.
Site open for day use only.

HOUSTON LOOP
Stephen F. Austin State Park

#91

GPS ⊕ **29.818, -96.113**

JUST OFF FM331 NORTH OF SAN FELIPE, TEXAS

KEY BIRDS
Pileated woodpecker, red-headed woodpecker

BEST SEASON
Migrations and winter

AREA DESCRIPTION
Brazos River bottomland forests, including wetland, aquatic, and hardwood forest

This beautiful 664-acre recreation park occupies the moss-draped pecan bottoms along the Brazos River and the Mexican land granted to Stephen F. Austin, "Father of Texas," for the first Anglo colony in Texas. The habitat in this state park is similar to that found along Harper's Church Road (Brazos River bottomland forests).

Birders may spot nesting pileated woodpeckers, as well as many other nesting species.

Information and prices are subject to change. Please call the park or park information (1-800-792-1112) for the latest updates. The daily entrance fee is charged in addition to any facility fees, unless otherwise stated. A Texas State Park Pass will allow you and your guests to enjoy unlimited visits for one year to more than 90 state parks, without paying the daily entrance fee, in addition to other benefits.

Red-headed Woodpecker

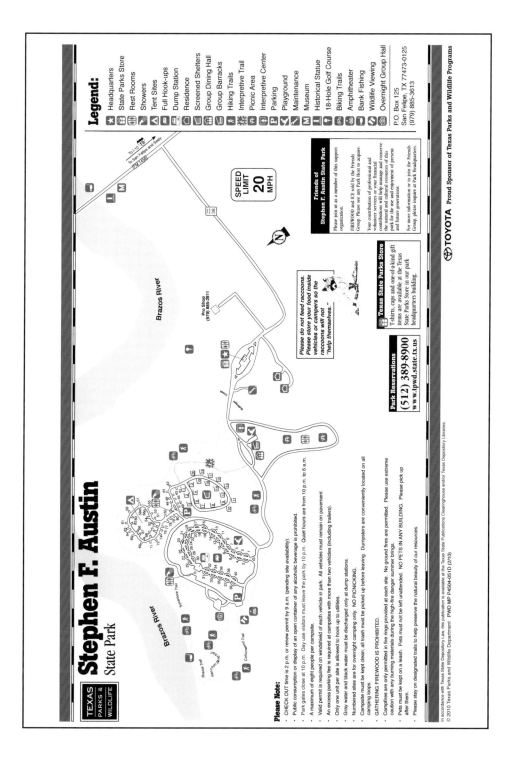

TEXAS PARKS & WILDLIFE

Stephen F. Austin
State Park

Legend:

- Headquarters
- State Parks Store
- Rest Rooms
- Showers
- Tent Sites
- Full Hook-ups
- Dump Station
- Residence
- Screened Shelters
- Group Dining Hall
- Group Barracks
- Hiking Trails
- Interpretive Trail
- Picnic Area
- Interpretive Center
- Parking
- Playground
- Maintenance
- Museum
- Historical Statue
- 18-Hole Golf Course
- Biking Trails
- Amphitheater
- Bank Fishing
- Wildlife Viewing
- Overnight Group Hall

P.O. Box 125
San Felipe, TX 77473-0125
(979) 885-3613

Brazos River

To I-10
To San Felipe and Sealy
FM 1458

SPEED LIMIT **20** MPH

Brazos River

Pro Shop
(979) 885-2811

**Friends of
Stephen F. Austin State Park**

Please join us as a member of this support organization.

FIREWOOD and ICE sold by the Friends Group. Please see any Park Host to acquire.

Your contribution of professional and volunteer services or your financial contributions will help manage and conserve the natural and cultural resources of this park for the use and enjoyment of present and future generations.

For more information or to join the Friends Group, please inquire at Park headquarters.

Please do not feed raccoons. Please store your food inside vehicles or campers so the raccoons will not "help themselves."

Texas State Parks Store

T-shirts, caps and one-of-a-kind gift items are available at the Texas State Parks Store in our park headquarters building.

Park Reservations
(512) 389-8900
www.tpwd.state.tx.us

TOYOTA Proud Sponsor of Texas Parks and Wildlife Programs

Please Note:

- CHECK OUT time is 2 p.m. or renew permit by 9 a.m. (pending site availability).
- Public consumption or display of an open container of any alcoholic beverage is prohibited.
- Park gates close at 10 p.m. Day use visitors must leave the park by 10 p.m. Quiet hours are from 10 p.m. to 6 a.m.
- A maximum of eight people per campsite.
- Valid permit is required on windshield of each vehicle in park. All vehicles must remain on pavement
- An excess parking fee is required at campsites with more than two vehicles (including trailers).
- Only one unit per site is allowed to hook up to utilities.
- Gray water and black water must be discharged only at dump stations.
- Numbered sites are for overnight camping only. NO PICNICKING.
- Campsite must be kept clean; all trash must be picked up before leaving. Dumpsters are conveniently located on all camping loops.
- GATHERING FIREWOOD IS PROHIBITED.
- Campfires are only permitted in fire rings provided at each site. No ground fires are permitted. Please use extreme caution with any burning materials during the high-fire danger summer brings.
- Pets must be kept on a leash. Pets must not be left unattended. NO PETS IN ANY BUILDING. Please pick up after them.
- Please stay on designated trails to help preserve the natural beauty of our resources.

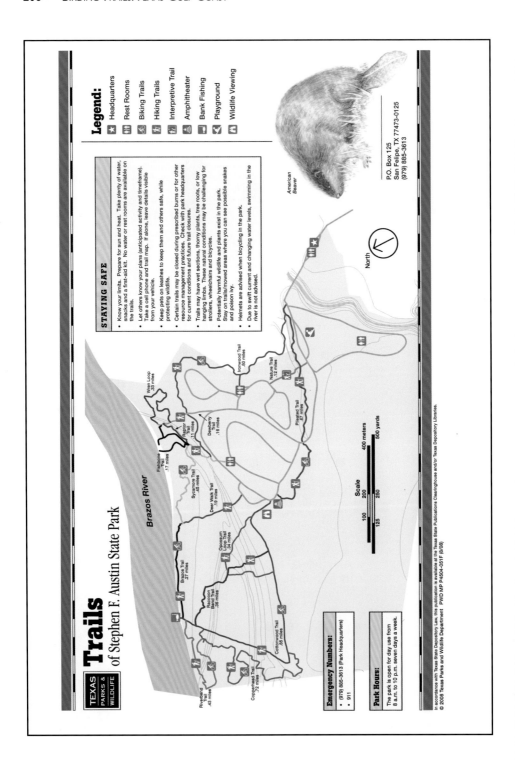

Trails
of Stephen F. Austin State Park

TEXAS PARKS & WILDLIFE

Legend:

- ★ Headquarters
- 👥 Rest Rooms
- 🚲 Biking Trails
- 🥾 Hiking Trails
- 👁 Interpretive Trail
- 📢 Amphitheater
- 🎣 Bank Fishing
- 🛝 Playground
- 🔭 Wildlife Viewing

STAYING SAFE

- Know your limits. Prepare for sun and heat. Take plenty of water, snacks and a first-aid kit. No water or rest rooms are available on the trails.
- Let others know your plans (anticipated activity and timeframe). Take a cell phone and trail map. If alone, leave details visible from your vehicle.
- Keep pets on leashes to keep them and others safe, while protecting wildlife.
- Certain trails may be closed during prescribed burns or for other resource management practices. Check with park headquarters for current conditions and future trail closures.
- Trails may have wet sections, thorny plants, tree roots, or low hanging limbs. These natural conditions may be challenging for strollers, wheelchairs and bicycles.
- Potentially harmful wildlife and plants exist in the park. Stay on trails/mowed areas where you can see possible snakes and poison ivy.
- Helmets are advised when bicycling in the park.
- Due to swift current and changing water levels, swimming in the river is not advised.

American Beaver

P.O. Box 125
San Felipe, TX 77473-0125
(979) 885-3613

North

Brazos River

Wren Loop .33 miles

Fishbone Trail .17 miles

Raptor Trail .11 miles

Dewberry Trail .16 miles

Ironwood Trail .80 miles

Nature Trail .12 miles

Pileated Trail .67 miles

Sycamore Trail .45 miles

Deer Walk Trail .19 miles

Opossum Loop Trail .34 miles

Brazos Trail .27 miles

Raccoon Bend Trail .38 miles

Cottonwood Trail .85 miles

Riverbend Trail .43 miles

Copperhead Trail .72 miles

Scale

100 200 400 meters
125 250 500 yards

Emergency Numbers:
- (979) 885-3613 (Park Headquarters)
- 911

Park Hours:
The park is open for day use from 8 a.m. to 10 p.m. seven days a week.

In accordance with Texas State Depository Law, this publication is available at the Texas State Publications Clearinghouse and/or Texas Depository Libraries.

© 2008 Texas Parks and Wildlife Department   PWD MP P4504–051F (8/08)

DIRECTIONS

From Harper's Church Road drive west on FM 529 to FM 331, then south on FM 331 to Stephen F. Austin SP. Watch for the signs directing you to the park.

CONTACT INFORMATION

P O Box 125, San Felipe TX, 77473-0125
Phone: 979-885-3613
Web Site: http://www.tpwd.state.tx.us/business/park_reservations/#alert

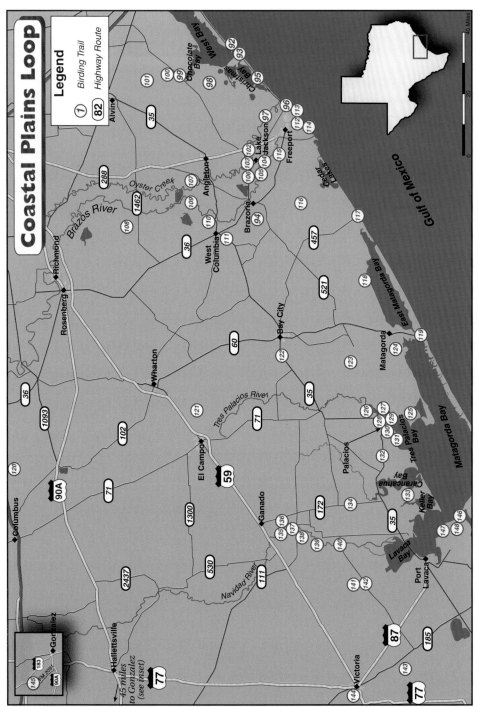

Coastal Plains Loop

Legend

1 Birding Trail

82 Highway Route

Gulf of Mexico

© Wilderness Adventures Press

40 Miles

Coastal Plains

One of my favorite birding areas in Texas reaches as far north as the town of Gonzales then to the southern stretches of Port Lavaca and Matagorda Bay. Driving either Highway 59 or Texas 35 along the coast and stopping to explore the various locations, the birds are everywhere.

Birders will find that some of the national and state wildlife management areas will have periods where they are closed for hunting. A minor inconvenience when you consider that hunter's dollars paid for these areas.

Leaving the Rosenberg area on Highway 59 South, visit the locations south of Ganado on the way to the coast. This is a great area and you will not be disappointed with the birds spotted here.

A word to the wise, there are two ways to drive. First there is driving to get somewhere, observing the speed limit signs. And second, driving to bird an area, which means slowing down and taking your time watching the fences, trees, shrubs, and water edges as you go. The Coastal Plains Loop is great for the latter.

Coastal Plains Locations

92. San Luis Pass County Park
93. San Luis Pass
94. Christmas Bay - Follett's Island
95. Bluewater Highway
96. Surfside Jetty Park
97. Village of Oyster Creek Municipal Park
98. Brazoria NWR
99. Amoco (Chocolate Bayou) Nature Trail
100. UTC Amoco Wetlands Trail
101. Solutia Prairie
102. Brazosport Nature Center and Planetarium Nature Trail
103. Brazosport Dow Chemical Plant Access
104. Sea Center Texas
105. Dow Centennial Bottomlands Park
106. Lake Jackson Wilderness Park
107. Brazos River County Park
108. Brazos Bend State Park
109. Manor and Eagle Nest Lakes
110. Varner-Hogg Plantation
111. Hanson Riverside County Park
112. Quintana Neotropical Bird Sanctuary
113. Quintana Beach County Park
114. UTC Bryan Beach
115. Justin Hurst WMA
116. San Bernard NWR
117. Sargent Beach
118. Big Boggy National Wildlife Refuge
119. Matagorda County Jetty Park/Lower Colorado River Authority
120. Attwater Prairie Chicken National Wildlife Refuge

Coastal Plains Locations

121. Texas R.I.C.E. /Pierce Ranch Waterbird Viewing Site
122. Matagorda County Birding and Nature Center
123. South Texas Project Prairie Wetlands
124. Mad Island WMA, Clive Runnells Family Mad Island Marsh Preserve
125. Oyster Lake Road
126. Cash Creek
127. Bayshore Drive
128. Trull Marsh
129. Palacios Waterfront and Texas Baptist Encampment
130. Lookout Point
131. Palacios Marine Education Center Nature Trail
132. Perry R. Bass State Marine Fisheries Research Station
133. Port Alto and Olivia
134. Formosa-Tejano Wetlands
135. Lake Texana Mustang Creek Boat Ramp
136. Mustang Creek Recreation Area
137. Lake Texana Park and Campground
138. Brackenridge Plantation Park and Campground
139. Palmetto Bend Dam
140. Lavaca/Navidad Estuary
141. Bennett Park
142. Garcitas Creek Boat Ramp
143. Dupont Wetlands
144. Riverside Park and Athey Nature Sanctuary
145. Palmetto State Park
146. Port Lavaca Bird Sanctuary
147. Magnolia Beach
148. Magic Ridge

COASTAL PLAINS

San Luis Pass County Park

GPS 29.079, -95.131

14001 CR 257 (BLUE WATER HIGHWAY) FREEPORT, TX 77541

KEY BIRDS
Northern gannet, gulls, terns, and magnificent frigatebird

BEST SEASON
All seasons

AREA DESCRIPTION
Beach and sand flats

This 15-acre county park offers birders another view of San Luis Pass including the sand flats, which are often the site of flocks of gulls and terns. Northern gannets often venture into the swift waters of San Luis Pass to fish. Glass the air above the beach and near-shore waters in summer and fall for magnificent frigatebirds.

A few of the species also found in and around this park are common goldeneye, red-breasted merganser, common loon, reddish egret, American oystercatcher, marbled godwit, black skimmer, plus several species of gulls and terns. Both Nelson's, sharp-tailed, and seaside sparrows may also be found in the area near the edge of the bay.

Immature Ring-billed Gull

The park offers overnight accommodations in cabins and with a full-service, paved RV campsite. Fees are charged.

DIRECTIONS

Driving from Galveston, cross San Luis Pass on the toll bridge and continue southwest on the Bluewater Highway (Brazoria CR 257). Immediately after crossing the bridge, exit west for San Luis Pass County Park.

CONTACT INFORMATION

Phone: 979-233-6026 or 800-372-7578
Email: sanluis@brazoria-county.com
Park office hours are 8:00am to 5:00pm; closed 12:00pm to 1:00pm for lunch. Office is closed on Mondays.

COASTAL PLAINS
San Luis Pass

#93

GPS 29.081, -95.123

SOUTHWESTERN END OF GALVESTON ISLAND

KEY BIRDS
Least tern, black skimmer, both species of pelican, red-breasted merganser, and Bonaparte's gull

BEST SEASON
All seasons

AREA DESCRIPTION
Saltwater beaches and open pastureland

San Luis Pass is a strait of water at the southwestern end of Galveston Island off the shores of Texas. It connects the sheltered waters of West Bay to the open Gulf of Mexico. Only the Bolivar Flats can challenge the number of species available to birders that can be seen at San Luis Pass. Birders can expect to spot waterbirds in seemingly endless numbers on the sand flats and extending into the bay.

Watch for both species of pelican as well as Bonaparte's gulls and red-breasted mergansers feeding in the pass during the winter months. When the tides are changing, this pass attracts large numbers of shorebirds feeding on baitfish being carried through the pass.

Snowy and piping plovers are common during the cooler months while least terns and black skimmers will try to nest on the sand. Wilson's plovers as well as horned larks will be seen nesting the sand dunes.

Please, avoid disturbing the birds during nesting season.

Over 25,000 black terns stage here in late summer - August through early September - and magnificent frigatebirds roost on the pilings in West Bay from late April through late September.

Most beaches are closed to vehicles, but San Luis Pass is the exception, so this makes birding even all the more enjoyable. Check the many miles of open pastureland for feeding shorebirds and waders on west FM 3005.

Warning: *The sand here can be extremely soft, so please be careful when driving on the flats.*

Black Skimmer

DIRECTIONS
Drive west on FM 3005 to the west end of Galveston Island and San Luis Pass. You may access the flats by exiting FM 3005 immediately before the toll bridge.

CONTACT INFORMATION
No contact information available at this time. Birders may try the web site: http://www.galveston.com/birding/
Site open for day use only.

COASTAL PLAINS

#94 Christmas Bay – Follett's Island

GPS ⊕ 29.0256, -95.623

ON THE BLUEWATER HIGHWAY NORTHEAST OF FREEPORT, TEXAS

KEY BIRDS
Snowy and piping plovers, gulls, and terns

BEST SEASON
All seasons

AREA DESCRIPTION
Gulf prairies and marshes

Follett's Island is the thin strip of land separating Christmas Bay from the mainland. Caution should be taken however if the tide is low; driving carefully on the hard-packed sand beaches is allowed. Birders must obtain a beach pass.

Christmas Bay is a high quality subsystem estuary and has not been greatly altered by human activity. The prairies have extensive fresh and saline marshes and are transected by meandering streams that flow southeast into the western bay estuary.

The waters of Christmas Bay to the mean high tide line constitute the preserve of approximately 4,173 acres. The preserve is one of the most ecologically productive bays of the Galveston complex.

Royal Tern

Attracted to the bay are large numbers of redhead ducks that winter on this bay. Birders should also watch for Wilson's plovers and horned larks that will nest in the dunes near the shore. With a current beach pass (required) birders may drive the beach from this point to Surfside. On the drive, birders will see several species of gulls, terns, and shorebirds. During migration, red knots may be spotted along this beach. Slow down and see more birds.

There are five beach-access roads along the beach. Birders should watch for gulls, snowy and piping plovers, and terns all along the beaches and water. Other interesting birds along this stretch of beach are royal and sandwich terns. In 1999, Texas' only yellow-footed gull was seen near Beach Access Road number five.

The numerous brown pelicans – one of the two species of pelican – may be seen diving into schools of menhaden. This also is a good area to spot several varieties of sea ducks that at times will be close to the beach.

DIRECTIONS

Drive southwest on the Bluewater Highway to Christmas Bay and the Christmas Bay Scenic View located 3.2 miles from San Luis Pass.

CONTACT INFORMATION

Brazoria County Parks Department Administrative Offices, 313 W. Mulberry, Angleton, TX 77515
Phone: 979-864-1541
Site open for day use only.

COASTAL PLAINS
Bluewater Highway

#95

GPS 29.022, -95.195

BLUEWATER HIGHWAY EXTENDS FROM SURFSIDE BEACH TO GALVESTON

KEY BIRDS
Yellow-headed blackbird, American kestrel, peregrine falcon, merlin, and willet

BEST SEASON
All seasons, weather permitting

AREA DESCRIPTION
Sandy beaches and dunes

This is a 40-mile drive along the Texas Coast from Surfside Beach to the bustling port and tourist center of Galveston. The drive follows the coast, starting in a section that is relatively empty and quiet and ending in the city of Galveston. As along most of the Texas Coast, there are only a few trees near the shore except where they have been planted.

Wind, salt, and occasional hurricanes make it difficult for trees to become established. But the beaches and dunes have a stark beauty of their own. Behind the beaches are low dune ridges that are often covered with flowers, such as the purple goat-foot morning glory. Marshes flank the back bays and harbor a tremendous variety of birds, fish, and other creatures.

Willet

Peregrine falcon, merlin, and American kestrel are commonly seen along the beach during both migrations. Birders should watch for the yellow-headed blackbird mixed in with other species of blackbirds that flock along this road during migration. According to some birders and TPW, bobolinks have been spotted in pastures with fields of spiderwort.

DIRECTIONS

Drive southwest on Bluewater Highway to TX 332 in Surfside. The bay may be accessed by driving to the Swan Lake Boat Ramp or the Lazy Palms Boat Ramp.

CONTACT INFORMATION

Texas Department of Transportation
125 East 11th Street
Austin, TX 78701
Phone: 512-305-9500

COASTAL PLAINS
Surfside Jetty Park

GPS 28.938, -95.295

301 PARKVIEW RD.
FREEPORT, TX 77541

KEY BIRDS
Northern gannet, scoter, mergansers, and other water birds and waders

BEST SEASON
Winter

AREA DESCRIPTION
Open water-front park with palm trees and shoreline habitats with rocky jetties and low tide beaches

There has been considerable work done expanding this jetty. The hike along the jetty to its end may now be accomplished with secure footing.

These mostly protected and calm waters are where birders have seen northern gannets while birding the jetties. The rare scoter and some fish-eating mergansers can also be viewed feeding here.

DIRECTIONS
From the intersection of the Bluewater Highway and TX 332 in Surfside, continue southwest across TX 332 on Fort Velasco Drive to Parkview Road. Go south on Parkview Road to Surfside Jetty Park.

CONTACT INFORMATION
Phone: 979-239-3547 or contact the Brazoria County Parks Department Administrative Offices at 313 W. Mulberry, Angleton, TX 77515
Phone: 979-864-1541
Site open for day use only.

Common Merganser

COASTAL PLAINS

#97 Village of Oyster Creek Municipal Park/Trail

GPS⊕ 29.001, -95.328

Oyster Creek, Texas

Key Birds
Red-shouldered hawk, belted kingfisher

Best Season
Migrations

Area Description
Waterfront habitat with some low brush and open pastures with some manicured areas and houses

Driving from Lexington Boulevard, the three-mile hike and bike trail is accessible on Dulles Avenue. The Greenbelt Trail has a rock-lined waterfall feature and a pond. These features are located adjacent to Oyster Creek and near the Hwy 6 entrance to the park.

Watch the trees along Oyster Creek for migrants as you make the drive to Brazoria NWR. Take this drive slowly and watch power poles around the parking area for red-shouldered hawks seen on the telephone lines.

Directions
From Surfside, drive west on TX 332 to FM 523, then go north on FM 523 to Village of Oyster Creek Municipal Park.

Contact Information
Alvin-Manvel Area Chamber of Commerce
Phone: 281-331-3944
Web Site: www.ci.alvin.tx.us/
Or contact: The Oyster Creek Parks and Recreation Department
Phone: 281- 275-2885
Email: pab@sugarlandtx.gov
Site open for day use only.

Belted Kingfisher

COASTAL PLAINS
#98 Brazoria National Wildlife Refuge

GPS 29.153, -95.299

ON THE SHORES OF BASTROP, CHRISTMAS, AND DRUM BAYS NORTHEAST OF FREEPORT, TEXAS

KEY BIRDS
Dowitchers, dunlin, lesser yellowlegs, semipalmated and western sandpipers

BEST SEASON
All seasons

AREA DESCRIPTION
Coastal grassland, bluestem prairie, mud flats, fresh and saltwater marshes, and a bewildering assortment of potholes, lakes, and streams

This is a refuge that fully endorses the concepts of the Federal Waterfowl Stamp by providing duck and goose hunting as a large part of their management plan. Birders may use the waterfowl stamp as their entry method instead of cash. These stamps are what pay for this and other National Wildlife Refuges.
Birders will enjoy the gravel Big Slough Auto Route, a 7.5-mile

Long-billed Dowitchers

car tour that runs through the Big Slough Recreation Area, the heart of Brazoria. It wraps around Olney and Teal Ponds and accesses Big Slough and Rogers Pond. Here again, slow is best. The road is also open to biking.

There is a new observation platform built by the Friends of the Brazoria NWR that overlooks Teal Pond and allows close views of the waterfowl that rest and feed there. Geese and sandhill cranes will also be found on the pond or along the shallows.

The refuge has also built a nature trail across Big Slough, behind the visitor's pavilion. The refuge hosts open houses throughout the year from 8:00am to 4:00pm on the first full weekend of each month and on the third weekend of each month from November through April. Otherwise, access to the refuge is restricted.

In addition to the remarkable diversity of waterbirds and waterfowl that reside here, this refuge contains over 5,000 acres of native bluestem prairie. Watch here for sedge wren and Le Conte's, Henslow's, and grasshopper sparrows.

Larger birds include white-tailed kites and white-tailed hawks that will frequent these prairies in the winter. The tidal flats at low tide often overflow with shorebirds.

The Western Hemisphere Shorebird Reserve Network recently designated the Brazoria Refuge Complex as an internationally significant shorebird site. The refuge has hosted over 100,000 shorebirds during spring migrations as well as semipalmated and lesser yellowlegs, dowitchers, western sandpiper, and dunlin.

Large numbers of shorebirds and waterfowl are seen along the shallow water shorelines, marshes, and freshwater ponds. Snow geese rest and feed here. They flourish on the roots of Olney's bulrush and other salt marsh plants. They rest in shallow waters with a clear view of their predators. Flights and roosting areas of snow geese can be watched in the winter.

Many years, the refuge will be the host for a warbler "fallout" during the early spring. This is because of its bottomland forests and willow trees. If the weather is warm, it will cause the moist air heading north to collide with cold dry air heading south, causing heavy rains and wind. This causes the small birds to fall out of the sky to find shelter in the trees. Hundreds of birds and dozens of species fall into a single area of trees.

About half or less of the 43,388-acre refuge is open to the public, leaving a vast landscape as wildlife sanctuary. A hike on one of the three hiking trails and the three-mile auto tour will allow birders a full day of watching. The three-mile auto tour is at the entrance from County Road 227 and passes through private lands.

DIRECTIONS
Travel north on FM 523 to CR 227, then east on CR 227 to Brazoria NWR.

CONTACT INFORMATION
Brazoria National Wildlife Refuge 24907 FM 2004, Angleton, TX 77515
E-mail: jamesdingee@fws.gov
Phone: 979-964-4011
Brazoria and San Bernard National Wildlife Refuges, 1212 North Velasco, Suite 200, Angleton, Texas 77515
Email: R2RW_BRZ@mail.fws.gov
Web Site: http://sturgeon.irm1.r2.fws.gov:80/u2/refuges/texas/brazoria.html
Phone: 409-849-7771
Site access restricted. Call ahead.

COASTAL PLAINS

#99 Amoco (Chocolate Bayou) Nature Trail

GPS⊕ 29.236, -95.181

ON TEXAS FM 2004 EAST OF ANGLETON, TEXAS

KEY BIRDS
American golden-plover, whimbrel, and buff-breasted sandpiper

BEST SEASON
All seasons

AREA DESCRIPTION
Flooded rice fields with some trees and small wooded areas

All along CR 227 and FM 2004 there are grasslands that give cover and feeding to several species of prey animals. These open areas of grass and the abundance of prey bring in several species of raptors. Birders should pay special attention to the white-tailed hawks that have been spotted across FM 2004 from the Amoco plant. They have also nested in this same area.

Least Grebes

Visiting birders are quite impressed when they spot crested caracaras along the road, known as the bird on the Mexican National flag. In fact, the crested caracara is more of a vulture than a bird of prey. This may be confirmed by watching to see how many of this species you spot in one location. Experts have said, "If you see more than one caracara in a single location, there is a better than not chance something is dead."

During the fall and winter the rice fields in this area are flooded. Birds attracted to these flooded fields are whimbrels, buff-breasted sandpipers, and American golden-plovers.

To access the nature trail – owned by Amoco Company – birders should park on the west side of FM 2004 near the Mustang Bayou Bridge. Amoco has been developed for bird watching, knowing the trees here along Mustang Bayou attract migrating birds.

DIRECTIONS
Drive northeast on CR 227 to FM 2004. Travel northeast on FM 2004 to the Amoco (Chocolate Bayou) Nature Trail.

CONTACT INFORMATION
No contact information available at this time.
Site open for day use only.

COASTAL PLAINS

#100 UTC Amoco Wetlands Trail

GPS 29.257, -95.186

ON FM2917, EAST OF ANGLETON, TEXAS

KEY BIRDS
American bittern and green heron

BEST SEASON
All seasons

AREA DESCRIPTION
Prairie habitat with ponds and wetlands habitat

The wetland ponds are located by following the road to an observation platform that has been built for birders. Hikers can pass through a sizable prairie, and birders would be well advised to listen for sedge wrens in the spring by carefully approaching the pond and its surrounding wetlands.

Migrant water birds and waders are often spotted feeding in the wetlands. Green heron, killdeer, greater yellowlegs, lesser yellowlegs, American bittern, common snipe, rock dove, mourning dove, Inca dove, black-necked stilt and belted kingfisher can be seen if you watch carefully.

DIRECTIONS
Continue northeast on FM 2004 to FM 2917, and then go 1.1 miles northwest on FM 2917 to the Amoco Wetlands Trail.

CONTACT INFORMATION
Site open for day use only.

Green Heron

COASTAL PLAINS
Solutia Prairie

#101

GPS 29.269, -95.191

ON CHOCOLATE BAYOU JUST OFF TX 332

KEY BIRDS
Kestrels, bluebirds, raptors, sedge wren, and Le Conte's sparrow

BEST SEASON
Migrations and winter

AREA DESCRIPTION
Native prairie habitat

Covering 2,500-acres, the Chocolate Bayou Facility is made up of a selected 500 acres of managed habitat. Among its goals, the program works for the expansion of bird species, the reestablishment of a prairie environment, establishing native trees of the east bank of New Bayou, and the reestablishment of the native wildflower population which is known to attract wild birds. This program hopes to create an increased facility, community awareness, and sensitivity to the wildlife portion of the project.

In 2000, a prescribed burn of 80 acres of native prairie habitat was conducted. Part of the overall plan was to eliminate the invasive Chinese tallow tree. Raptor perches and kestrel nesting boxes have been added to the already existing bluebird, purple martin, and owl boxes/houses.

There is also a tract of coastal prairie where sedge wrens and Le Conte's sparrows are seen and heard on a semi-regular basis.

DIRECTIONS
Drive on FM 2917 to the Solutia Prairie - 2 miles from FM 2004.

CONTACT INFORMATION
The Wildlife Habitat Council, 8737 Colesville Road, Suite 800, Silver Spring, MD 20910
Phone: 301-588-8994
Email: whc@wildlifehc.org
Site open for day use only.

American Kestrel

COASTAL PLAINS
#102 Brazosport Nature Center and Planetarium Nature Trail

GPS 29.046, -95.407

ON THE EAST CAMPUS OF THE BRAZOSPORT COLLEGE IN CLUTE, TEXAS

KEY BIRDS
Quail, wading birds, and waterfowl

BEST SEASON
Migrations and winter

AREA DESCRIPTION
A mosaic of coastal grasslands, marshes, swamps, beach, and open Gulf waters

The Texas cities of Clute, Lake Jackson, Oyster Creek, Freeport, and Jones Creek combined to make up what is called the Brazosport Area. What these towns have in common is they are all located at or near the mouth of the Brazos River.

Bordering the Brazos are tall river trees that need a steady supply of water. The river works together with swamps, beaches, coastal grasslands, marshes, and open Gulf waters to make the correct habitats for local and migrating species.

Birders should note that the Freeport Christmas Bird Count takes place normally near the end of December. The Freeport count has recorded more species of birds that rank them high in the national bird counts and has frequently led the nation in the number of species recorded. Birders should look into the Migration Celebration held in the spring.

The trail begins across from the nature center and winds along the river bottom through the trees. This particular area is located on Oyster Creek.

DIRECTIONS
From the intersection of FM 523 and TX 332, travel west on TX 332 to BUS 288. Go north on BUS 288 to College Blvd., then west on College Blvd. to Brazosport College. Take the first entrance, and park at the Brazosport Arts and Sciences Center. This is where the NCAP is housed.

CONTACT INFORMATION
Contact the Brazosport Convention and Visitors Council for information about the Migration Celebration annual festival.
Website: http://www.visitbrazosport.com/
Site open for day use only.

Snowy Egret

COASTAL PLAINS
#103 Brazosport Dow Chemical Plant Access

GPS 29.044, -95.453

400 COLLEGE DRIVE
LAKE JACKSON, TX 77566

KEY BIRDS
Black skimmers

BEST SEASON
Nesting season

AREA DESCRIPTION
Mosaic of coastal grasslands, marshes, swamps, beach, and open Gulf waters

The parking lots within the plant have been taken over by colonies of least and gull-billed terns, as well as a larger number of black skimmers.

Dow Chemical has preserved these sites for the nesting birds since 1968. During nesting season, tours are conducted by Dow personnel so birders can watch these colonies. The tour may be joined each Wednesday at 2:00pm during nesting season. The tours start at the Dow administrative building located about 0.8 mile south of the intersection of BUS 288 and TX 332.

Birders should also check out if other tours are available.

DIRECTIONS
Return to the intersection of BUS 288 and TX 332, and then continue south on BUS 288 to Dow Chemical.

CONTACT INFORMATION
Phone: 409-265-3376
Web Site: tgn.net/~snark/ncap/ncap2.html
Reservations for the bus tours are required. Call: 409-238-2323.

Black Skimmer

COASTAL PLAINS

#104 Sea Center Texas

GPS ⊕ 29.017, -95.445

300 MEDICAL CENTER DRIVE
LAKE JACKSON, TX 77566

KEY BIRDS
Mostly waterbirds

BEST SEASON
All seasons

AREA DESCRIPTION
A marine ecosystem with two wetlands, a 3.78-acre freshwater marsh, and a 1.31-acre saltwater marsh

The Gulf Coast Conservation Association, in cooperation with Texas Parks and Wildlife and Dow Chemical built this facility for an aquarium and also a marine education center.

The hatchery is capable of producing over 20 million fingerlings annually, mostly spotted sea trout and red drum to be released into Texas baywaters.

In spite of the general purpose of Sea Center to be a marine ecosystem, there are two small wetlands that have been made that attract many species of waterbirds.

The center also has an outdoor interpretive building, a boardwalk, as well as the indoor aquaria for visitors to enjoy.

DIRECTIONS
Drive west on TX 332 to Plantation Drive in Lake Jackson, and then go south on Plantation Drive to Medical Drive.

CONTACT INFORMATION
Phone: 409-292-0100
Site open for day use only.

Stilt Sandpiper

COASTAL PLAINS
#105 Dow Centennial Bottomlands Park

GPS 29.026, -95.46

93 LAKE ROAD
LAKE JACKSON, TX 77566

KEY BIRDS
Migrating species

BEST SEASON
Migrations and winter

AREA DESCRIPTION
Bottomland forests

Dow Chemical donated this 240-acre tract to Lake Jackson to commemorate the company's 100th anniversary. Located behind the MacLean Park Pavilion, the preserve, with its extensive bottomland forests, is dedicated as a nature sanctuary.

The Columbia Bottomlands forests are found along the Brazos River. Many birders and scientists know this as area one of the most important migratory vectors for landbirds in this country.

Migrants pass through these woodlands each spring by the millions as the trans-Gulf migratory species near the end of their travels. Birders will need to be here at the right time – Lady Luck comes into play. Without the correct timing, birders may see only a small number of migrating birds.

American Robin

DIRECTIONS

Drive west on TX 332 to Oak Drive, and then go south on Oak Drive to MacLean Park and the entrance to Dow Centennial Bottomlands Park.

CONTACT INFORMATION

Phone 979-297-4533
Website:
http://www.ci.lake-jackson.tx.us/city_dept/parks_dowcentennial.html
Site open for day use only.

COASTAL PLAINS

#106 Lake Jackson Wilderness Park

GPS 29.049, -95.478

ON LAKE JACKSON WILDERNESS PARK ROAD, APPROXIMATELY 1.5 MILES WEST OF OAK DRIVE

KEY BIRDS
Neotropical migrants

BEST SEASON
Migrations and winter

AREA DESCRIPTION
Dense thickets, bottomland forest, and evergreen bottomlands

Birders should be cautioned that the road leading into the park is unpaved. However, it will take you into dense thickets and bottomland forests where a slow trip allows entry into this area. The pools located on the roadside may permit birders to spot a colorful wood duck.

These lush, mostly evergreen bottomlands that cover 477 acres will stay green during the winter, and birders may find a number of neotropical migrant birds spending the winter and feeding on numerous species of insects. These birds normally would continue on to their wintering areas in Central and South America.

DIRECTIONS
Drive west on Lake Jackson Wilderness Park Rd., which is located approximately 1.5 miles west of Oak Drive.

CONTACT INFORMATION
Phone 979-297-4533
Website: http://www.ci.lake-jackson.tx.us/city_dept/parks_dowcentennial.html
Site open for day use only.

Female Painted Bunting

COASTAL PLAINS

#107 Brazos River County Park

GPS 29.204, -95.506

3035 COUNTY ROAD 30, WEST OF ANGLETON, TEXAS

KEY BIRDS
Wood duck, yellow-crowned night-heron

BEST SEASON
All seasons

AREA DESCRIPTION
Brazos riverside habitats

This county park is a 40-acre day-use wooded park located on the north side of Planters Point Subdivision on the Brazos River. The park features paved parking, restrooms, a canoe launch, and a walking trail through the trees.

Duckweed grows in profusion here and at times covers the ponds. Duckweed is an excellent wild food for wood ducks and other waterfowl. Wading birds like yellow-crowned night-herons may be spotted in their semi-frozen positions along the shoreline, waiting for a snake, frog, or small fish.

After arriving at the park, use the boardwalk winding along the Brazos and watch for Mississippi kites, which will at times nest in these trees. Don't strain your neck as you watch the treetops carefully during the summer for the hard-to-spot pileated woodpecker.

Wood Duck

DIRECTIONS

Drive west on TX 332 to TX 521, and then continue north on TX 521 to TX 35. Continue north on TX 521 to CR 30 (approximately 5 miles north of TX 35), and then go west on CR 30 to Planter's Point. Enter Planter's Point and follow Colony Lane to Brazos River County Park.

CONTACT INFORMATION

Brazoria County Parks Department, 313 W. Mulberry, Angleton, TX 77515
Phone: 979-864-1541
Web Site: http://www.brazoriacounty.com/parks/Brazos_River/brazos_river.html
Site open for day use only.

COASTAL PLAINS

#108 Brazos Bend State Park

GPS 29.371, -95.641

21901 FM 762
NEEDVILLE, TX 77461

KEY BIRDS
Prothonotary warbler, vermilion flycatcher, purple gallinule, and least bittern

BEST SEASON
All seasons

AREA DESCRIPTION
A mixture of coastal prairies, swales, oxbow lakes, freshwater marshes, and dense riparian woodlands

This is a very popular park due to its location less than 30 miles southwest of Houston. Located in the Brazos River floodplain, the park consists of freshwater marshes, oxbow lakes, coastal prairies, and thick riparian woods. It covers 4,897 acres, with an eastern boundary of 3.2 miles fronting on the Brazos River.

Birders can watch the open water habitat at 40 Acre Lake. Big Creek crosses the park with its rattle bean groves giving birds a place to perch as well as to feed on the mature beans. While birding the parking area at the lake watch for both water and land birds.

A hike to the observation platform located between Pilant and 40 Acre Lakes may allow you to spot prothonotary warblers, purple gallinules, and least bitterns. Pay special attention to the marshes if your visit coincides with the nesting season. Watch the willows along the levee for nesting birds.

A quick birders note: The barred owl has now been proven to be one of the chief causes of the demise of the spotted owl. Bigger, faster, and more aggressive, the little spotted owl is mostly the loser in owl-to-owl confrontations.

DIRECTIONS
From Angleton, drive north on TX 521 to FM 1462. Go west on FM 1462 to TX 762, then north on TX 762 to PR 72 and Brazos Bend State Park.

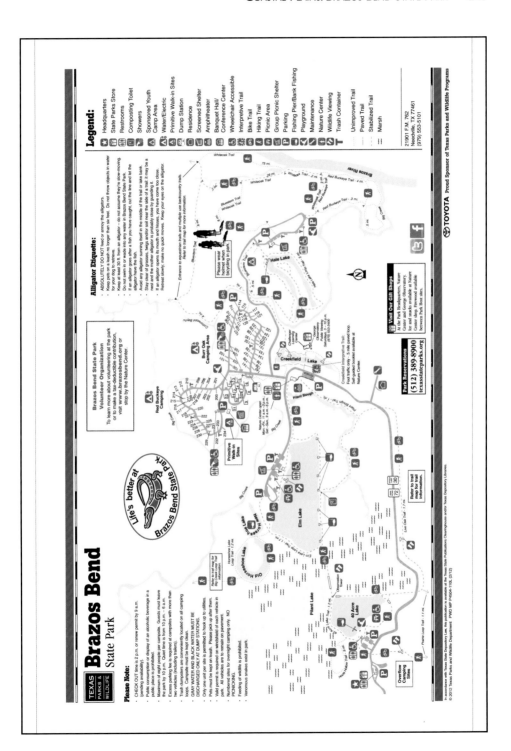

Brazos Bend State Park

Please Note:

- CHECK OUT time is 2 p.m. or renew permit by 9 a.m. (pending availability).
- Public consumption or display of an alcoholic beverage in a public place is prohibited.
- Maximum of eight people per campsite. Guests must leave the park by 10 p.m. Quiet time is from 10 p.m.– 6 a.m.
- Excess parking fee is required at campsites with more than two vehicles (including trailers).
- Trash dumpsters are conveniently located on all camping loops. Campsite must be kept clean.
- GRAY WATER AND BLACK WATER MUST BE DISCHARGED ONLY AT DUMP STATIONS.
- Only one unit per site is permitted to hook up to utilities.
- Pets must be kept on leash. Please pick up after them.
- Valid permit is required on windshield of each vehicle in park. All vehicles are to remain on pavement.
- Numbered sites for overnight camping only. NO PICNICKING.
- Feeding of wildlife is prohibited.
- Venomous snakes exist in park.

Brazos Bend State Park Volunteer Organization

To learn more about volunteering at the park or to make a tax-deductible contribution, visit www.brazosbend.org or stop by the Nature Center.

Alligator Etiquette:

- ABSOLUTELY DO NOT feed or annoy the alligators.
- Keep pets on a leash no longer than six feet. Do not throw objects in water for your dog to retrieve.
- Keep at least 30 ft. from an alligator - do not assume they're slow-moving.
- Do not swim in or wade into any water in Brazos Bend State Park.
- If an alligator goes after a fish you have caught, cut the line and let the alligator have the fish.
- Avoid any alligator sunning itself in the middle of the trail or side of a trail. It may be a nest and the mother alligator is probably close by guarding it.
- If an alligator opens its mouth and hisses, you have come too close. Retreat slowly, make no quick moves. Keep your eyes on the alligator.

Legend:

- Headquarters
- State Parks Store
- Restrooms
- Composting Toilet
- Showers
- Sponsored Youth Camp Area
- Water/Electric
- Primitive Walk-in Sites
- Dump Station
- Residence
- Amphitheater
- Screened Shelter
- Banquet Hall/Conference Center
- Wheelchair Accessible
- Interpretive Trail
- Bike Trail
- Hiking Trail
- Picnic Area
- Group Picnic Shelter
- Parking
- Fishing Pier/Bank Fishing
- Playground
- Maintenance
- Nature Center
- Wildlife Viewing
- Trash Container
- Unimproved Trail
- Paved Trail
- Stabilized Trail
- Marsh

21901 F.M. 762
Needville, TX 77461
(979) 553-5101

Park Reservations
(512) 389-8900
texasstateparks.org

Visit Our Gift Shops

At the Park Headquarters, Nature Center and George Observatory for and snacks available at Nature Center shop. Firewood available between Park host sites.

TOYOTA Proud Sponsor of Texas Parks and Wildlife Programs

Purple Gallinule

CONTACT INFORMATION
Phone: 409-553-5101
Site open daily. Developed camping available. Fee charged.

BONUS SITE
As you leave Brazos Bend State Park, drive farther north on TX 762 to Davis Estates Road (approximately 2.1 miles from PR 72). This road, much of it unpaved, is favored by local birders for its tendency to lure unusual species. Golden eagles and tundra swans have been found here in the past, and wood storks are often seen in the shallow ponds that border the road.

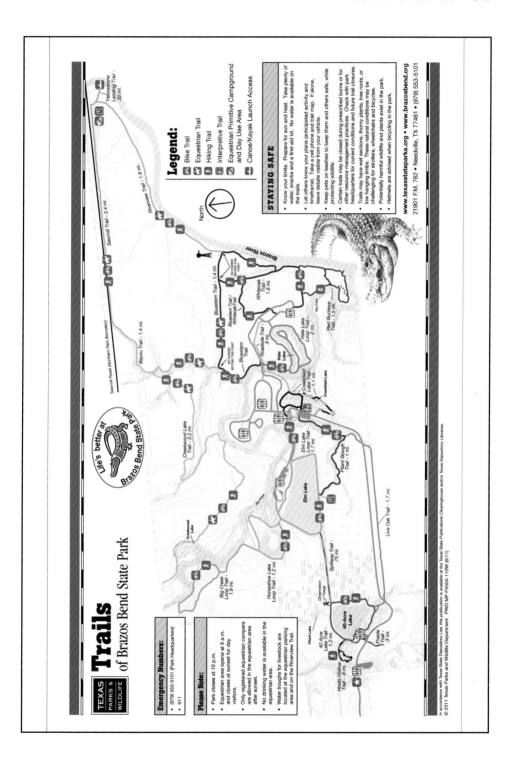

COASTAL PLAINS
Manor Lake and Eagle Nest Lake

#109

GPS | **MANOR LAKE: 29.218, -95.579**
EAGLE NEST LAKE: 29.224, -95.61

ON CR 24, BETWEEN HOUSTON AND LAKE JACKSON, TEXAS

KEY BIRDS
Eastern bluebird, least bittern, yellow-crowned night-heron, purple gallinule, and common moorhen

BEST SEASON
All seasons

AREA DESCRIPTION
Marshy, lakeside habitats with some wooded areas

Manor and Eagle Nest Lakes are both 40-acre lakes, with Manor Lake offering the best birding. After a day driving and watching for birds, this is a great location to slow down (as if I haven't written that before) and pay attention to the miles of pasture where you will find sandhill cranes during the winter.

Watch the fields along CR 25 for crested caracaras and ferruginous hawks. Manor Lake is usually the best for birders. It has extensive marshes pulling in a diversity of waterbirds, some of which are purple gallinule, yellow-crowned night-heron, common moorhen, and least bittern.

Birders listening for birdcalls may hear the gurgling and raspy call of marsh wrens in late spring and summer during the breeding season.

Bald eagles are known to nest here and are seen perched near the water or flying over the water in search of fish. As you leave Manor Lake on CR 27, watch the trees and brush for eastern bluebirds. These are some of the prettiest birds, and are seen in the pecan trees or picking up small stones on the gravel road. Closer to the river watch the trees and you may spot a pileated woodpecker. This area is one of the best locations to see this big woodpecker.

Yellow-crowned Night-heron

DIRECTIONS
Return to FM 1462, and continue east 0.8 mile to Cow Creek Road. Travel south on Cow Creek Road (becoming CR 25 at the county line) to Manor and Eagle Nest Lakes.

CONTACT INFORMATION
No contact information available at this time.
Site open for day use only.

COASTAL PLAINS

#110 Varner-Hogg Plantation

GPS⊕ 29.163, -95.64

1702 NORTH 13TH STREET
WEST COLUMBIA, TX 77486

KEY BIRDS
Eastern bluebird

BEST SEASON
Many species during migrations

AREA DESCRIPTION
River habitats and wooded areas supporting wildlife

Located on 66-acres and on the Brazos River, 50 miles to the south of Houston in Brazoria County, this site was at one time, but is no longer, a state park. It is a State Historic Site and a Texas Historical Commission property.

Managed as basically a historical site, this site offers limited birding opportunities. However, the 66-acre park supports a healthy population of eastern bluebirds, and the woodlands here should be inspected in spring for migrants.

DIRECTIONS
Continue south on CR 25 to TX 35, and then go west on TX 35 to FM 2852. Travel north on FM 2852 to Varner-Hogg Plantation.

CONTACT INFORMATION
Varner-Hogg Plantation State Historic Site, P.O. Box 696, West Columbia, TX 77486
Site Staff Phone: 979-345-4656
Email: varner-hogg@thc.state.tx.us
Texas Historical Commission Phone: 512-463-7948
Email: historic-sites@thc.state.tx.us
Site open for day use only.

Eastern Bluebird

COASTAL PLAINS

Hanson Riverside County Park

#111

GPS $\oplus$ **29.112, -95.675**

ALONG THE SAN BERNARD RIVER NEAR WEST COLUMBIA, TEXAS

KEY BIRDS
Black-necked stilt, white-faced ibis, yellow-crowned night-heron, killdeer, common snipe, greater yellowlegs, lesser yellowlegs, mourning dove

BEST SEASON
Migration and winter

AREA DESCRIPTION
Native hardwood trees and river habitats

Birders should pay close attention to this 35-acre area of woodlands during the spring for eastern woodland birds and migrant species. The park features an extended trail system as well as an observation platform, covered pavilion, picnic tables, and grills.

DIRECTIONS
Continue west on TX 35 through West Columbia to Hanson Riverside County Park.

Black-necked Stilt

CONTACT INFORMATION
Brazoria County Parks Department Administrative Offices, 313 W. Mulberry, Angleton, TX 77515
Phone: 979-864-1541
Site open for day use only.

COASTAL PLAINS
#112 Quintana Neotropical Bird Sanctuary

GPS 28.933, -95.308

814 LAMAR STREET
QUINTANA, TX 77541

KEY BIRDS
Warblers, vireos, buntings, thrushes, and hummingbirds

BEST SEASON
Migrations

AREA DESCRIPTION
Reclaimed overgrown salt cedar lot, with park-like amenities

The area is very industrial, with chemical plants and busy seaports. It was an overgrown salt cedar lot, but now it has been improved, adding a nature trail, benches, and an observation tower along with water features. Funding for this project came from the local chemical companies who also furnished volunteer labor. Damaged in September 2008 by Hurricane Ike, the sanctuary lost a number of the trees. Volunteers cleaned up the sanctuary and have worked hard preparing for the migration. The work was completed in time and just keeps improving.

Today the small grove of salt cedars has become a birding hotspot as migrant birds often rest and recuperate for a few days here after crossing the Gulf of Mexico in March and April. The bird that is responsible for promoting the location with birders is the yellow-green vireo that flew in during the spring of 1998. As a bonus, a king eider was seen during the Great Texas Birding Classic of 1998 on a nearby beach.

Painted Bunting

Throughout April, the Quintana Spring Fling trailer is staffed every day from 9:00am until 4:00pm to greet visitors, answer questions, help with bird IDs, provide cold drinks, or a needed field guide.

DIRECTIONS
From Freeport, drive south on FM 1495 across the Gulf Intracoastal Waterway to CR 723 (Lamar Street). Turn left on CR 723 to proceed 2.1 miles to the Quintana Neotropical Bird Sanctuary.

CONTACT INFORMATION
Gulf Coast Bird Observatory
Phone: 979-480-0999
Website: www.gcbo.org
Site open for day use only.

COASTAL PLAINS
#113 Quintana Beach County Park

GPS 28.934, -95.302

330 5TH STREET
FREEPORT, TX 77541

KEY BIRDS
The occasional jaeger or gannet and a variety of terns

BEST SEASON
All seasons

AREA DESCRIPTION
Waterfront habitat

This 51-acre beachfront park offers birders both day use as well as overnight and camping facilities. There's a paved full-service RV area as well as cabins for rent and space for tent camping. It has restrooms, showers, covered pavilions, as well as beach access.

After birding this park, the Quintana Jetty may be reached by a short hiking trail. When birding the jetties, watch the offshore waters for gulls, terns, and an occasional jaeger or gannet.

DIRECTIONS
From Houston, take Hwy. 288 south to Freeport, until it dead ends. Turn right on FM 1495 and cross the bridge. Turn left on CR 723 (2 miles). Turn right at dead end at park entrance.

CONTACT INFORMATION
Day-use hours: 8:00am to dusk. Developed camping available. Fee charged.
Phone: 979-233-1461 or 800-872-7578
Email: quintana@brazoria-county.com

Caspian Tern

COASTAL PLAINS

#114 UTC Bryan Beach

GPS 28.898, -95.35

FOUR MILES SOUTH OF FREEPORT ON THE GULF ON FARM ROAD 1495

KEY BIRDS
American avocets, piping and snowy plovers

BEST SEASON
All seasons

AREA DESCRIPTION
Beach habitats and open areas of sand grass

Bryan Beach is a very small coastal village just a few miles south of Freeport, Texas. Bryan Beach State Recreation Area, an 878-acre park located a couple of miles down the beach, opened in 1973.

The unit is undeveloped yet, in some ways, this unspoiled condition adds to the appeal of this location. Flocks of waterbirds crowd the sand flats at the mouth of the river, and gangs of American avocets often swirl through the shallow waters here. Piping and snowy plovers chase the water's edge, and merlins eye them while perched on the driftwood that litters the dunes.

DIRECTIONS
On FM 1495, turn south on CR 750. Proceed south to the beach, and drive southwest along the beach until reaching the mouth of the Brazos River and the Bryan Beach Unit of the Justin Hurst WMA.

CONTACT INFORMATION
Phone: 979-233-3526.
Site open for day use only.

American Avocet

COASTAL PLAINS
#115 Justin Hurst WMA

GPS 28.969, -95.444

WEST OF FREEPORT, TEXAS NEAR JONES CREEK

KEY BIRDS
Neotropical migrants

BEST SEASON
Migrations and winter

AREA DESCRIPTION
Oak and hackberry mottes, adjacent grasslands and wetlands

The 10,311-acre Justin Hurst WMA was purchased using waterfowl stamp funds from 1985 to 1987. In 1988, an additional 1,627 acres were purchased.

Most of this wildlife management area consists of either coastal prairie or coastal marshes that are inaccessible to the public. Nature trails have been created to provide birders with the chance to bird the hackberry and oak stands as well as adjoining grassland areas.

The Live Oak Loop and the Jones Creek Trail are found in a small picnic area that may be entered 0.2 mile from TX 36.

The WMA owns a 40-acre tract of live oaks located behind the Jones Creek municipal building on Stephen F. Austin Drive. This location is open to the public year round. This location is near the Little Ridge entrance to the WMA.

Many of the neotropical migrants in this part of the coast may be found in this location.

DIRECTIONS
Return to the intersection of FM 1495 and TX 36, and continue northwest on TX 36 to the TPWD Justin Hurst WMA.

CONTACT INFORMATION
Justin Hurst WMA offices, County Courthouse Room 101, Bay City, TX 77414
Phone: 409-244-7697
Web Site: www.tpwd.state.tx.us/huntwild/hunt/wma/find_a_wma/list/?id=41
Site open for day use only.

COASTAL PLAINS
San Bernard NWR
#116

GPS 28.913, -95.578

TWELVE MILES WEST OF FREEPORT, TEXAS

KEY BIRDS
Snow goose, warblers, many fall-out birds during spring and fall migrations

BEST SEASON
All seasons

AREA DESCRIPTION
Coastal prairie, both salt and freshwater marshes, freshwater lakes, and scattered woodlands

Covering all of 27,414-acres, this national refuge is located in Brazoria and Matagorda Counties, 12 miles west of Freeport.

The refuge is one of the best locations to watch lesser snow geese both roost and feed. Snow geese flourish on the roots of Olney bulrush and other salt marsh plants. They rest in shallow waters within clear view of their predators and the numerous bird watchers.

If the warm and normally moist air heading north from the

Tennessee Warbler

Gulf collides with cold dry air heading south, the resulting weather conditions will create a major warbler "fallout".

Birders should pay close attention as well as spend some time glassing or scoping the bottomland trees and willows on the sides of the tour road. This area may attract high numbers of migrating warblers heading north.

Although the majority of the refuge is worth birding many times, certain parts are just not accessible. There is a three-mile Moccasin Pond driving loop and Scissor-tail Trail. Hiking the Bobcat Woods Trail with an elevated boardwalk gives birders a great view of Cocklebur Slough.

DIRECTIONS
Drive northwest on TX 36 to FM 2611, then west on FM 2611 to FM 2918. Proceed south on FM 2918 to CR 306, then west on CR 306 to San Bernard NWR.

CONTACT INFORMATION
Shane Kasson, Refuge Manager, 6801 County Road 306, Brazoria, TX 77422
Phone: 979-964-3639
Email: R2RW_SNB@mail.fws.gov
http://sturgeon.irm1.r2.fws.gov:80/u2/refuges/texas/sanbern.html
For information about the Texas Mid-Coast NWR Complex, please contact Tom Schneider, Outdoor Recreation Planner, tom_schneider@fws.gov
Phone: 979-849-6062
Site open for day use only.

COASTAL PLAINS
Sargent Beach
#117

GPS 28.768, -95.619

SOUTH ON FM 457 FROM BAY CITY, TEXAS

KEY BIRDS
White-tailed kite, northern harrier, sandhill crane, eastern bluebird, and Swainson's warbler

BEST SEASON
Winter and migrations

AREA DESCRIPTION
Beachfront habitat with tall trees along Caney Creek

Located past the intersection of FM 457 and FM 521, mostly the birding is along the public roads, beaches, and along Caney Creek. **BIRDERS NOTE:** Please, bird Caney Creek only from the public roads. Also explore the coastal grasslands and marshes along FM 457 as you are approaching the coast.

Birders should be on the lookout for white-tailed kite, northern harrier, and sandhill crane during in winter. Glass the beach for shorebirds such as black-bellied plover, piping plover, ruddy turnstone, and sanderling.

Bird the along Caney Creek to the southwest of Sargent. This area is the home to many songbirds and waterbirds as well. Many of the eastern species may be found here. Watch for the pileated woodpecker and the eastern bluebird. At times, in the forests along this waterway, birders will see Swainson's warblers.

Sandhill Cranes

As a special note, the pileated woodpecker can at times be hard to spot. Birders should listen for the sound of pecking or sounding or the call that is somewhat like a flicker. These woodpeckers love dead or dying trees.

DIRECTIONS
Drive south on FM 457 from the intersection with FM 521 in Matagorda County to Sargent Beach.

CONTACT INFORMATION
Bay City Chamber of Commerce P. O. Box 768 Bay City, Texas 77404
Phone: 979-245-8333
Site open for day use only.

COASTAL PLAINS
#118 Big Boggy
National Wildlife Refuge

GPS 28.753, -95.809

LOCATED ON THE COAST BETWEEN SARGENT AND MATAGORDA, TEXAS

KEY BIRDS
Yellow-crowned night-heron, white-faced ibis, wood stork, wood duck, mallard, gadwall, northern pintail, American wigeon, northern shoveler, blue-winged teal, green-winged teal, ring-necked duck

BEST SEASON
Winter

AREA DESCRIPTION
Combination of low brush, marshy areas, and freshwater and brackish ponds

At this time this refuge is closed to the Public. But, in spite of this, the refuge staff periodically will offer day trips. Contact the Brazoria NWR staff in Angleton for information about arranging for visitation.

DIRECTIONS
Drive west on FM 521 from Sargent until reaching Chinquapin Road, turn left (south) on Chinquapin Road, and then drive by Big Boggy NWR to Chinquapin Landing.

CONTACT INFORMATION
Big Boggy National Wildlife Refuge, 1212 N. Velasco, Suite 200, Angleton, Texas 77515
Phone: 409-849-6062
Site access restricted. Call ahead.

American Wigeons

COASTAL PLAINS
#119 Matagorda County Jetty Park/Lower Colorado River Authority

GPS⊕ **28.597, -95.977**

6430 FM 2031
MATAGORDA, TX 77457

KEY BIRDS
White-tailed hawk

BEST SEASON
Winter and migrations

AREA DESCRIPTION
Coastal and river habitats

The grasslands along FM 521 between Sargent and Matagorda offer a fine opportunity to see the white-tailed hawk, which has become a south Texas specialty.

Located at the mouth of the Colorado River on the Matagorda Peninsula and described as one of the best birding areas in the nation, this 1,600-acre park follows roughly two miles of the Gulf of Mexico coastline. In addition, there are two miles of river frontage including hundreds of acres of coastal marshes and dunes.

The groups of trees within the city of Matagorda were all planted with several species of exotic trees and shrubs for the purpose of attracting neotropical migrants. Birders should also take note of the many hummingbird feeders supported by the city. While you are visiting the city, watch for hummers near some of the accessible feeders. Wintering hummingbirds are great to watch, but please respect private property.

This city is also an important location of the Mad Island Marsh Christmas Bird Count (CBC). To reach the count area, drive south on FM 2031, and then follow the Colorado River to the Gulf. Numerous pull-outs make this road easier and safer to bird. Watch the marshes adjacent to this road for wading birds such as the roseate spoonbill, white ibis, white-faced ibis, and salt marsh species such as seaside sparrow and the clapper rail.

A pier is also located here and will get birders closer to birds such as scoters or jaegers, and northern gannet. In the summer, birders should watch for magnificent frigatebirds flying over the water. At the mouth of the river, adjacent to the pier, birders may see a shorebird roost as well as terns and gulls. Bird this beach carefully and you may see a piping or snowy plover, maybe both.

There is a small store located within the park where birders/campers may rent a canoe, bathrooms and showers, as well as a coin-operated laundry.

DIRECTIONS

Continue west on FM 521 to the intersection with TX 60 at Wadsworth, proceed south on TX 60 to Matagorda.

CONTACT INFORMATION

Phone for camp & RV Park: 800-776-LCRA(5272), Ext. 4778
Phone for Natural Science Center: 800-776-5272, Ext. 4740
E-mail for Natural Science Center: matagordabay@lcra.org

Site open for day use only. Day-use visitors are allowed in the park from dawn to dusk. Overnight campers must be registered at the park.

Immature Red-tailed Hawk

COASTAL PLAINS

#120 Attwater Prairie Chicken National Wildlife Refuge

GPS 29.684, -96.288

APPROXIMATELY SIX MILES NORTHEAST OF EAGLE LAKE, TEXAS

KEY BIRDS
Attwater prairie chicken, dark-eyed junco, ferruginous hawk, Sprague's pipit, sedge wren, grasshopper sparrow, Leconte's sparrow, and Harris' sparrow

BEST SEASON
Winter and migrations

AREA DESCRIPTION
Mostly grasslands with a little low brush and trees

This is another refuge established with funds from the Federal Waterfowl stamp. It was created in order to protect the Attwater's greater prairie chicken. In addition, this refuge shelters and feeds many species of birds that depend on these grasslands. Local farming practices over the years have become detrimental to several species.

With over 10,000 acres, the Attwater Prairie Chicken NWR takes in some of the largest tracts of native grasslands remaining in Colorado County. It is some of the last remaining coastal prairie habitat for this bird.

Birders may also find birds such as Sprague's pipit, white-tailed hawk, ferruginous hawk, grasshopper sparrow,

Dark-eyed Junco

sedge wren, Leconte's sparrow, and Harris' sparrow species, most likely to be seen in this area during the winter months.

A few rare species have been seen here also, such as golden eagle, prairie falcon, masked duck, zone-tailed hawk, least grebe, and Say's phoebe.

Eagle Lake is host to a prairie-chicken festival each spring, so check with the Chamber of Commerce in Eagle Lake for the dates. In addition, the Attwater Prairie-Chicken NWR CBC is held each year in late December.

DIRECTIONS

Travel north on TX 60 from Matagorda to Wharton, take FM 102 north to its merger with FM 3013, and then take FM 3013 east to the refuge entrance (approximately six miles northeast of Eagle Lake).

CONTACT INFORMATION

Attwater Prairie Chicken National Wildlife Refuge, P.O. Box 519, Eagle Lake, Texas 77434
Phone: 409-234-3021
Access to this refuge is restricted; however the site may be open for day use.

COASTAL PLAINS

#121 Texas R.I.C.E/Pierce Ranch Waterbird Viewing Site

GPS 29.187, -96.174

On Pierce West Road (FM 421), southwest of Pierce, Texas

Key Birds
Geese, ducks, and king, Virginia, sora, and yellow rails

Best Season
October through early March

Area Description
Mostly rice fields with some higher areas for viewing

A great advantage for birders, the viewing sites here are well-marked and many are reached directly from the road. The Texas R.I.C.E. is composed of rice growers, individuals who have gathered to help maintain and improve working relationships between the rice business people, conservationists, and interested groups.

Normally during the month of October, after the rice growers have harvested their second crop, these fields are managed for the use of roosting geese, cranes, ducks, and wading birds. Here again, the largest majority of the available property is private, please respect property rights.

As they cut the rice, harvesting machinery will flush birds from the location of the harvesters. Birders may see species such as rails – king, yellow, Virginia, and sora – flushing just ahead of the harvesters.

The Karankawa Plains Outfitting Company is located on the Pierce Ranch and offers birding tours. They charge $40 for a half day of birding, including breakfast and $65 for a full day, including breakfast and lunch. There is a limit of four persons per guide. For additional information, go to their website at www.karankawa.com or call them at 979-578-0100.

Directions
From Wharton, drive southwest on US 59 to Pierce. Continue on US 59 past Pierce, then exit on Pierce West Road and travel south for four miles to the viewing sites.

CONTACT INFORMATION

El Campo Chamber of Commerce, P. O. Box 1400 El Campo, Texas 77437
Phone: 979-543-2713
Email: ecc@elcampochamber.com
Site open for day use only.

Green-winged Teal

COASTAL PLAINS
Matagorda County Birding and Nature Center

GPS 28.983, -96.012

ON THE COLORADO RIVER, NEAR WHARTON, TEXAS

KEY BIRDS
American crow, barn swallow, purple martin, gray-cheeked thrush, eastern bluebird, tufted titmouse, American robin, northern mockingbird

BEST SEASON
All seasons

AREA DESCRIPTION
Wetlands, native grasslands, and bottomlands along the river

One of the popular features of this location, the Nature Center, is the outdoor learning center. Other areas that attract birders are the well-maintained hummingbird and butterfly gardens. On the 34 acres of this site, birders will enjoy several accessible trails, observation bridges, and raised platforms providing access and viewing of the native grasslands, wetlands, and the riverside habitats along the Colorado River.

Birders should watch for other species such as the eastern bluebird, American crow, barn swallow, purple martin, house finch, tufted titmouse, American robin, northern mockingbird, cedar waxwing, summer tanager, northern cardinal, blue grosbeak, indigo bunting, painted bunting, roseate spoonbill, gray-cheeked thrush, brown-headed cowbird, and the American goldfinch.

DIRECTIONS
Return to Wharton and take TX 60 south to Bay City, and then take TX35 south 1.7 miles to the nature center's entrance.

CONTACT INFORMATION
Address: P.O. Box 2212
Bay City, TX 77404-2212
Call: 979-245-3336
Entrance Fees: $3.00 per person or $5.00 per carload
Web site of http://mcbnc.org
Site open for day use only.

Northern Mockingbird

COASTAL PLAINS

#123 South Texas Project Prairie Wetlands

GPS 28.793, -96.043

OFF FM 521 SOUTHWEST OF BAY CITY, TEXAS

KEY BIRDS
White-faced ibis, wood stork, wood duck, mallard, gadwall, northern pintail, American wigeon, northern shoveler, blue-winged teal, green-winged teal, ring-necked duck, bufflehead, hooded merganser, ruddy duck

BEST SEASON
Fall through spring

AREA DESCRIPTION
Seasonally flooded wetlands habitat

This 110-acre project involves three seasonally-flooded wetlands known to attract many species of waterfowl and roosting geese. During the spring months, watch the water's edges for migrant shorebirds and wading birds. Parking is available near the observation area.

DIRECTIONS
Return to the intersection of FM 521 and TX 60 and travel west two miles past the Colorado River to the South Texas Project.

CONTACT INFORMATION
For a tour of the site, contact the Visitors Center
Phone: 361-972-3611).
Site open for day use only.

Ruddy Duck

COASTAL PLAINS

#124 Mad Island WMA, Clive Runnells Family Mad Island Marsh Preserve

GPS⊕ **28.663, -96.004**

WEST OF MATAGORDA AND EAST OF COLLEGEPORT, TEXAS

KEY BIRDS
Puddle and diver ducks, sandhill crane, mottled duck

BEST SEASON
Fall through spring

AREA DESCRIPTION
Fresh to brackish marshland with sparse brush and flat coastal prairie

The 7,200-acre Mad Island Wildlife Management Area is managed by Texas Parks and Wildlife, while The Clive Runnells Family Mad Island Marsh Preserve is owned and managed by The Nature Conservancy of Texas. This area has been closed to the public, so call ahead for current information.

Access may be arranged through the managing agencies and organizations on special occasions. In addition to the seasonal public trips, the Mad Island Marsh Christmas Bird Count happens in December

Mottled Duck

of each year. More information on the bird count is available by calling Texas Parks and Wildlife or The Nature Conservancy of Texas if you would like to join the count.

The annual Mad Island Christmas Bird Count has ranked in the top five national counts since its inception in 1993.

This location has attracted nearly 250 species of birds. A few of these species are first migrating and resident songbirds. Wading birds are spotted using this spot for feeding, resting, and roosting. There are also colonial nesting birds and waterfowl including 16 species of ducks and four species of geese.

Many birders will visit this site to see the large and at times noisy sandhill cranes using these wetlands for feeding and roosting. Also watch for several species of wading birds on the Mad Island Marsh Preserve at some point during the year.

DIRECTIONS
From the South Texas Project, take FM 521 west to FM 1095, then take FM 1095 left (south) toward Collegeport and its intersection with Brazos Tower Road. Turn left (south) on Brazos Tower Road, and then left (east) on A-P Ranch Road. After two miles, the gate marks the entrances.

CONTACT INFORMATION
Lang Alford, 2200 7th Street, 3rd Floor, Bay City, TX 77414
Phone: 979-323-9579
OR: Mad Island Office: The Nature Conservancy of Texas 4, P.O. Box 163, Collegeport, Texas 77428-016
Phone: 361-972-2615
This site is access restricted, please call ahead.

COASTAL PLAINS
#125 Oyster Lake Road

GPS 28.644, -96.2

OFF FM 1095, SOUTHEAST OF COLLEGEPORT, TEXAS

KEY BIRDS
American oystercatcher, golden plover, Hudsonian godwit, Baird's sandpiper, white-rumped sandpiper

BEST SEASON
Winter and migrations

AREA DESCRIPTION
Extensive salt marsh on both sides of the road

Oyster Lake Road winds its way to Matagorda Bay, and is a gravel road for several miles. During most normal weather conditions this road is passable, however be cautious during heavy rains.

Birders will drive through a salt marsh where many species of wading birds may be viewed. Watch for Nelson's sharp-tailed sparrow, clapper rail, and seaside sparrow.

Use your binoculars or spotting scope to watch the shoreline for redhead, common goldeneye, red-breasted merganser, bufflehead, and American oystercatcher.

If you are birding during the migrations, pay attention to the scrubby trees along the road as they may harbor several species of migrants. Without straining your neck or falling over backwards, keep an eye out for raptors and swallows.

American Oystercatcher

Rice fields border the northern part of Oyster Lake Road and Franzen Road. Driving these in spring will allow you to spot migrant species such as Hudsonian godwit, golden plover, white-rumped sandpiper, and Baird's sandpiper.

Both snow geese and sandhill cranes are in this location during the winter months. Remember to examine each snow goose flock for a smaller Ross' goose mixed in with the larger snows. Driving back to Brazos Tower Road, drive west to near Collegeport. Birders should park at the end of the pavement and watch the bay edges for ducks, grebes, and loons.

DIRECTIONS
From the intersection of A-P Ranch Road and Brazos Tower Road, continue west on Franzen Road. Turn south onto Oyster Lake Road.

CONTACT INFORMATION
Palacios Chamber of Commerce, 312 Main Street Palacios, Texas 77465
Phone: 361-972-2615
Site open for day use only.

COASTAL PLAINS
#126 Cash Creek

GPS 28.764, -96.193

JUST OFF FM 2853, NORTH OF PALACIOS, TEXAS

KEY BIRDS
Geese, sandhill crane, and several species of ducks

BEST SEASON
Winter and migrations

AREA DESCRIPTION
Agricultural fields and freshwater marshes along the creek

The fields in this area are mostly agricultural, growing crops such as rice. The large fields are flooded after harvest to attract large flights of sandhill cranes, ducks, and geese. Field counts have reported over two million snow geese wintering along the Texas Coast between Corpus Christi and the Sabine River.

Birders should watch the snow goose flocks carefully for the Ross' goose, which is becoming a regular visitor, arriving in the fall then heading north in the early spring to nest.

The freshwater marshes along the creek can be viewed from the shoulder of the bridge where Cash Creek crosses FM 2853. Be quiet and you will see cliff swallows that will nest under the bridge.

White-tailed hawks and other raptors are seen hunting the grass pastures and fields along FM 2853.

Sandhill Cranes

DIRECTIONS

From Collegeport, take FM 1095 to FM 521, go west on FM 521 to FM 2853, and then take FM 2853 south.

CONTACT INFORMATION

Palacios Chamber of Commerce 312 Main Street, Palacios, Texas 77465
Phone: 361-972-2615
Site open for day use only.

Eared Grebe

COASTAL PLAINS
#127 Bayshore Drive

GPS 28.711, -96.207

PALACIOS, TEXAS

KEY BIRDS
Common loon, eared grebe, common goldeneye, red-breasted merganser

BEST SEASON
Winter

AREA DESCRIPTION
Bayside and wetlands

This drive offers visiting birders the chance to bird Tres Palacios Bay. A slow drive through the bordering marshes will produce the spotting of many water birds including eared grebe, common loon, and diving ducks like the red-breasted merganser, redhead, and common goldeneye.

Rarities for this area include three species of scoters, oldsquaw, and the pacific loon during the winter months.

DIRECTIONS
Drive south on FM 2853 1.3 miles to Bayshore Drive. FM 2853 parallels Tres Palacios Bay to Business 35/1st Street.

CONTACT INFORMATION
No contact information available.
Site open for day use only.

COASTAL PLAINS
Trull Marsh

#128

GPS 28.711, -96.211

PALACIOS, TEXAS

KEY BIRDS
Ring-necked duck, lesser scaup, black-necked stilt

BEST SEASON
All seasons

AREA DESCRIPTION
A roadway with viewing habitats on either side with some improvements in the marsh

Where the highway shoulder ends, the water will begins. Birders may view ducks at times only a few feet from the car like lesser scaup, ring-necked and bufflehead ducks, along with the black-necked stilt that at times will nest in this area. Wading birds like the long-billed dowitcher and greater yellowlegs are spotted wading the shallow edges.

The observation deck located at the Trull Marsh allows birders to get close for spotting and photography with large numbers of shorebirds, egrets, herons, ibis, as well as several waterfowl species, all trying to feed.

Both sites, both sides of the road, will be improved for birders with projects during the future years.

DIRECTIONS
This location extends for two blocks north of the intersection of Business 35 and Bayshore Drive, with Trull Marsh on the west and Brookings on the east of Business 35/1st Street.

CONTACT INFORMATION
No contact information available.
Site open for day use only.

Black-necked Stilt

COASTAL PLAINS

#129 Palacios Waterfront and Texas Baptist Encampment

GPS 28.7, -96.21

100 1ST STREET
PALACIOS, TX 77465

KEY BIRDS
Waterfowl and shorebirds

BEST SEASON
Winter

AREA DESCRIPTION
A waterfront and bay environment within the city limits

Park near the fishing pier along Bay Drive. Birders should take a slow walk along the Tres Palacios Bay watching for pelicans, loons, grebes, common goldeneye, gulls, and terns. If your birding time allows, bird on both Bayshore Drive and Lookout Point. It will be well worth the time spent here watching for many species of waterbirds.

DIRECTIONS
The Texas Baptist Encampment is situated on a point of land (Hamilton's Point) near the conjunction of East and South Bay Boulevards, and may be reached by continuing south three blocks on Business 35 from Trull Marsh and turning left on East Bay Boulevard.

Willet

CONTACT INFORMATION
Palacios Chamber of Commerce, 312 Main Street, Palacios, Texas
Phone: 361-972-2615 (Texas Baptist Encampment)
Site open for day use only.

COASTAL PLAINS
#130 Lookout Point

GPS 28.696, -96.231

END OF MARGERUM ROAD, PALACIOS, TEXAS

KEY BIRDS
Waterfowl, Bonaparte's, laughing, ring-billed, and herring gulls

BEST SEASON
Winter

AREA DESCRIPTION
Bayside habitats

Park at the end of Margerum Road and carefully watch the bay for waterfowl and other wetland species. In addition, pay close attention to the various gulls that congregate around the fishing boats docked in the harbor.

Each year a few oddities like the glaucous, lesser black-backed, and black-legged kittiwake, and laughing, Bonaparte's, ring-billed, and herring gulls are often seen here.

DIRECTIONS
Drive west on Business 35 past the turning basins, then turn left or south on Margerum Road toward Tres Palacios Bay.

CONTACT INFORMATION
Palacios Chamber of Commerce 312 Main Street, Palacios, Texas 77465
Phone: 361-972-2615
Site open for day use only.

Ring-billed Gull

COASTAL PLAINS

Palacios Marine Education Center Nature Trail

#131

GPS 28.695, -96.24

WEST OF PALACIOS, TEXAS

KEY BIRDS
Egrets, clapper rail, seaside sparrow, Nelson's sharp-tailed sparrow

BEST SEASON
All seasons

AREA DESCRIPTION
Shoreline of Palacios Bay

A parking lot is provided for birders who wish to view the 27 acres of shoreline here. The nature trail begins just to the left of the pier. During the spring, the scrub brush and bushes along the trail are where to walk slow and watch for buntings, warblers, migrant vireos, and orioles.

Included in the center's wetlands is a 1.25-mile nature trail with an elevated platform, a 700-foot by 20-foot pier, a saltwater marshland, as well as over 2,000 feet right on the beach. Birding from the observation deck is only a short distance from Tres Palacios Bay and its array of waterbirds.

Walk quietly and glass the pond carefully for egrets, bitterns, and herons. The marsh nearly surrounds the observation deck, making it a super location to see seaside and Nelson's sharp-tailed sparrows and clapper rail.

DIRECTIONS
Drive to the intersection of Margerum Road and Business 35, turn west for 0.6 mile to Camp Hulen Road and then go south 0.7 mile to the entrance gate.

CONTACT INFORMATION
The Marine Center is open Monday through Friday, 8:00am to 4:00pm. Phone: 361-972-3774.
Site open for day use only.

Great Egret

COASTAL PLAINS
#132 Perry R. Bass State Marine Fisheries Research Station

GPS ⊕ 28.718, -96.325

ON FM 3280 WEST OF PALACIOS, TEXAS

KEY BIRDS
Northern harrier, sandhill crane, loons, and grebes

BEST SEASON
All seasons

AREA DESCRIPTION
Prairies and marshes

This research facility maintains a science staff that is divided into two groups, the life history staff and the genetics staff. The genetics staff consists of a lead geneticist and three genetics biologists. The Perry R. Bass Marine Fisheries Research Station was not built for birders, but birders are welcome.

The prairies and marshes located on FM 3280 attract coastal grassland species such as short-eared owl, northern harrier, and sandhill crane. Birders would be well advised to glass the gulf at road's end mainly for ducks, grebes, loons, gulls, and terns. Glass the beaches for ruddy turnstones, sanderling, and other shorebirds.

During migrations, watch the fences and hedges for migrants such as scissor-tailed flycatcher, eastern and western kingbirds, and dickcissel.

DIRECTIONS
Stay on TX 35 from Palacios for 7.5 miles, then turn left or south for 5.5 miles on FM 3280 to the Perry R. Bass State Marine Fisheries Research Station.

CONTACT INFORMATION
Address: FM 3280, Palacios, TX 77465
Phone: 361-972-5483
Email: Mark.Fisher@tpwd.state.tx.us
Web Site: http://www.tpwd.state.tx.us/fishboat/fish/management/hatcheries/prb.phtml
Site open for day use only.

Pie-billed Grebe

COASTAL PLAINS
#133 Port Alto and Olivia

GPS | PORT ALTO: 28.66, -96.416
Olivia: 28.645, -96.453

ON THE BAYS IN SOUTHERN JACKSON COUNTY

KEY BIRDS
Rails and shorebirds, Cassin's sparrow

BEST SEASON
Winter and migrations

AREA DESCRIPTION
Bayside habitat and park habitat area with Tamaulipan scrub along the road

This is not a major stop for many birders. However, birders have a chance to have some great bird watching. Drive west on TX 35 to Carancahua Bay. Park near the boat ramp, and glass the bay for bufflehead and redhead ducks, and the red-breasted merganser. With proximity to the water, birders may see an osprey. As you drive from one location to another, watch for osprey nesting platforms on poles or in trees.

From the end of TX 172 south in Olivia, watch Keller Bay for bay ducks, loons, and grebes. Pay close attention to the marshes and watch for rails and shorebirds.

CR 314 will wind the through Tamaulipan scrub brush and is an excellent place to watch for warblers during spring fallout. This road is also a great place to find a Cassin's sparrow in the summer.

After reaching the western shore of Carancahua Bay, watch the water for waterfowl and shorebirds at low tide. Don't overlook the brush along M. Johnson Avenue for Bewick's wren and curve-billed thrasher. These birds will rarely be found farther north than this location.

DIRECTIONS
From Palacios, drive west on TX 35 to the intersection with TX 172. Before entering the Texana Loop to the north, turn south on TX 172 toward Port Alto and Olivia. Travel east from Olivia on CR 314 toward Carancahua Bay and Port Alto. Turn north and take M. Johnson Ave. toward Port Alto, then return to TX 172 on Spur 159, checking the fields for sandhill cranes in winter and grassland shorebirds in spring.

CONTACT INFORMATION

Palacios Chamber of Commerce 312 Main Street, Palacios, Texas 77465
Phone: 361-972-2615
Site open for day use only.

Common Moorhen

COASTAL PLAINS

#134 Formosa-Tejano Wetlands

GPS 28.82, -96.464

Just off FM 172, north of Ganado, Texas

Key Birds
Ducks, geese, and large wading birds

Best Season
Winter and migrations

Area Description
245 acres; Ponds, permanent wetlands, and coastal prairie, plus woodland habitats

This 245-acre site, owned by Formosa Plastics Corp, consists of several ponds, permanent wetlands, and coastal prairie, plus some woodlands that will attract neotropical migrants and native birds alike.

Increased water depths are provided for the flocks of ducks and geese, large waders, and shorebirds that spend the winter in this location. There have been disputes of water uses here and also in other locations along the coast.

The Formosa-Tejano Wetlands is divided into six units, four of which are west of TX 172. These four are adjacent to a 100-acre reservoir providing wetlands habitat for wood storks, American white pelicans, and diving ducks. Other bird species found here are treated as a bonus by visiting birders. Birders will find parking at the north end of this site, west of TX 172 and at the south end of the two sites, east of TX 172.

Great Egret

DIRECTIONS

From the intersection of TX 35 and TX 172, travel north on TX 172 toward Ganado. Continue north 6.9 miles to the gate (left) of the Formosa-Tejano Wetlands.

CONTACT INFORMATION

Formosa Plastics Corporation, P.O. Box 700, 201 Formosa Drive, Point Comfort, TX 77978
Phone: 361-987-7000
Site open for day use only.

COASTAL PLAINS
#135 Lake Texana Mustang Creek Boat Ramp

GPS 28.981, -96.53

SOUTH OF GANADO, TEXAS ON MUSTANG CREEK

KEY BIRDS
Red-tailed hawk, pileated woodpecker, tufted titmouse, Carolina chickadee, wood duck

BEST SEASON
Winter and migrations

AREA DESCRIPTION
Creekside habitats and wet areas

The Mustang Creek boat ramp, owned and managed by the Lavaca Navidad River Authority near Ganado, offers birders a place to park and bird the nearby oak woods. These trees are common along the bottom areas of the rivers.

Species such as the pileated woodpecker, tufted titmouse, red-shouldered hawk, and Carolina chickadee are quite common at this site. In the flooded wooded areas watch for wood ducks early in the morning. The water near the boat ramp is a good place to spot dabbling ducks.

Photographers will find the boat ramp area a great place to photograph waterfowl.

DIRECTIONS
From Ganado, drive south on FM 172 to the entry sign for the entrance to the boat ramp.

CONTACT INFORMATION
Jackson County Chamber of Commerce P. O. Box 788, Edna, Texas 77957 / Phone: 361-782-7146
Email: jccc@ykc.com
Site open for day use only.

Red-tailed Hawk

COASTAL PLAINS
#136 Mustang Creek Recreation Area

GPS 28.891, -96.53

SOUTHWEST OF GANADO, TEXAS

KEY BIRDS
Eastern woodland birds and migration species

BEST SEASON
All seasons except for summer

AREA DESCRIPTION
A very forested area on the coast

Unspoiled and rarely visited, this wooded location offers the opportunity to watch a variety of eastern woodland birds that are identical to those spotted in the Lake Texana State Park area.

No one will ever know exactly what might be seen at any given location. Migrations tend to mix up species seen in this locality.

DIRECTIONS
In Ganado, drive west on Loop 522 W to FM 2982 S, then turn left (south) on FM 2982 to CR 249. Turn left (east) on CR 249, and drive straight to the entrance of the Mustang Creek Recreation Area.

CONTACT INFORMATION
Jackson County Chamber of Commerce P. O. Box 788, Edna, Texas 77957 / Phone: 361-782-7146
Email: jccc@ykc.com
Web Site: www.stxmaps.com/go/texas-coastal-birding-trail-mustang-creek-recreation-area.html
This site is open daily and there is some developed camping available, as well as wilderness camping.

Altamira Oriole

COASTAL PLAINS
#137 Lake Texana Park and Campground

GPS 28.957, -96.544

46 PARK ROAD 1
EDNA, TEXAS 77957

KEY BIRDS
Pileated woodpecker, golden-fronted woodpecker, Carolina chickadee, American crow

BEST SEASON
All seasons

AREA DESCRIPTION
Coastal grasslands, and some woodlands such as coastal riparian forest

Formerly a state park, this 575-acre area east of Edna is now under the management of the Lavaca-Navidad River Authority.

Prairie grasslands dominated the coastal landscape in early days, with forested areas only occurring along the rivers. This site is an example of that earlier landscape. Birders will find many of the woodland birds inhabiting this coastal area.

The park has equipment that can be rented, including hydrobikes, canoes, and single-person kayaks. Educational opportunities are available, including guided hikes and wildlife programs.

DIRECTIONS
Stay on US 59 and continue southwest on US 59 to Edna, then turn south on TX 111. Continue on TX 111 as it veers to the east until reaching the entrance to Lake Texana Park and Campground located approximately 6.5 miles from Edna.

CONTACT INFORMATION
Phone: 361-782-5718
Site open daily with developed camping available and fees are charged. The park offers overnight facilities (campsites with water and electrical hookups, showers, restrooms).

Golden-fronted Woodpecker

COASTAL PLAINS
#138 Brackenridge Plantation Park and Campground

GPS 28.948, -96.541

891 BRACKENRIDGE PARKWAY
EDNA, TX 77957

KEY BIRDS
Pileated, red-bellied, and downy woodpeckers, Carolina chickadee, American crow

BEST SEASON
All seasons

AREA DESCRIPTION
Coastal grasslands, and some woodlands such as coastal riparian forest

Considering the park's nearness to Lake Texana Park and Campground, the birds will be the same during all seasons. Brackenridge Plantation is a private facility. It has various camping facilities for rent, including full hook-ups. An elevated gazebo provides a nice place to watch for birds.

DIRECTIONS
Across the road from the Lake Texana Park and Campground as described in site #137.

CONTACT

INFORMATION
P.O. Box 487, Edna, Texas 77957
Phone: 361-782-5456 or 361-782-7272
Site open daily. Developed camping available. Fee charged.

American Crow

COASTAL PLAINS
#139 Palmetto Bend Dam

GPS 28.891, -96.583

ON FM 3131 AT LAKE TEXANA

KEY BIRDS
Western grebe, loons, grebes, diving ducks

BEST SEASON
Winter

AREA DESCRIPTION
Agricultural fields, grasslands, lakeside habitats

The agricultural fields along FM 3131 are known to attract shorebirds and small seed-eating birds during the spring. Birders should watch for long-billed curlews, American golden-plovers, and several species of upland sandpipers.

Park in the designated parking spaces at the Palmetto Bend Dam, then watch carefully for diving ducks, loons, and grebes. The Palmetto Bend Dam is among the best locations along the Texas Coast to spot a western grebe. Birders should listen for a variety of woodland birds in the woodlands below the dam. It is a project of the Bureau of Reclamation.

DIRECTIONS
Drive west on TX 111 to the intersection with FM 3131, drive south on FM 3131 as it turns east to Palmetto Bend Dam. Turn left (east) on CR 417, and continue to Lake Texana and Simon's Boat Ramp. Returning to FM 3131, continue 2 miles south to Palmetto Bend Dam.

Western Grebes

CONTACT INFORMATION
Oklahoma-Texas Area Office, 5316 Highway 290 West, Suite 110 Austin, TX 78735-8931 / Phone: 512-899-4150

COASTAL PLAINS
#140 Lavaca/Navidad Estuary

GPS 28.833, -96.577

ADJACENT TO THE NAVIDAD RIVER NEAR LOLITA, TEXAS

KEY BIRDS
Wood stork, anhinga, ducks, bitterns

BEST SEASON
All seasons

AREA DESCRIPTION
Riverside habitats with grassy areas and small brush in wetlands

I spent several hours here, and each time I thought I had seen all there was, something else caught my attention. This is a wading bird paradise. Birders will find herons, egrets, spoonbills, anhingas, ducks, bitterns, and shorebirds in, above, and around these marshes. The best times of the day are in the mornings and late afternoons.

In late summer and early fall look for wood stork, a wading bird that breeds in the tropics to our south but migrates north after nesting, to loaf along the Texas Coast.

Visitors will be pleased with the parking and the excellent view from the observation Platform.

DIRECTIONS
From Edna, drive east on FM 3131 to the intersection with FM 1593, then turn right (south) on FM 1593 until reaching FM 616 at Lolita. Turn right again (west) on FM 616, and proceed until reaching the observation deck on FM 616 that overlooks the Lavaca / Navidad estuary.

CONTACT INFORMATION
Jackson County Chamber of Commerce P.O. Box 788, Edna, TX 77957
Phone: 361-782-7146
Email: jccc@ykc.com
Site open for day use only.

Anhinga

COASTAL PLAINS
Bennett Park

#141

GPS 28.797, -96.702

NEAR LA SALLE, TEXAS

KEY BIRDS
Lesser yellowlegs, common snipe

BEST SEASON
Migration

AREA DESCRIPTION
40 acres; Coastal habitat but having palmettos and the Texas sabal palm trees

Bennett Park has become known by birders to be the best viewing site for migration birds within Jackson County. Of course, weather conditions will be the deciding factor as to the number of migrants seen in this 40-acre coastal park.

A few species to watch for are lesser yellowlegs, common snipe, mourning dove, Inca dove, rock dove, greater roadrunner, ruby-throated hummingbird, and belted kingfisher.

Texas sabal palms (*Sabal mexicanas*) also known as Mexican palmettos are located here. These sabal palms were thought to be found only in far south Texas. If unharmed, these palms will eventually grow to the size of the palms farther south.

DIRECTIONS
Drive west on FM 616 and turn right or north on CR 325 at LaSalle. Cross the tracks, and at the T-intersection (0.7 mile) follow CR 325 left. Turn left on CR 326 (1.3 miles) to the entrance to the park located about 1 mile from the intersection.

CONTACT INFORMATION
Jackson County Chamber of Commerce P.O. Box 788, Edna, TX 77957
Phone: 361-782-7146
Email: jccc@ykc.com
Site open for day use only.

Lesser Yellowlegs

COASTAL PLAINS
#142 Garcitas Creek Boat Ramp

GPS 28.778, -96.699

LOCATED ON FM 616 ON GARCITAS CREEK

KEY BIRDS
Blue jay, waterthrush during migrations, marsh wren

BEST SEASON
Migration

AREA DESCRIPTION
Same type habitat as Bennett Park without the palm trees

Parking is available at the boat ramp for birding the surrounding woodlands. The boat ramp offers birders habitat that is also found in Bennett Park. The changing weather during migrations will be the determining factor on the number of species visiting this location at any time.

The marsh next to the boat ramp is a great place to watch for the two species of waterthrush, as well as common yellowthroat and marsh wrens.

Adjacent property is private, so respect the wishes if the owners and do not cross fences or trespass.

DIRECTIONS
Return to FM 616 at LaSalle, and then continue west on FM 616 to the Garcitas Creek crossing.

CONTACT INFORMATION
Jackson County Chamber of Commerce, P.O. Box 788, Edna, TX 77957
Phone: 361-782-7146
Email: jccc@ykc.com
Site open for day use only.

Blue Jay

COASTAL PLAINS
#143 Dupont Wetlands

GPS 28.664, -96.945

SOUTH OF VICTORIA, TEXAS

KEY BIRDS
Double-crested cormorant, American bittern, great blue heron, cattle egret, yellow-crowned night-heron, white-faced ibis

BEST SEASON
All seasons

AREA DESCRIPTION
53 acres; Estuarine-tidal saltmarshes (brackish) and flats; managed impoundments of forested bottomlands and hardwoods

The treated wastewater from the chemical plant is cleaned by moving it slowly through the wetlands, and then returned to the Guadalupe River. The amenities in this wetlands project by Dupont Company include a Wetlab Education Center, a pier, walkways, decks, an observation blind, and a boardwalk.

Only a part of DuPont's $180 million dollar program was used to construct the wetlands. DuPont also constructed two raised observation areas for the birding public. These observation areas are located near the parking lot. Both the platform and the knoll allow birders to watch the birdlife on DuPont's 53-acre wetland. This wetlands system allows Du Pont to return millions of gallons of clean water back into the Guadalupe River.

DIRECTIONS
Drive west on FM 616 to the intersection with TX 185 in Bloomington. Go north on TX 185 to FM 1686. Go left (west) on FM 1686 0.7 mile to the T-intersection, turn left and go 1.4 miles to the 90° turn. It is another 0.7 mile to the DuPont Wetlands parking area.

CONTACT INFORMATION
Visitors wishing to tour the wetland interior should schedule in advance for a wetland escort (361-572-2137).
Site open for day use only; no fees are charged.

Great Blue Heron

COASTAL PLAINS
#144 Riverside Park and Athey Nature Sanctuary

GPS⊕ 28.816, -97.009

ALONG THE GUADALUPE RIVER IN VICTORIA, TEXAS

KEY BIRDS
Golden-crowned kinglet, sparrows, and winter wren

BEST SEASON
Winter and migration

AREA DESCRIPTION
Partially wooded with grass and pasture areas

Riverside Park is situated along the Guadalupe River adjacent to Athey Nature Sanctuary (continue west on Red River until reaching the park entrance). A trail has been created that connects Athey Nature Sanctuary and Riverside Park. Cross an old river channel or *resaca*, and visit Grover's and Fox's Bend which should yield a surprising variety of woodland birds.

Birders should watch for pine warbler, chipping sparrow, eastern bluebird, golden-crowned kinglet, and winter wren. There is also a good chance of seeing a green kingfisher.

DIRECTIONS
From the Dupont Wetlands, go east on FM 1686 to its intersection with US 87. Go north on US 87 to Victoria. From the intersection of US 59 and US 87 in Victoria, go north on US 87 to Red River, and turn left (west) and continue to Vine. Turn right (north) on Vine and continue to the Victoria South Texas Crossroads RV Park. Park near the entrance to the Athey Nature Sanctuary at the RV park and walk across the bridge to the gate into the park.

CONTACT INFORMATION
Site open for day use only.

Immature White-Crowned Sparrow

COASTAL PLAINS
Palmetto State Park

#145

GPS 29.593, -97.586

FOURTEEN MILES NORTHWEST OF GONZALES, TEXAS

KEY BIRDS
Kentucky warbler, northern parula, red-shouldered hawk

BEST SEASON
All seasons

AREA DESCRIPTION
Palmetto swamps of the San Marcos River

Besides birding, visitors will enjoy the history of this location. Well known as the Cradle of Texas Independence, it was here that the first shots were fired in 1835 in the fight for Texas independence.

The 270.3-acre Palmetto State Park is located within the palmetto swamps of the San Marcos River, just outside the city of Gonzales and offers a river-based habitat in contrast to the arid grass and brush country.

Over 240 species of birds have been observed within the park's boundaries. Some of the birds most often spotted include the crested caracara and red-shouldered hawk.

A number of eastern woodland species nest within the park, including prothonotary and Kentucky warblers, northern parula, and indigo and painted buntings. The chicken

Crested Caracara

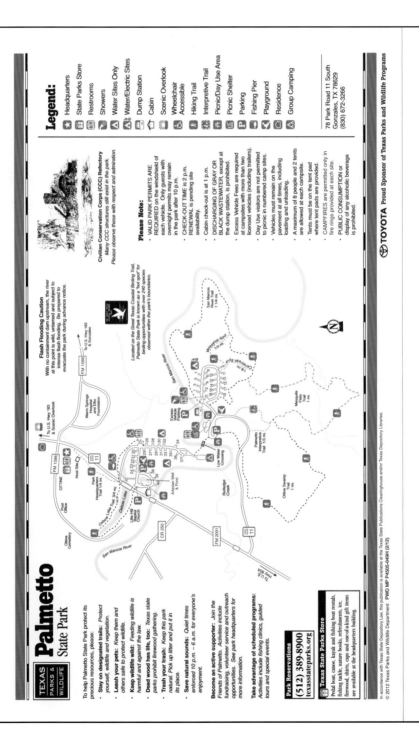

Palmetto State Park

To help Palmetto State Park protect its precious resources, please:

- **Stay on designated trails:** *Protect yourself, wildlife and vegetation.*
- **Leash your pets:** *Keep them and others safe to protect wildlife.*
- **Keep wildlife wild:** *Feeding wildlife is harmful and against the law.*
- **Dead wood has life, too:** *Texas state parks prohibit firewood gathering.*
- **Trash your trash:** *Keep this park natural. Pick up litter and put it in its place.*
- **Save natural sounds:** *Quiet times enforced 10 p.m. – 6 a.m. for everyone's enjoyment.*

Become an active supporter: *Join the Friends of Palmetto. Activities include fundraising, volunteer service and outreach opportunities. See park headquarters for more information.*

Take advantage of scheduled programs: *Activities include fishing clinics, guided tours and special events.*

Park Reservations
(512) 389-8900
texasstateparks.org

Texas State Parks Store
Pedal boat, canoe, kayak and fishing boat rentals; fishing tackle, nature books, refreshments, ice, firewood, shirts, caps and one-of-a-kind gift items are available at the headquarters building.

Flash Flooding Caution
With no containment dam upstream, the river at this point is wild, untamed and subject to intense flash flooding. Be prepared to evacuate the park during advance notice.

Located on the Great Texas Coastal Birding Trail, Palmetto State Park is known as a "hot spot" for birding opportunities with over 240 species observed within the park's boundaries.

Civilian Conservation Corps (CCC) Refectory
Many CCC structures still exist in the park. Please observe these with respect and admiration.

Please Note:

- VALID PARK PERMITS ARE REQUIRED on the windshield of each vehicle. Only guests with overnight permits may remain in the park after 10 p.m.
- CHECK-OUT TIME is 2 p.m. RENEWAL is pending site availability.
- Cabin check-out is at 1 p.m.
- DISCHARGING OF GRAY OR BLACK WASTEWATER, except at the dump station, is prohibited.
- Excess Vehicle Fees are required at campsites with more than two licensed vehicles (including trailers).
- Day Use visitors are not permitted to picnic in numbered camp sites.
- Vehicles must remain on the pavement at all times, including loading and unloading.
- A maximum of 8 people and 2 tents are allowed at each campsite.
- Tents must be on the tent pad where tent pads are provided.
- CAMPFIRES are permitted only in fire rings provided at each site.
- PUBLIC CONSUMPTION or display of any alcoholic beverage is prohibited.

Legend:

- Headquarters
- State Parks Store
- Restrooms
- Showers
- Water Sites Only
- Water/Electric Sites
- Dump Station
- Cabin
- Scenic Overlook
- Wheelchair Accessible
- Hiking Trail
- Interpretive Trail
- Picnic/Day Use Area
- Picnic Shelter
- Parking
- Fishing Pier
- Playground
- Residence
- Group Camping

78 Park Road 11 South
Gonzales, TX 78629
(830) 672-3266

In accordance with Texas State Depository Law, this publication is available at the Texas State Publications Clearinghouse and/or Texas Depository Libraries.
© 2012 Texas Parks and Wildlife Department   PWD MP P4505-049H (2/12)

farms in Gonzales County attract numbers of crested caracara. This attraction also accounts for the roosting caracaras in the park and the surrounding trees.

Canoe and paddle boat rentals are available. Campsites are also available, as well as one cabin.

DIRECTIONS
From Cuero, drive north on US 183 to Gonzales. Continue another 14 miles north of Gonzales on US 183 to the park.

CONTACT INFORMATION
Palmetto State Park, Route 5, Box 201 Gonzales, TX 78629
Phone: 830-672-3266
Web Site: http://www.tpwd.state.tx.us/spdest/findadest/parks/palmetto/

COASTAL PLAINS

#146 Port Lavaca Bird Sanctuary

GPS 28.517, -96.495

ON THE MATAGORDA BAY IN PORT LAVACA, TEXAS

KEY BIRDS
Nelson's sharp-tailed sparrow, common goldeneye, American oystercatcher

BEST SEASON
Winter and migration

AREA DESCRIPTION
A marshy coastal wetlands area with some trees, brush, and grassy feeding areas

Walk out on the Formosa Wetlands Walkway to the Alcoa Birding Tower. Birders should watch the marshlands along the walkway for Nelson's sharp-tailed and seaside sparrow, along with the clapper rail. The best viewing for these species will be in the winter and early spring months.

Birders who may also be "green inclined" should note that the pathway is constructed of recycled plastic with the major contribution coming from Formosa Plastics. The tower was built and paid for by the people of Port Lavaca and the Alcoa Corporation.

From the birding tower, birders should watch for a variety of gulls and terns and the now recovered brown pelican. Visitors should also enjoy a slow drive east across the Lavaca Bay bridge toward Point Comfort to enjoy the many species of birds along the old causeway.

Pay close attention to the bay waters and spoil islands for common goldeneye, American oystercatcher, common loon (quite uncommon), horned grebe, and osprey.

DIRECTIONS
From the intersection of US 87 and TX 35 in Port Lavaca, and go east on TX 35 a short distance to the Port Lavaca Lighthouse Beach and Bird Sanctuary. Take the exit to your right immediately before the bridge across Lavaca Bay.

CONTACT INFORMATION
Port Lavaca/Calhoun County Chamber of Commerce & Agriculture, P. O. Box 528, Port Lavaca, Texas 77979 / Phone: 361-552-2959
Site open for day use only.

Barrow's Goldeneye

COASTAL PLAINS
#147 Magnolia Beach

GPS 28.56, -96.542

SOUTHEAST OF PORT LAVACA, TEXAS

KEY BIRDS
Wilson's phalarope, Hudsonian godwit, and buff-breasted sandpiper

BEST SEASON
Winter and migration

AREA DESCRIPTION
Prairie habitat with scattered rice fields, and beach habitats

The prairies here are composed mainly of scattered rice fields, which will attract a variety of hawks, including the numerous white-tailed hawks, as well as sandhill cranes and a large number of snow geese. Glass the rice fields for spring migrating shorebirds. Some of these species are Hudsonian godwit, buff-breasted sandpiper, and Wilson's phalarope.

Rails are quite common along the marshes as you near the end of the road. Pay close attention as you near the Magnolia and the LaSalle Monuments. While birding along Magnolia Beach north along the bay, glass both the beach and bay for some of the more interesting gulls as well as the three species of scoters.

DIRECTIONS
Driving from Port Lavaca, go west on TX 35 to the intersection with FM 2433. Turn left and continue to the intersection with TX 238. At this point you will veer right on TX 238 and travel a short distance to the intersection with TX 316. Continue straight on TX 316 and follow the signs to Magnolia Beach and Indianola.

CONTACT INFORMATION
None available
Site open for day use only.

Wilson's Phalaropes

COASTAL PLAINS
#148 Magic Ridge

GPS ⊕ 28.519, -96.509

JUST OFF THE BEACH AT INDIANOLA, TEXAS

KEY BIRDS
Ruby-throated hummingbird, whistling duck, boat-tailed grackle, various gulls and terns, roseate spoonbill

BEST SEASON
Winter and migration

AREA DESCRIPTION
A shell ridge covered with one of the northernmost stands of native Tamaulipan scrub

Indianola was the major Texas seaport until devastating hurricanes in the late 19th century led to its abandonment. Mostly the town is nonexistent and hard to find.

The shell-covered ridge, named Magic Ridge, has the northernmost stands of native Tamaulipan scrub. The 78-acre location is now an avian sanctuary owned by the Texas Ornithological Society. The tract is bisected by Zimmerman Road.

The Golden Crescent Nature Club ranks this site and the adjoining land within the top five birding destinations near Victoria.

This is the site where Calhoun County was able to amass 243 species during a spring migration count. This area is commonly known as "Zimmerman Road", "Cemetery Road", or "Magic Road" by birders that are familiar with the area.

Boat-tailed Grackle

Area birders for years have frequented this site and birded from the two public access points: the county road and the Old Town Cemetery. This site is a well-known site for watching for neotropical migratory songbirds, shorebirds, as well as some south Texas species on the northern edge of their range.

All along Zimmerman Road, north to the gate and then south back to the cattle guard, pay attention to the scrub brush and the wet areas along the road. The areas off the road are private property, so please accomplish your birding from the road to both protect the habitat and to avoid trespassing.

Birders should spot scrub birds such as long-billed and curve-billed thrashers, Bewick's wren and, during migrations, many species of songbirds as well as ruby-throated hummingbirds. Watch the water along the road for boat-tailed grackle, whistling duck, roseate spoonbill, gulls and terns, wood stork, and reddish egret.

The mouth of Powderhorn Lake is an excellent place to see roosting American oystercatcher and other waterbirds.

DIRECTIONS
From Magnolia Beach, continue south along Lavaca Bay to Indianola Beach. Turn right on FM 316; continue about 1/4 mile, then turn right onto Zimmerman Road. Cross the cattle guard and continue toward the Old Town Cemetery. At the cemetery you are at Magic Ridge. From Zimmerman Road, continue straight to Powderhorn Lake and Indianola.

CONTACT INFORMATION
Texas Ornithological Society (TOS)
Phone: 281-440-6364
Site open for day use only.

BIRDING TRAILS: TEXAS GULF COAST

Rockport/Port Aransas Loop

As many birders know this coastal refuge, The Aransas National Wildlife Refuge is the southern migration point of the much endangered whooping crane. These large birds can be seen from the Rockport area north to the refuge and many parts in between.

One of our nation's National Seashores is located just south of Corpus Christi, and watching the shore and wading birds will keep new birders reaching for their bird books.

Don't leave out Seabrook on your tour of this loop, and pay special attention to Port Aransas and Mustang Island as you drive slowly on Highway 361. Port Aransas is the home of the Whooping Crane Festival each February.

Inland there are several sites worth visiting near Victoria and Goliad with more than a little Texas history thrown in for good measure. US 77 will take you through some interesting habitat and leave you wishing you had more time with the birds.

All in all, the Rockport/Port Aransas Loop will keep you as busy as you want to be. However the Texas Coastal Area is a large part of the state, so relax and enjoy adding that new bird to your life list.

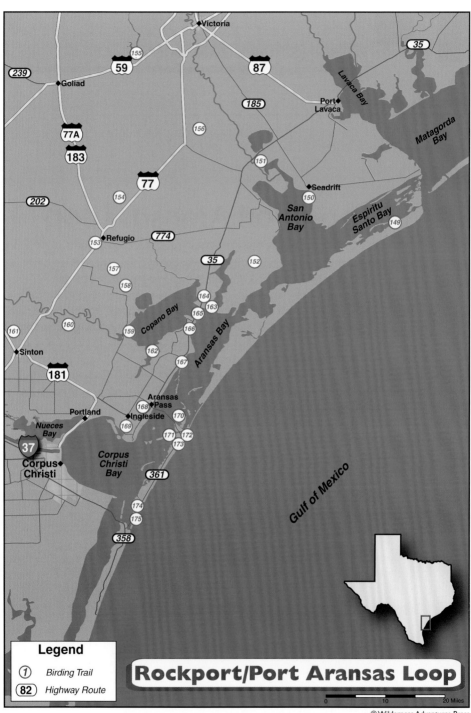

Victoria

35

155
59

239

Goliad

87

Port
Lavaca

Lavaca Bay

185

Matagorda
Bay

156

77A

183

151

202

77

154

Seadrift

150

San
Antonio
Bay

Espiritu
Santo Bay

149

153 Refugio

774

35

152

157

158

164

163

161

160

159

Copano Bay

165

166

Aransas Bay

Sinton

162

167

181

Aransas
Pass
168

Portland

Ingleside

170

Nueces
Bay

169

171 172

37

173

Corpus
Christi

Corpus
Christi
Bay

361

Gulf of Mexico

174

175

358

Legend

1   *Birding Trail*

82   *Highway Route*

Rockport/Port Aransas Loop

0   10   20 Miles

Rockport/Port Aransas Locations

149. Port O'Connor/Matagorda Island State Wildlife Area
150. Seadrift/Swan Point
151. Guadalupe Delta Wildlife Management Area
152. Aransas National Wildlife Refuge
153. Lion's /Shelley Park
154. Golidad State Park
155. Coleto Creek Reservoir and Park
156. Rio Vista Bluff Ranch
157. Fennessey Ranch
158. Mission River Flats
159. Copano Bay
160. Welder Park
161. Rob and Bessie Welder Park
162. Aransas Woods
163. Goose Island State Park
164. Big Tree
165. Copano Bay State Fishing Pier
166. Rockport Demo Bird Garden
167. Connie Hagar Sanctuaries
168. Newbury Park Hummingbird Garden
169. Live Oak Park
170. Aransas Pass Wetlands
171. Leonabelle Turnbull Birding Center
172. Port Aransas Jetty
173. Port Aransas Wetland Park
174. Mustang Island State Park
175. Corpus Christi Pass

ROCKPORT/PORT ARANSAS LOOP

#149 Port O'Connor/Matagorda Island State Wildlife Area

GPS 28.328, -96.478

ON MATAGORDA BAY

KEY BIRDS
White-tailed hawk, whooping crane, brown pelican, peregrine falcon

BEST SEASON
All seasons

AREA DESCRIPTION
Barrier island habitat

Port O'Connor is the port of embarkation for Matagorda Island Park. The dock and ferry service is operated by TPW and is located at 16th and Maple in Port O'Connor. The ferry operates to allow pedestrians to reach the island.

This wildlife area is really located on an offshore barrier island that creates several bayside marshes and consists of 56,688 acres. It is no longer in the state park system. It is operated and jointly owned by the Texas General Land Office and the U.S. Fish and Wildlife Service. This site is managed as the Matagorda Island National Wildlife Refuge and Texas State Natural Area. TPW manages the area for public use, while the Fish and Wildlife Service has the responsibility for managing the wildlife and habitat on the island.

The 38-mile long island changes from less than a mile to about four and a half miles in width.

Whooping Crane

This is the place for birders to see a wide variety of migratory birds. It must be noted that this location attracts some 19 state or federally listed threatened or endangered species. Birders should also keep a wary watch for alligators.

History buffs birding this location will find an old lighthouse dating back to 1852 on the north end of the island.

No island on the Texas Coast with public access is as unspoiled as Matagorda, and no visitor to Texas should leave without experiencing the breathtaking scenery and birdlife to be found here.

White-tailed hawk, whooping crane, brown pelican, peregrine falcon, and a host of shorebirds are some of the over 320 species catalogued by TPW and the USFWS. Best viewing time is in the morning, so leave for this location in the dark. Don't miss the sunrise, with birds taking off for a new day along the coast.

While in Port O'Connor, bird the mudflats on the north end of Washington Street. The best birding will be at low tide.

DIRECTIONS
Travel to the intersection of FM 1289 and TX 185, then go left (southeast) on TX 185 to Port O'Connor.

CONTACT INFORMATION
Matagorda Island Park, P.O. Box 117, Port O'Connor, Texas 77982
Phone: 361-983-2215 or 361-983-4358
Call TPW ahead for information and to reserve space on the ferry. This location is access restricted; please call ahead.

ROCKPORT/PORT ARANSAS LOOP
#150 Seadrift/Swan Point

GPS 28.389, -96.71

CLOSE TO THE SAN ANTONIO BAY NEAR SEADRIFT, TEXAS

KEY BIRDS
Scoters, oldsquaw, a variety of bay ducks

BEST SEASON
Winter and migration

AREA DESCRIPTION
Bayside and beachfront habitats

This location is an excellent place to glass San Antonio Bay. Scoters, oldsquaw, and a variety of bay ducks have been seen in this area, so inspect the bay waters closely.

After a visit to Swan Point go back to Seadrift, and drive along the bay front. During the winter months numerous waterfowl, gulls, and terns may be found here. During the winter of 1995 an oldsquaw was seen here.

DIRECTIONS
Drive west on TX 185 to Seadrift and Swan Point. To reach Swan Point follow the signs to the public boat ramp one mile east of Seadrift off of TX 185.

CONTACT INFORMATION
Seadrift Chamber of Commerce,
Mailing address: PO Box 3
Seadrift, Texas, 77983
Phone: 361-237-0406
Site open for day use only.

Lesser Scaup

ROCKPORT/PORT ARANSAS LOOP
#151 Guadalupe Delta Wildlife Management Area

GPS 28.472, -96.828

NORTH OF SEADRIFT, TEXAS BORDERING TX 35

KEY BIRDS
Herons, egrets, and wading birds, white-faced ibis, roseate spoonbill, wood stork

BEST SEASON
Winter and migration

AREA DESCRIPTION
Freshwater lake and marsh habitats, along with coastal marshes

Guadalupe Delta WMA consists of four units: Mission Lake Unit with 4,447 acres, the Hynes Bay Unit with 1,007.72 acres, the Guadalupe River Unit with 1,138 acres, and the San Antonio Unit with 818 acres. It is within the delta of the Guadalupe River. It's a combination of natural and manmade wetland areas.

The observation deck or the platform is located on the south side of TX 35 and is open throughout the year, but the WMA itself is closed and is accessible only during scheduled events.

The freshwater lake and marshes at Guadalupe Delta are seasonally swamped with floodwaters that attract waterfowl, shorebirds, and a variety of herons, egrets, and wading birds.

In late summer and early fall, wood storks may be spotted in this location. The wetlands around Buffalo Lake offer great places to view roseate spoonbills, herons, egrets, white-faced ibis, and the least bittern.

Roseate Spoonbill

During the late spring, birders should watch and listen for the call of the marsh wren. Guided tours in both the spring and fall will take birders into the Guadalupe Delta. These tours are part of the Texas Conservation Passport Program conducted by the Texas Parks and Wildlife.

DIRECTIONS
From Seadrift, travel north on TX 185 back to TX 35, then turn left (west) on TX 35. Continue until reaching the Guadalupe Delta WMA entrance.

CONTACT INFORMATION
Guadalupe Delta WMA, Texas Parks and Wildlife, 2601 N. Azalea, Suite 31, Victoria, TX 77901
Phone: 361-576-0022 or 361-790-0308 is the regional office
Site open for day use only.

ROCKPORT/PORT ARANSAS LOOP
#152 Aransas National Wildlife Refuge

GPS 28.233, -96.9002

SOUTH OF AUSTWELL, TEXAS

KEY BIRDS
Whooping crane, crested caracara, buff-bellied hummingbird

BEST SEASON
Winter and migration

AREA DESCRIPTION
Oak woodlands, bayside and Intracoastal habitats, mesquite and south Texas brush

No single location along the Texas Coast captures the traveler's interest more than does this refuge — best known as the winter home of the endangered whooping crane. The arrival of the cranes marks the end of their 2,500-mile flight from Canada.

The search for wintering cranes should begin from the observation tower located on the Tour Loop Drive. Seeing an exceptional variety of both resident and transient birds is worth the trip. The number of species seen at Aransas is rapidly nearing the 400 mark.

Watch the shallow waters along the margins of San Antonio Bay and from the Jones Lake viewing platform for both white and white-faced ibis, reddish egret, roseate spoonbill, and a wide variety of ducks, grebes, and many shorebirds.

Whooping Cranes

The oak woodlands are an excellent location to see buff-bellied hummingbirds from late spring through fall. Hiking the birding trail immediately past the heron flats parking area is especially favorable for migrant landbirds.

Birders searching for purple gallinule and common moorhen along the water's edges will be well rewarded. Birds such as ducks and grebes are common winter visitors. Birders driving the tour road will find the best times will be in the early morning and late evening. Watch for crested caracara perching in the upper branches of the ever-present mesquite trees.

The wildlife interpretive center is located near the entrance of the refuge. Birders should ask for a map and bird checklist when they are checking in. The center also has a well-stocked book store. A number of valuable reference books and field guides may be purchased here, including this book.

DIRECTIONS

To reach the entrance to the refuge, continue south on TX 35 until reaching the intersection with TX 239, then turn left (east) and follow the signs through Austwell.

CONTACT INFORMATION

Aransas National Wildlife Refuge, P.O. Box 100, Austwell, Texas 77950
Phone: 361-286-3559; 361-286-3533
Site open for day use only. The refuge is open daily from sunrise to sunset; the wildlife interpretive center hours are 8:30am to 4:30pm.

ROCKPORT/PORT ARANSAS LOOP
#153 Lion's/Shelley Park

GPS 28.296, -97.28

ON THE MISSION RIVER IN REFUGIO, TEXAS

KEY BIRDS
Crested caracara, white-tailed hawk, herons

BEST SEASON
Migrations

AREA DESCRIPTION
Bottomland forests, the coastal prairie is now either in agriculture or brush

Birders should enter the park slowly and glass the power poles and lines as well as the brush for raptors. Some of these may be white-tailed hawk, red-tailed hawk, and the crested caracara. Lucky birders may spot a Harris's Hawk.

Shelley Park is located on the Mission River, and the bottomland forests here will oftentimes attract migrant birds in spring and fall. Riparian woodlands here may draw the migrants into the trees. The surrounding habitats are coastal prairie that is now mainly agriculture or brush. This fact is generally inhospitable to forest species. Watch the trees carefully along the river for green kingfisher, a South Texas specialty.

DIRECTIONS
From TX 35 and FM 774, travel west to Refugio. Continue on FM 774 across US 77 and into Lion's / Shelley Park.

CONTACT INFORMATION
Refugio County Chamber of Commerce
Phone 361 526-2835
Site open for day use only.

Little Blue Heron

ROCKPORT/PORT ARANSAS LOOP
Goliad State Park

#154

GPS 28.391, -97.225

ON US 183 JUST SOUTH OF GOLIAD, TEXAS

KEY BIRDS
White-tailed hawk, scissor-tailed flycatcher, loggerhead shrike

BEST SEASON
All seasons

AREA DESCRIPTION
A mix of three ecological zones and located on the San Antonio River

Goliad is one of the most hallowed of Texas cities, with the Mission Espiritu Santo, the General Zaragoza birthplace, and the grave of Col. James W. Fannin and his soldiers.

A visit to 188-acre Goliad State Park, therefore, presents the rare opportunity to simultaneously experience human as well as natural history. Goliad is situated within a transition zone, where broad ecological influences join at a biological juncture.

Nature trails here traverse a selection of upland and bottomland habitats. This is a pleasant mix of eastern, western, and south Texas thorn-scrub species that will attract birds and birders, making an early morning hike very productive. Some of the species encountered may be scissor-tailed flycatcher, white-tailed hawk, crested caracara, and a loggerhead shrike, as well as the tufted titmouse, American crow, purple martin, and the barn swallow.

Scissor-tailed Flycatcher

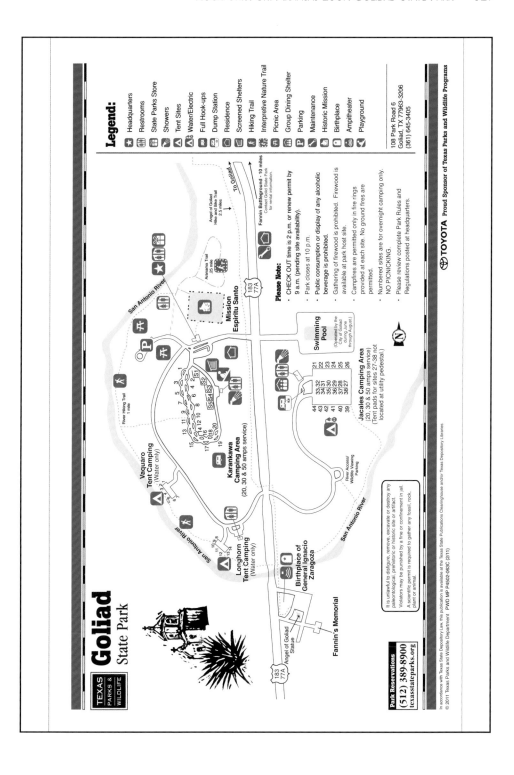

Goliad
State Park

TEXAS PARKS & WILDLIFE

Park Reservations
(512) 389-8900
texasstateparks.org

Fannin's Memorial

Angel of Goliad Statue

Birthplace of General Ignacio Zaragoza

Longhorn Tent Camping (Water only)

Vaquero Tent Camping (Water only)

River Hiking Trail 1 mile

San Antonio River

Karankawa Camping Area (20, 30 & 50 amps service)

River Access/ Wildlife Viewing Parking

San Antonio River

Mission Espiritu Santo

Swimming Pool (Operated by the City of Goliad during June through August.)

Jacales Camping Area (20, 30 & 50 amps service) (Tent pads for sites 27-38 not located at utility pedestal.)

Aranama Trail .25 mile

Angel of Goliad Hike and Bike Trail 2.5 miles

Fannin Battleground - 10 miles Contact Gold State Park for rental information.

To Goliad

183 77A

It is unlawful to disfigure, remove, excavate or destroy any paleontological, prehistoric or historic site or artifact.
Violators may be punished by a fine or confinement in jail.
A scientific permit is required to gather any fossil, rock, plant or animal.

Please Note:

- CHECK OUT time is 2 p.m. or renew permit by 9 a.m. (pending site availability).
- Park closes at 10 p.m.
- Public consumption or display of any alcoholic beverage is prohibited.
- Gathering of firewood is prohibited. Firewood is available at park host site.
- Campfires are permitted only in fire rings provided at each site. No ground fires are permitted.
- Numbered sites are for overnight camping only. NO PICNICKING.
- Please review complete Park Rules and Regulations posted at headquarters.

Legend:

★ Headquarters		🚻 Restrooms	
🏪 State Parks Store		🚿 Showers	
🏕 Tent Sites		Water/Electric	
Full Hook-ups		Dump Station	
Residence		Screened Shelters	
Hiking Trail		Interpretive Nature Trail	
Picnic Area		Group Dining Shelter	
🅿 Parking		Maintenance	
Historic Mission		Birthplace	
Amphitheater		Playground	

108 Park Road 6
Goliad, TX 77963-3206
(361) 645-3405

TOYOTA Proud Sponsor of Texas Parks and Wildlife Programs

In accordance with Texas State Depository Law, this publication is available at the Texas State Publications Clearinghouse and/or Texas Depository Libraries.
© 2011 Texas Parks and Wildlife Department   PWD MP P4502-063C (2/11)

DIRECTIONS

Starting from Refugio, take US 183 north toward Goliad, and continue until reaching the entrance to Goliad State Park located on US 183 just south of Goliad.

CONTACT INFORMATION

Goliad State Park, P.O. Box 727, Goliad, TX 77963
Phone: 361-645-3405
This site is open daily with developed camping available. Fees to enter and camp are charged.

ROCKPORT/PORT ARANSAS LOOP
Coleto Creek Reservoir and Park

#155

GPS | **28.722, -97.176**

ON US 59 BETWEEN GOLIAD AND VICTORIA, TEXAS

KEY BIRDS
Bald eagle, osprey, waterfowl

BEST SEASON
Winter

AREA DESCRIPTION
Open grassy and wooded lakeside areas

This multi-use facility is operated by the Guadalupe-Blanco River Authority and contains camping and picnic sites, restrooms, nature trails, and a variety of other day-use opportunities within its 190 acres. Approximately 40 acres have been developed.

Birding is generally best around the reservoir, so scan the lake for osprey, bald eagle, grebes, waterfowl, and cormorants. Most any inland reservoir in the state may lure in an odd gull, grebe, or duck during the winter, so glass the lake carefully. Cormorants are usually found in water with a population of fish.

DIRECTIONS
Drive east on US 59 from Goliad to the entrance to Coleto Creek Reservoir and Park. The park is approximately 12 miles southwest of Victoria on US 59.

CONTACT INFORMATION
Coleto Creek Park, P.O. Box 68, Fannin, TX 77960 / Phone: 361-575-6367
E-mail: svazquez@gbra.org
Website: http://www.gbra.org/coletocreekpark
Site open daily with developed camping available for a fee.

Bald Eagle

ROCKPORT/PORT ARANSAS LOOP
Rio Vista Bluff Ranch

#156

GPS⊕ 28.554, -97.015

NEAR MCFADDIN, TEXAS – 16 MILES SOUTH OF VICTORIA

KEY BIRDS
Mourning dove, Inca dove, rock dove, greater roadrunner

BEST SEASON
All seasons

AREA DESCRIPTION
Cypress swamp, coastal prairie wetlands, mesquite savannah, lakes, ponds and riparian woodlands

Over 350 bird species have been sighted on the 2,800-acre ranch. Habitats include coastal prairie wetlands, mesquite savannah, cypress swamp, lakes, ponds and woodlands located mostly along the Guadalupe River.

Wildlife is abundant on this historic working ranch. Facilities include hiking trails and observation stands, some of which are wheelchair accessible.

Species to watch for are mourning dove, Inca dove, rock dove, greater roadrunner, ruby-throated hummingbird, and belted kingfisher.

A friendly birder passed this along: Be sure to visit the McFaddin Café located in the town of McFaddin. Visitors will learn about area ranching history. Then open the menu and order some of great food, especially some pie. As a bonus, the McFadden Café people can direct you to some great birding sites, as well as some that are usually overlooked.

CONTACT INFORMATION
Ranch web site: www.riovistaranchtx.com
Phone: 361-935-6216 for reservations and directions.
Email: snipes10@viptx.net.
This site is access restricted, so please all ahead for reservations

Roadrunner

ROCKPORT/PORT ARANSAS LOOP
Fennessey Ranch

#157

GPS 28.23, -97.246

SOUTH OF REFUGIO, TEXAS

KEY BIRDS
Black-bellied whistling duck and mottled duck

BEST SEASON
All seasons

AREA DESCRIPTION
Inland marsh, riparian woodland, coastal grassland, thorn-scrub brush

The Fennessey Ranch is a private ranch, and visitation must be arranged through Fennessey Ranch Nature Tours using the phone number listed in the contact information.

Inland marsh, riparian woodland, coastal grassland, thorn-scrub brush are some of the ranch habitats on this 3,500 acres. The Fennessey Ranch is blessed with numerous bird species and other wildlife.

Black-bellied whistling-duck and mottled duck, sometimes called Texas mallard, will nest in the marshes as do least bittern, purple gallinule, common moorhen, and marsh wren. The masked duck has appeared here in the recent past.

The winter will bring sparrows to the grasslands and Sprague's pipits, that will launch into the air in front of your hiking boots.

Birders should make it a point to glass the riparian forest along the Mission River. This area attracts migrant landbirds moving inland

Black-bellied Whistling Duck

in spring and toward the coast in fall. Hummingbirds will gather here in numbers and in migration, the trees vibrate from the sound of hummingbirds feeding on turk's cap and hawking insects.

Thousands of sandhill cranes, geese, and waterfowl all add to a spectacular sunset at the ranch. Just watching the numbers of birds flying back to their roosts is spectacular.

DIRECTIONS

Driving from Refugio, take FM 774 east 2 miles to the intersection with FM 2678. Turn right on FM 2678 and drive 4.6 miles south to the entrance of the Fennessey Ranch. A large sign marks the entrance gate.

CONTACT INFORMATION

Fennessey Ranch Nature Tours, P.O. Box 99, Bayside, TX 78340
Phone: 361-529-6600
Web Site: http://fennesseyranch.com/
This site is access restricted, so please call ahead for reservations. A fee is charged.

ROCKPORT/PORT ARANSAS LOOP
Mission River Flats

#158

GPS 28.184, -97.214

LOCATED ON FM 2678 NEAR BAYSIDE, TEXAS

KEY BIRDS
Wood stork, American avocet

BEST SEASON
Winter and migration

AREA DESCRIPTION
Roadside habitats with large expanses of mud flats during the spring

When the road crosses the Mission River bridge, find a good place to park safely on the shoulder. The Mission River Flats may be birded from the shoulder of the road. Please use extreme caution and watch for traffic that has speed on their minds and not birds.

In late summer and early fall wood storks may be seen here, and waterfowl flocks in the winter may be prodigious. Low water levels in spring may expose vast expanses of mudflats, and migratory shorebirds will concentrate in the shallow waters. This is a great place to watch for American avocet during the winter months.

DIRECTIONS
Continue south on FM 2678 toward Bayside. When the road crosses the Mission River you are there.

CONTACT INFORMATION
City of Bayside phone: 361-529-6520

American Avocets

ROCKPORT/PORT ARANSAS LOOP

#159 Copano Bay/Black Point

GPS 28.132, -97.034

NEAR BAYSIDE, TEXAS ON A BLUFF OVERLOOKING COPANO BAY

KEY BIRDS
Cooper's and sharp-shinned hawks, all three falcons, American kestrel, merlin, peregrine

BEST SEASON
All seasons, especially migration

AREA DESCRIPTION
Bayside habitats and sand and mud flats

Inspect the flats south of Bayside for pelicans, waterfowl, herons, egrets, and shorebirds. In the shallows, birders will find the reddish egret. Watch the flats at low tide for a multitude of shorebirds.

Perched upon a bluff over Copano Bay is the town of Bayside. At times, especially during migrations, several species of hawks will be seen from this ridge. Local birders say this is a great place to see raptors such as Cooper's and sharp-shinned hawk, American kestrel, merlin, peregrine, and the northern harrier hawk at almost eye level.

Bird this area in fall during the passage of cold fronts to enjoy the peak times of raptor movements.

DIRECTIONS
From Mission River Flats, stay on FM 2678 which becomes FM 136 immediately south of the Mission River and on to Bayside.

CONTACT INFORMATION
Refugio County Chamber of Commerce
P. O. Box 127
Refugio, Texas 78377
Phone: 361-526-2835
Site open for day use only.

American Kestrel

ROCKPORT/PORT ARANSAS LOOP
#160 Welder Park

GPS 28.107, -97.377

OFF US HWY 77 NORTH OF SINTON, TEXAS

KEY BIRDS
Waterthrush, prothonotary warbler, common yellowthroat

BEST SEASON
Winter and migration

AREA DESCRIPTION
A wooded area with immense trees along the creek

Welder is a great birding location mostly overlooked by birders and not often listed in most of the field guides. So this location is rarely birded in spite of it being one of the better birding locations in the county. Located in a remote corner of Sinton, the park is closed to vehicular traffic, which improves the birding considerably. Visitors should leave their cars and walk into the park.

Welder attracts many species of migrating birds. The large trees located on the creek can attract many of these migrants during the spring. Birders should watch for prothonotary warbler, waterthrush, or the common yellowthroat. In the densest growth, watch for worm eating, hooded, and mourning warblers.

Mesquite scrub brush lining the park entrance may warrant a brief stop at the fence's edge. Birders may see a number of species like the Bewick's wren and the blue-gray gnatcatcher. These species are not normally found inside the more open park.

DIRECTIONS
Drive south on FM 136 to the intersection with TX 188. Turn west on TX 188, and continue to Sinton and US 181. Welder Park (not to be confused with the Rob and Bessie Welder Park) may be reached off US 181 on N. Rachal in Sinton. From the intersection with N. Rachal, turn right and look for the sign to the Wayne Hitt Law Enforcement Center. Stay on N. Rachal across Chiltipin Creek to the entrance to the park at 700 North Rachal Avenue.

CONTACT INFORMATION

Welder Park, P. O. Box 1400, Sinton, TX 78387
Phone: 361-364-2643
URL: www.welderwildlife.org
Site open for day use only.

Bewick's Wren

ROCKPORT/PORT ARANSAS LOOP

Rob and Bessie Welder Park

#161

GPS 28.068, -97.528

ON US 181, JUST NORTHWEST OF SINTON, TEXAS

KEY BIRDS
Common yellowthroat and marsh wren, along with migrating species

BEST SEASON
Winter and migration

AREA DESCRIPTION
Open grasslands with scattered trees near a densely vegetated pond

This park is a multi-use facility in the City of Sinton. Of the approximately 300 acres of the park, Sinton has recently dedicated about 45 acres to remain as a natural preserve.

To access the nature trail, as birders enter the park, stay to the right past the ballparks until reaching the parking lot. This trail circles through open grasslands with scattered trees, and eventually passes by an observation platform overlooking a densely vegetated pond.

Watch the cattails carefully for yellowthroat and marsh wrens, as well as yellow-headed blackbirds. Watch the trees around the pond for migrants. As the habitat grows older it should improve greatly.

DIRECTIONS
The Rob and Bessie Welder Wildlife Foundation is located approximately 8 miles north of Sinton on US 77. The refuge is open to the public each Thursday at 3:00pm. Contact the Welder Wildlife Foundation for a bird checklist and information about public access.

CONTACT INFORMATION
Welder Wildlife Foundation, P.O. Drawer 1400, Sinton, TX 78387
Phone: 361-364-2643
Site open for day use only.

Yellow-headed Blackbird

ROCKPORT/PORT ARANSAS LOOP
Aransas Woods

#162

GPS 28.026, -97.145

NEAR PORT BAY ON TX 35

KEY BIRDS
Waterfowl and wading birds

BEST SEASON
Winter and migration

AREA DESCRIPTION
Grassland, oak mottes, and shallow wetlands

At Port Bay, scan the bay for waterfowl and wading birds, and inspect the mudflats for shorebirds before arriving at the Aransas Woods. Park at the gate and enter the woods.

During "fallouts" the coastal mottes, like Aransas Woods, provide protection and food to the thousands of migrating and tired birds. These birds could die unless they find safe roosting trees, if inland forests are not within a reasonable distance.

These three areas – Aransas Woods, Connie Hagar Sanctuary, and Goose Island State Park – are well located to help migrating birds. If you find yourself close to these three areas in the spring, make sure you spend a day or so birding here. You will not be sorry. Birders will enjoy the observation platform located on the site which was donated by the Robert M. Latimer family.

From the platform birders may glass over the oak mottes, grasslands, and shallow wetlands. A number of birds may be watched here, making this site one you should not miss.

American Bittern

Direction

Depart Sinton on TX 188, travel east toward Rockport. After crossing the intersection with TX 136, continue east and stop at Port Bay. Continue east to the intersection with TX 35 Bypass, and turn left (north) and travel for 1.6 miles to the entrance to Aransas Woods. The entrance will be on your right.

Contact Information

None available
Site open for day use only.

ROCKPORT/PORT ARANSAS LOOP
Goose Island State Park

#163

GPS 28.138, -96.986

In Lamar, Texas off of TX 35 on Park Road 13

Key Birds
Waterfowl, loons, grebes, common goldeneye, red-breasted merganser, redhead duck

Best Season
Winter and migration

Area Description
321 acres; Bay side habitats with large live oak trees and smaller scrub brush

The live oaks along the roads as you approach the park during a spring cold spell may be full of migrant birds. According to the Texas Parks and Wildlife the "groundings" or "fallouts" here on the southern tip of the Lamar Peninsula are well known and recorded.

At the end of the road, turn right for the park and left on 12th Street to get to the Big Tree, which is the national champion live oak that is thought to be better than 1,000 years old.

Lamar Beach Blvd. will take you to St. Charles Bay. Turn left and drive along the bay front. Most birders in the winter will stop to view the flocks of waterfowl such as the red-breasted merganser, common goldeneye, and redhead duck. Other species which may be seen are loons and grebes. Park Road 13 will be straight ahead and will take you to the park entrance.

Pick up a park bird checklist at the entrance. A slow drive of this

Redhead Ducks

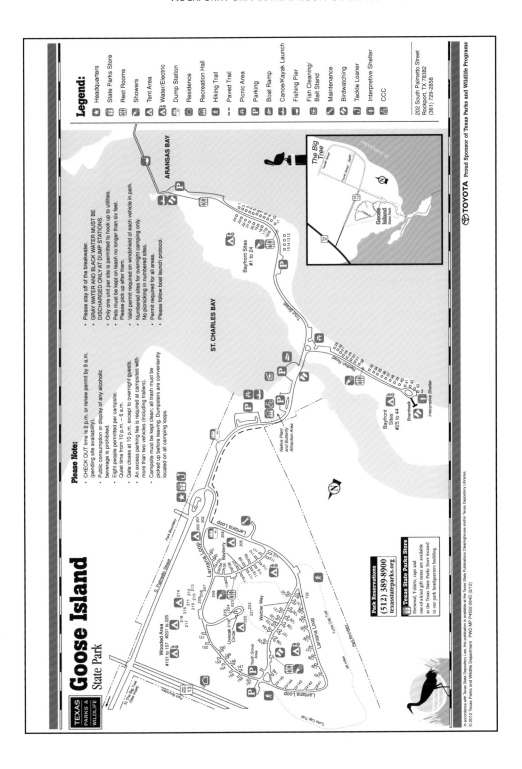

Goose Island
State Park

Please Note:

- CHECK OUT time is 2 p.m. or renew permit by 9 a.m. (pending site availability).
- Public consumption or display of any alcoholic beverage is prohibited.
- Eight people permitted per campsite.
- Quiet time from 10 p.m. – 6 a.m.
- Gate closes at 10 p.m. except to overnight guests.
- An excess parking fee is required at campsites with more than two vehicles (including trailers).
- Campsite must be kept clean; all trash must be picked up before leaving. Dumpsters are conveniently located on all camping loops.
- Please stay off of the breakwater.
- GRAY WATER AND BLACK WATER MUST BE DISCHARGED ONLY AT DUMP STATIONS.
- Only one unit per site is permitted to hook up to utilities.
- Pets must be kept on leash no longer than six feet. Please pick up after them.
- Valid permit required on windshield of each vehicle in park.
- Numbered sites for overnight camping only. No picnicking on numbered sites.
- Permit required for all areas.
- Please follow boat launch protocol.

Legend:

- Headquarters
- State Parks Store
- Rest Rooms
- Showers
- Tent Area
- Water/Electric
- Dump Station
- Residence
- Recreation Hall
- Hiking Trail
- Paved Trail
- Picnic Area
- Parking
- Boat Ramp
- Canoe/Kayak Launch
- Fishing Pier
- Fish Cleaning/Bait Stand
- Maintenance
- Birdwatching
- Tackle Loaner
- Interpretive Shelter
- CCC

Park Reservations
(512) 389-8900
texasstateparks.org

Texas State Parks Store
Firewood, T-shirts, caps and one-of-a-kind gift items are available at the Texas State Parks Store located in our park headquarters building.

ARANSAS BAY

ST. CHARLES BAY

The Big Tree

202 South Palmetto Street
Rockport, TX 78382
(361) 729-2858

TOYOTA Proud Sponsor of **Texas Parks and Wildlife Programs**

321-acre area will let you see migrants in the live oaks. Glass the marshes for gallinules, marsh wrens, rails, and the common yellowthroat. Over 300 varieties of birds have been seen in the park.

There is also a nature trail located in the park and a slow hike will allow birders to enjoy the beauty of the bay and the wind-sculpted oaks along the shore.

Another feature of the park is the number of bird specialists living in the park that conduct birding walks and presentations in the evenings.

DIRECTIONS
Stay on TX 35 Bypass until it dead ends at FM 3036. Turn right or to the east, and continue until the intersection with TX 35, where you will turn north. You will cross Copano Bay on the Lyndon B. Johnson Causeway. In Lamar, turn right on Main Street just past the Sea-Gun Resort. Stay on main to Park Road 13 and the entrance to Goose Island State Park.

CONTACT INFORMATION
Goose Island State Park, Star Route 1, Box 105, Rockport, Texas 78382
Phone: 361-729-2858
This site is open daily with developed camping available for a fee.

ROCKPORT/PORT ARANSAS LOOP
#164 Big Tree

GPS 28.139, -96.988

IN GOOSE ISLAND STATE PARK

KEY BIRDS
Whooping crane, sandhill crane, and migrating birds of several species such as warblers and wrens

BEST SEASON
Fall migration

AREA DESCRIPTION
There is a willow-grove and wet slough in this location

The Big Tree is the national champion live oak, thought to be better than 1,000 years old.
  This is where I photographed the whooping cranes that are featured on the cover of this book. Watch for the cranes in the field across the road from the Big Tree and the adjoining yards nearby. Many of these cranes have been close enough for great photography. There is also a road around the pasture on three sides. Again, please respect the area someone may have taken before you. Mind your manners and don't move in on a birder or photographer set up on some whooping crane.

DIRECTIONS
From Highway 35 go left on Main Street. Just over the bridge from Rockport, turn left on 12th Street. Follow the signs to the Big Tree. Turn right for the park and left for big tree.

CONTACT INFORMATION
Rockport Fulton Chamber of Commerce, 319 Broadway St, Rockport, TX 78382
Phone: 361-729-6445
Website: www.rockportfulton.org
This site is for day use only.

Whooping Cranes

A Word About the Whooping Crane

The U.S. Fish and Wildlife Service (USFWS) is the principal Federal Agency responsible for conserving, protecting and enhancing fish, wildlife, and plants and their habitats for the continuing benefit of the American people.

The USFWS manages the 97-million-acre National Wildlife Refuge System, which encompasses 547 national wildlife refuges, thousands of small wetlands and other special management areas.

The USFWS also oversees the Federal Assistance program, which distributes hundreds of millions of dollars in excise taxes on fishing and hunting equipment to state fish and wildlife agencies.

It must be noted and remembered that the largest majority of the funds for these refuges came from sportsmen by way of the Waterfowl Stamp hunters must buy to hunt waterfowl. For many years, non-hunters would not buy the stamps but continued to visit the refuges. This mindset must change.

WHOOPING CRANES

The whooping crane is one of the rarest birds in North America. It is also the tallest, with adults approaching five feet in height. Males are slightly larger than females. Whooping cranes mate for life and can live nearly 30 years in the wild, and 35 to 40 years in captivity. Adult whooping cranes have snow-white plumage with black wingtips. Their bills are dark olive-gray, which becomes lighter during the breeding season. All of the whooping cranes alive today – both wild and captive – are descendants of the last 15 remaining cranes that were found wintering in Texas in 1941.

In the freshwater and brackish marshes of South Texas, a distinct and wild trumpeting call can be heard across the marsh. It is the whooping crane, *Grus Americana*, and the rarest crane species.

These are magnificent birds, unique to North America. Whooping Cranes are considered one of the best known of all endangered species, and they symbolize the struggle to maintain the vanishing creatures of this world.

They are the tallest bird in North America, standing nearly five feet tall, with a seven-foot wingspan. Their snow-white body feathers are accented by jet-black wing tips and a crescent of black feathers with a patch of red skin on the head. In the fall, juveniles have a rusty brown plumage with some white adult feathers just beginning to appear. By the time they leave Aransas, the juveniles are white.

The only natural wild flock of whooping cranes nests in Wood Buffalo National Park in the Northwest Territories of Canada. These large birds mate for life, but have been known to re-mate following the death of their mate. They may survive up to 25 years in the wild and 35 to 40 years in captivity. Adults generally begin to produce eggs when they reach four or five years of age and then will lay two eggs, usually rearing only one chick.

In late spring and summer, their nests are built on small islands of bulrushes, cattails, and sedges. Dry years can result in heavy predation with few young surviving. In the fall, migration begins. Whoppers fly 2,500 miles from Wood Buffalo National Park to their wintering grounds at Aransas NWR.

They travel as a single pair, family group, or in small flocks, sometimes accompanying sandhill cranes. They migrate during daylight hours and making regular stops. By December, all or nearly all have reached the marshes in and around Aransas.

Over the 2004-2005 winter, 216 birds stayed in the area feeding on blue crabs, wolfberries, crayfish, frogs, large insects, and roasted acorns from prescribed burns. As spring arrives with warmer weather and longer days, the cranes will prepare for the trip back to Wood Buffalo by increasing their food intake to fatten up for the long return flight.

Courtship behavior consists of calling, wing flapping, head bowing and astonishing leaps into the air by both birds. These dances begin in late winter as prelude to mating, but may occur at other times as the birds defend their territories or play.

This writer is not alone in objecting to the USFWS trying to create another flock from man-raised cranes that must be lead, unsuccessfully I might add, both north and south. These funds should be spent on helping the only wild flock remaining.

GENERAL VIEWING INFORMATION

A pair or family (three) of whooping cranes can usually be seen from the observation tower generally from mid-October through March. They feed in the marsh during daylight hours. During the winter 2011, I photographed a three-bird family unit near the Big Tree close to Goose Island State Park across the bridge from Rockport.

Be sure to ask at the visitor center front desk for the latest sightings.

The very best way to see quite a few whoopers in a day is to take a boat trip out of Port Aransas or Rockport.

Call the Port Aransas Chamber of Commerce at, 361-749-5919 or look for them on the web at: http://www.portaransas.org/.

The Rockport Chamber of Commerce at 361-729-6445 or 1-800-242-0071 (in Texas). Out of state, call 1-800-826-6441. Their website is www.rockport-fulton.org.

Reference: International Crane Foundation Brochure

ROCKPORT/PORT ARANSAS LOOP
#165 Copano Bay State Fishing Pier

GPS 28.124, -97.016

THE PIER IS LOCATED CLOSE TO FULTON, AT THE BASE OF THE LYNDON B. JOHNSON CAUSEWAY

KEY BIRDS
Peregrine falcon, merlin, osprey, and swallow-tailed kite

BEST SEASON
Winter and migration

AREA DESCRIPTION
Pier and gulf water habitats

A slow walk along the fishing pier with binoculars and a spotting scope should be very productive for grebes, loons, and diving ducks in the bay.

Watch for the American oystercatcher on the shell spoil islands. Be particularly observant to birds close to the southeast corner of the causeway. Also bird the causeway itself, watching for migrating hawks mostly during the spring and fall.

Spotting hawks and other raptors at times gives you excellent watching and photographic chances. At times these birds (raptors) will fly over and along the causeway rather than over the open bay. During migrations you may spot osprey, merlin, and peregrine falcon. A rare sighting of a swallow-tailed kite is possible but quite rare. Pacific loons were seen near the south end of the causeway during the 1995 migration.

DIRECTIONS
From Goose Island State Park go back to TX 35 and turn left (south) toward Fulton. The Copano Bay State Fishing Pier extends from the tip of Lamar Peninsula to Fulton, and may be accessed (for a fee) from the base of the Lyndon B. Johnson Causeway.

CONTACT INFORMATION

Aransas County Navigation District, 911 Navigation Circle, and Rockport, Texas 78382
Phone: 361-729-6661
Copano Causeway North Phone: 361-425-8325
Copano Causeway South Phone: 361-425-8326
Email: aransasnav1@yahoo.com
This site is open daily with developed camping available for a fee.

Osprey

ROCKPORT/PORT ARANSAS LOOP

#166 Rockport Demo Bird Garden and Wetlands Pond

GPS 28.048, -97.042

TXDOT HIGHWAY REST AREA NEAR ROCKPORT, TEXAS

KEY BIRDS
Ruby-throated hummingbird

BEST SEASON
Fall and migration

AREA DESCRIPTION
There is a willow grove and wet slough in this location

Park and walk around the hummingbird garden jointly developed and maintained by Texas Department of Transportation and the community of Rockport. There is a boardwalk and an observation platform.

Beginning about the middle of September, birders may witness hundreds and maybe thousands of mostly ruby-throated hummingbirds, as well as other species as they migrate through Rockport.

This is a special event for the town as well as attracting numerous visitors and birders. The community holds their annual Rockport Hummer/Bird Celebration. Information for each year's event is available at the Rockport-Fulton Area Chamber of Commerce.

Birders may watch these little birds closely to learn their feeding habits as well as to notice the native plants that attract these diminutive birds.

Broad-tailed Hummingbird

A boardwalk literally covered with trumpet creeper vines produces flowers that attract hummingbirds to the blooms. Birders should continue on the boardwalk through the willow grove and wet slough for migrating species.

DIRECTIONS
Drive south on TX 35 toward Rockport, and stop at the TXDOT highway rest area on the left, 0.9-mile south of the intersection of TX 35 and FM 3036.

CONTACT INFORMATION
Rockport Fulton Chamber of Commerce, 319 Broadway St, Rockport, TX 78382
Phone: 361-729-6445
Website: www.rockportfulton.org
This site is for day use only.

ROCKPORT/PORT ARANSAS LOOP
#167 Connie Hagar Sanctuaries

GPS 28.009, -97.059

FIRST AND CHURCH STREETS IN ROCKPORT, TEXAS

KEY BIRDS
Grebes, pelicans, and waterfowl, with concentrations of redhead ducks

BEST SEASON
Migrations

AREA DESCRIPTION
Pond, kiosk, all-weather trail

A small motel owned and operated here by Connie Hagar and her husband, Jack, and called the Rockport Cottages was once the pride of the ornithological world dating back to the 1930s.

Connie Hagar was responsible for putting this site on the birders' maps and letting the national birding community know about the large bird migrations along the coast of Texas.

Maintained by the Friends of Connie Hagar, the sanctuary was established to keep alive her memory and provide a resting and feeding area for the many migrants flying into the Rockport area.

Located on six acres, the Connie Hagar Cottage Sanctuary is made up of many types of habitats. Birders should be attentive and may see grosbeaks, flycatchers, vireos, warblers, and thrushes. These species are especially prevalent

White Pelicans

during a spring grounding and fallout. Glass the adjoining grasslands for visiting buntings, dickcissels, and several species of sparrows.

Birders will find a daily bird list posted in the kiosk listing birds seen prior to their arrival.

The town of Rockport is a bayside city and harbors several boats used to see the feeding areas of the endangered whooping crane in the Aransas NWR during the winter months. During the boat ride out, birders may see nesting islands for colonial waterbirds. Seeing the "whoopers" by boat is the best way. There is also a chance to see family groups in the previously mentioned area near the Big Tree.

DIRECTIONS

Drive south on TX 35, and stop at the Connie Hagar Wildlife Sanctuary. Then continue south on TX 35, staying in the left lane. Pass through the Rockport business district on Loop 70. Continue on Loop 70 (E. Market) to S. Church. Turn left on S. Church, and continue until reaching the Connie Hagar Cottage Sanctuary at E. First. Turn right on E. First, and enter the sanctuary through the entrance on your right.

CONTACT INFORMATION

Friends of Connie Hagar Foundation, PO Box 2465, Rockport, TX 78381
Phone: 361-729-2780
Website: www.birdrockport.com/connie_hagar_cottage_sanctuary.htm
Sites are open for day use only.

SEE THE "WHOOPERS" BY BOAT

Airboat Adventures — Capt. David Nesloney — 361-557-1048
Aransas Bay Birding Charters "Jack Flash" Capt. Kevin Sims 361-790-3746
Capt. Tommy Moore — 361-727-0643 - 1-877-892-4737
Captain Eddie Polhemus, Rockport Harbor Phone: 316-749-5448
The Wharf Cat, Rockport Harbor Phone: 800-605-5448 or 361-729-GULL

ROCKPORT/PORT ARANSAS LOOP

#168 Newbury Park Hummingbird Garden

GPS 27.543, -97.857

ON LAMONT STREET IN ARANSAS PASS, TEXAS

KEY BIRDS
Hummingbirds

BEST SEASON
Winter and migration

AREA DESCRIPTION
Coastal live oak habitat

Surrounded by its fringe of coastal live oaks, this small city of Aransas Pass community park is operated in cooperation with TPW and Texas Department of Transportation. Birders should make a note to spend some time glassing the hummingbird garden.

Built with funds from the Trail Project, the Newbury Park Hummingbird Garden is a striking example of wildlife habitat created within an urban setting. It is the largest outdoor hummingbird garden in the state.

The hummingbird garden plays host to thousands of hummingbirds passing through the Aransas Pass area during migration. This garden provides an intimate and relaxing spot to watch and enjoy these tiny migratory birds.

Also watch the park's oaks for other migrant species, particularly during spring cold fronts.

DIRECTIONS
As you leave the Connie Hagar Cottage Sanctuary, drive west on E. First to where it dead ends into TX 35. Turn left or south on TX 35 and travel to Aransas Pass. Continue into Aransas Pass to the intersection of TX 35 and Loop 90, and then veer right on Business 35 to Lamont. When approaching the intersection on Business 35, you may turn left on Lamont at the Dairy Queen and continue straight into Newbury Park.

CONTACT INFORMATION
Aransas Pass Chamber of Commerce, 130 Goodnight, Aransas Pass, TX 78336
Phone: 361-758-2750
Site open for day use only.

Rufous Hummingbird

ROCKPORT/PORT ARANSAS LOOP
Live Oak Park
#169

GPS 27.854, -97.213

ON SHERRY STREET IN INGLESIDE, TEXAS

KEY BIRDS
Thrushes, thrashers, and ground-dwelling warblers, black-crested titmouse and long-billed thrasher

BEST SEASON
Migration

AREA DESCRIPTION
Large open areas with some oak mottes

Located in the remainder of a dense oak motte, Live Oak Park is a community facility that provides outdoor recreational opportunities as well as a nature trail.

Live Oak Park is a small remnant of the extensive oak forest that once covered the coast bordering Redfish Bay. Walk the nature trail and notice the dense red bay understory that dominates this woodland.

The deep layer of fallen leaves on the forest floor is attractive to thrashers, thrushes, and several species of ground-dwelling warblers such as hooded, worm eating, and Swanson's warbler, as well as the ovenbird.

There are two ponds located on the north side of the park. These ponds are both great birding spots (when they have water) where birders may spot mottled ducks and the black-bellied whistling duck. The fulvous whistling duck may be seen during migrations, but your chances are slim.

Black-crested Titmouse

DIRECTIONS

Drive on TX 361 to Ingleside and the intersection with FM 1069. As you enter Ingleside TX 361 will swing to the west toward Gregory. Turn left on FM 1069 and continue to Sherry Street and the sign to Live Oak Park. Turn left on Sherry and enter Live Oak Park.

CONTACT INFORMATION

Gina Graham, Parks Coordinator, City Hall, 2671 San Angelo Street, Ingleside, TX 78362
Phone: 361-776-3438
Site open for day use only.

ROCKPORT/PORT ARANSAS LOOP
#170 Aransas Pass Wetlands

GPS 27.87, -97.069

ON THE NORTH END OF MUSTANG ISLAND

KEY BIRDS
Sooty tern, loons, grebes, diving ducks, and pelicans

BEST SEASON
All seasons, especially the winter

AREA DESCRIPTION
Tidal wetlands

On the way to Port Aransas, birders should not overlook the Conn Brown Harbor. The road is rough but could be well worth the drive. Scan the waters here for grebes, diving ducks, loons, and the seemingly ever-present pelicans. Drive back to TX 361, and drive east toward Port Aransas.

The stretch of TX 361 between Aransas Pass and Port Aransas is bordered by Redfish Bay. Watch for loons, grebes, diving ducks, and pelicans.

This road is also called the Dale Miller Causeway and a great place to watch for shorebirds, waterfowl, grebes, loons, American oystercatcher, snowy plover, and wading birds. If you are extremely lucky, you may see a sooty tern during the summer months.

DIRECTIONS
From Live Oak Park, drive on FM 1069 to the intersection with FM 2725, turn left on FM 2725 and travel to the intersection with TX 361. Turn right on TX 361, and continue north to the intersection where TX 361 will swing to the right. Turn right and continue toward Port Aransas. Before crossing the bridge, turn left at the sign into Conn Brown Harbor and go left on the dirt road and right on the paved road that proceeds into the harbor.

CONTACT INFORMATION
Aransas Pass Chamber of Commerce 130 Goodnight St., Aransas Pass, TX 78336
Phone: 361-758-2750
Site open for day use only.

Brown Pelicans

ROCKPORT/PORT ARANSAS LOOP

#171 Leonabelle Turnbull Birding Center

GPS⊕ 27.827, -97.078

1399 ROSS AVENUE
PORT ARANSAS, TEXAS

KEY BIRDS
Black-bellied whistling duck, cinnamon teal, herons, cormorants, egrets, and grebes including least

BEST SEASON
Winter and migration

AREA DESCRIPTION
Brush and some trees leading to the boardwalk over the marsh

This birding facility is a vivid example of what a community can do to attract birds and birders alike. The boardwalk extends into a freshwater marsh associated with the adjoining wastewater treatment plant.

This location has a consistent supply of fresh water for a wide variety of wetland birds. Walk slowly down the boardwalk for a closer sighting of several bird species.

Birding from the platform is the best idea and you will spot several species of waterfowl, for example cinnamon teal, black-bellied whistling duck, least and other grebes, herons and egrets, brown pelican, cormorants, and shorebirds, such as roseate spoonbills and black-necked stilt.

All along the parking lot and the walkway to the water, birders will notice the many flowering native plants attracting local and migrating birds.

DIRECTIONS
Stay on TX 361 to the ferry landing. While crossing on the free ferry, enjoy the bottle-nosed dolphins and brown pelicans during the short ride. Depart from the ferry and follow the signs to the Port Aransas Birding Center, taking the cut-off to the right on to Ross Avenue.

CONTACT INFORMATION

Visitors Office, 403 W. Cotter, Port Aransas, TX 78373

Phone: 361-749-5919

Site open for day use only.

Tri-colored Heron

ROCKPORT/PORT ARANSAS LOOP
Port Aransas Jetty

#172

GPS 27.835, -97.046

LOCATED ON ALISTER ROAD IN PORT ARANSAS PARK

KEY BIRDS
Magnificent frigatebird, masked and brown boobies

BEST SEASON
All seasons

AREA DESCRIPTION
Park habitat with a rock jetty extending into the Gulf

The jetty extends for several hundred yards into the Gulf, and furnishes an excellent vantage point from which to look for a variety of open water species.

Along the base of the jetties, gulls and terns have found excellent roosting areas. Watch for shorebirds feeding along the beach. During the winter months, watch the Gulf for Bonaparte's gull, jaegers, and the northern gannet. During the summer months, watch for magnificent frigatebird, brown and masked boobies, and sooty tern sometimes seen resting on the jetty.

If your luck holds and not many anglers arrive at the dock, birders might catch a ride as an observer on one of the commercial fishing boats. Port Aransas is the home of several snapper boats that head out to deep water for a day of fishing. In the fall, quite a few pelagic species such as jaegers, shearwaters, and boobies may be spotted.

Magnificent Frigatebird

Contact the Fisherman's Wharf in Port Aransas at 361-749-5760 or 361-749-5448 for information about offshore birding opportunities. In addition, boat trips to The Nature Conservancy of Texas Shamrock Island may be arranged by contacting the Port Aransas Area Chamber of Commerce. The island hosts immense numbers of nesting herons, egrets, and spoonbills in the summer.

DIRECTIONS
From Cut-Off Road, turn right and drive to Alister, then turn left and continue north to Port Aransas Park and the Port Aransas Jetty.

CONTACT INFORMATION
Visitors Office, 403 W. Cotter, Port Aransas, TX 78373
Phone: 361-749-5919
Day use is free, with a fee for overnight camping.

ROCKPORT/PORT ARANSAS LOOP
Port Aransas Wetland Park

#173

GPS 27.824, -97.071

OFF TX 361 IN PORT ARANSAS

KEY BIRDS
A variety of waterfowl and shorebirds

BEST SEASON
Winter and migration

AREA DESCRIPTION
Native dune community, freshwater habitat, scrubby vegetation, and grassy areas

This park is a joint project of the city of Port Aransas, TXDOT, and TPW. Along with parking, it is nicely landscaped and has a boardwalk and an observation platform.

Visiting this location can be a real treat for birders and nature watchers. With its freshwater, winter visitors will be surprised at the numbers and the variations of waterfowl species and the many shorebirds using the area during wet periods. The observation platform overlooks the area and provides a great place for both watchers as well as photographers.

Similar to the Port Aransas Birding Center, during drought times this location may often be the only freshwater habitat within miles. The city of Port Aransas has a raised wheelchair accessible boardwalk leading to a gazebo overlooking the flats.

This park has been mainly improved by landscaping to establish a native dune habitat. During migration, this vegetation and the grasses attract migrant birds.

DIRECTIONS
Return on TX 361 S to Cut-Off Road. Continue south on TX 361 for 0.3 mile from this intersection to the new Port Aransas Wetland Park. Watch for the sign that will be on your right.

CONTACT INFORMATION
Visitors Office, 403 W. Cotter, Port Aransas, TX 78373
Phone: 361-749-5919
Site open for day use only.

Blue-winged Teal

ROCKPORT/PORT ARANSAS LOOP
#174 Mustang Island State Park

GPS 27.671, -97.181

ON PR 53 OFF TX 361 SOUTH OF PORT ARANSAS

KEY BIRDS
Laughing and glaucous gulls, piping and snowy plovers, red knot

BEST SEASON
All seasons

AREA DESCRIPTION
Combination of sand dunes, coastal grasslands, marshes, bayside tidal flats, and sloughs

Approximately 14 miles south of Port Aransas, Mustang Island State Park is 3,954 acres with about five miles of beach on the Gulf of Mexico in Nueces County.

As you drive south along Mustang Island, use the access roads to the beach when you can, and enjoy watching for birds. Species seen most commonly are a variety of shorebirds, gulls, and terns. For well over a decade, there has been a lesser black-backed gull seen on the beach near Port Aransas.

During the early spring, watch for glaucous gulls which are seen here on a regular basis. During periods of high tide, glass the beach for small groups of snowy and piping plovers and, at times, there will be small groups of red knots.

Numerous waterfowl species and shorebirds are common. In addition there are several species of hawks and a wide variety of migratory songbirds.

Laughing Gulls

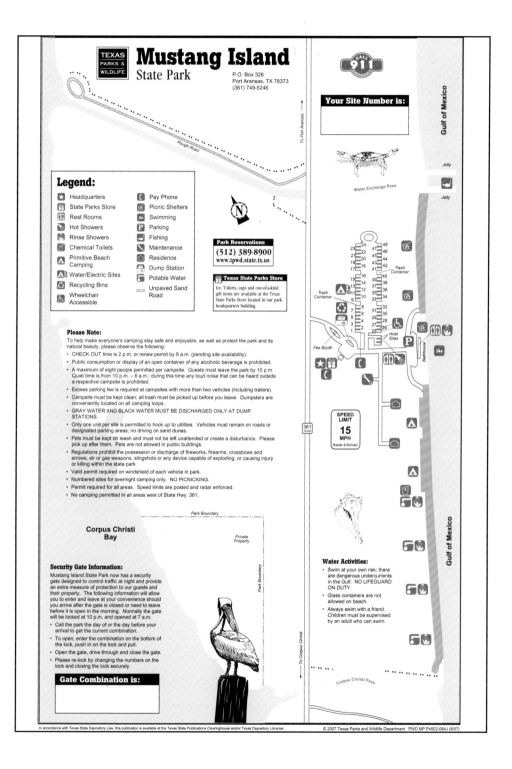

Mustang Island
State Park

TEXAS PARKS & WILDLIFE

P.O. Box 326
Port Aransas, TX 78373
(361) 749-5246

CALL 911 EMERGENCY

Your Site Number is:

Gulf of Mexico

Jetty

Water Exchange Pass

Jetty

Legend:

- ★ Headquarters
- State Parks Store
- Rest Rooms
- Hot Showers
- Rinse Showers
- Chemical Toilets
- Primitive Beach Camping
- Water/Electric Sites
- Recycling Bins
- Wheelchair Accessible
- Pay Phone
- Picnic Shelters
- Swimming
- P Parking
- Fishing
- Maintenance
- Residence
- Dump Station
- Potable Water
- Unpaved Sand Road

Rough Road

To Port Aransas

N

Park Reservations
(512) 389-8900
www.tpwd.state.tx.us

Texas State Parks Store
Ice, T-shirts, caps and one-of-a-kind gift items are available at the Texas State Parks Store located in our park headquarters building.

Please Note:
To help make everyone's camping stay safe and enjoyable, as well as protect the park and its natural beauty, please observe the following:

- CHECK OUT time is 2 p.m. or renew permit by 9 a.m. (pending site availability).
- Public consumption or display of an open container of any alcoholic beverage is prohibited.
- A maximum of eight people permitted per campsite. Guests must leave the park by 10 p.m. Quiet time is from 10 p.m. – 6 a.m.; during this time any loud noise that can be heard outside a respective campsite is prohibited.
- Excess parking fee is required at campsites with more than two vehicles (including trailers).
- Campsite must be kept clean; all trash must be picked up before you leave. Dumpsters are conveniently located on all camping loops.
- GRAY WATER AND BLACK WATER MUST BE DISCHARGED ONLY AT DUMP STATIONS.
- Only one unit per site is permitted to hook up to utilities. Vehicles must remain on roads or designated parking areas; no driving on sand dunes.
- Pets must be kept on leash and must not be left unattended or create a disturbance. Please pick up after them. Pets are not allowed in public buildings.
- Regulations prohibit the possession or discharge of fireworks, firearms, crossbows and arrows, air or gas weapons, slingshots or any device capable of exploding, or causing injury or killing within the state park.
- Valid permit required on windshield of each vehicle in park.
- Numbered sites are for overnight camping only. NO PICNICKING.
- Permit required for all areas. Speed limits are posted and radar enforced.
- No camping permitted in all areas west of State Hwy. 361.

Trash Container

Fee Booth

Host Sites

Bathhouse

P

SPEED LIMIT 15 MPH
Radar Enforced

361 TEXAS

Park Boundary

Corpus Christi Bay

Private Property

Park Boundary

Security Gate Information:
Mustang Island State Park now has a security gate designed to control traffic at night and provide an extra measure of protection to our guests and their property. The following information will allow you to enter and leave at your convenience should you arrive after the gate is closed or need to leave before it is open in the morning. Normally the gate will be locked at 10 p.m. and opened at 7 a.m.

- Call the park the day of or the day before your arrival to get the current combination.
- To open, enter the combination on the bottom of the lock, push in on the lock and pull.
- Open the gate, drive through and close the gate.
- Please re-lock by changing the numbers on the lock and closing the lock securely.

Gate Combination is:

Gulf of Mexico

Water Activities:
- Swim at your own risk; there are dangerous undercurrents in the Gulf. NO LIFEGUARD ON DUTY.
- Glass containers are not allowed on beach.
- Always swim with a friend. Children must be supervised by an adult who can swim.

To Corpus Christi

Corpus Christi Pass

Encompassing the entire barrier islands ecosystem, the state park takes in bayside tidal flats, sloughs, dunes, coastal grasslands, and marshes.

In the winter, watch for shorebirds as well as gulls and terns. Glass the Gulf for seabirds. The coastal grasslands should provide cover for LeConte's sparrow and the sedge wren. Wilson's plover is known to nest along the beach and will use the tidal flats in summer, along with the horned lark on the dunes habitat.

DIRECTIONS
Mustang Island SP is located on PR 53 off TX 361.

CONTACT INFORMATION
Mustang Island State Park, P O Box 326 Port Aransas, TX 78373
Phone: 361-749-5246
This site is open daily with developed camping available for a fee.

ROCKPORT/PORT ARANSAS LOOP
#175 Corpus Christi Pass

GPS 27.654, -97.194

LOCATED JUST PAST MUSTANG ISLAND STATE PARK ON MUSTANG ISLAND

KEY BIRDS
Piping plover and long-billed curlew

BEST SEASON
All seasons

AREA DESCRIPTION
Salt grass and island grasses with bayside habitats and shallow marshes

This is an area where you must slow down and pay attention. Driving south along Mustang Island toward Corpus Christi, there will be several hurricane wash-over sites where wading birds such as herons and egrets will be found. These passes have been cut through the island by past tropical storms. These cuts are common on coastal barrier islands and are worth glassing to spot several species of shore and waterbirds.

Corpus Christi Pass is located to the south of Mustang Island State Park; its bayside flats provide wintering areas for species like the piping plover and long-billed curlew. Glass these waters for hooded mergansers and green-winged teal. In the late spring, look here again for the nesting snowy plover.

Long-billed Curlew

DIRECTIONS

As you travel toward Corpus Christi, Corpus Christi Pass slices across the island south of Mustang Island State Park.

CONTACT INFORMATION

Visitors Office, 403 W. Cotter, Port Aransas, TX 78373
Phone: 361-749-5919
Site open for day use only.

BIRDING TRAILS: TEXAS GULF COAST

Coastal Bend Loop

Covering some of the best wetland and coastal birding in the state, the Coastal Bend Loop is where birders should plan on spending an appreciable amount of time.

Either entering the area on Highway 77 or on the Interstate system, there will be plenty of places to point your binoculars at our feathered friends. There are also numerous eating and lodging places for your birding comfort.

Centering around Corpus Christi - the largest city in the loop – birders will find dozens of locations only a short drive from the city center of Corpus. This includes Port Aransas with its annual Whooping Crane Festival with several exhibits and speakers on birding and crane topics.

Sites along the Laguna Madre are another attraction where spending time will be to the birder's advantage. These include Corpus Christi Bay and, of course, the Gulf of Mexico as seen from the beaches on Mustang Island.

Spend time on Nueces and Baffin Bays as well as the freshwater lakes including Lake Corpus Christi, Choke Canyon, and several of the rivers and creeks in this area.

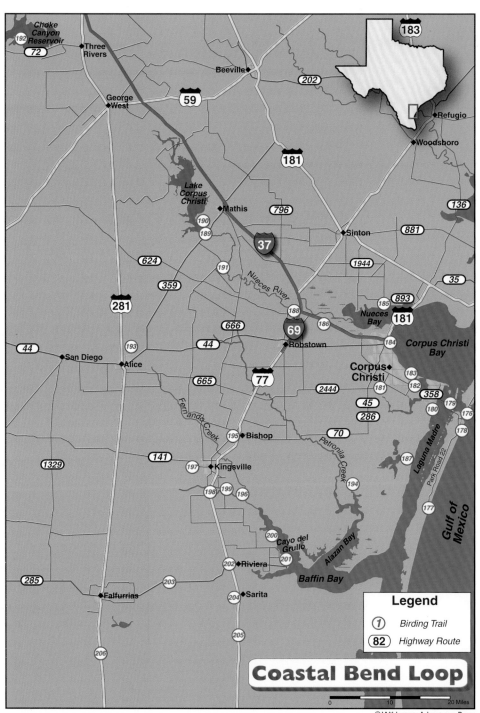

Coastal Bend Loop

Legend

(1)   *Birding Trail*

82   *Highway Route*

0   10   20 Miles

Coastal Bend Loop Locations

176. Packery Channel
177. Padre Island National Seashore
178. Packery Channel Park
179. JFK Causeway Wetlands
180. Redhead Pond Wildlife Management Area
181. South Texas Botanical Gardens
182. Oso Bay Park
183. Hans A. Suter Wildlife Area
184. Blucher Park
185. Fred Jones Nature Sanctuary
186. Hilltop Community Center
187. Pollywog Pond
188. Hazel Bazemore County Park
189. Wesley Seale Dam and the City of Corpus Christi Wildlife Sanctuary
190. Lake Corpus Christi State Park
191. Fort Lipantitlan State Historic Park
192. Choke Canyon State Park
193. Lake Findley (the former Lake Alice)
194. John J. Sablatura Nature Park
195. Bishop City Park
196. Santa Gertrudis Creek
197. King Ranch
198. Dick Kleberg Park
199. Santa Gertrudis Creek Bird Sanctuary
200. Drum Point & Kaufer-Hubert Memorial Park
201. Riviera Fishing Pier
202. Louise Trant Bird Sanctuary
203. Hawk Alley
204. Sarita/The Kenedy Ranch
205. TXDOT Sarita Rest Area
206. Brooks County Rest Area

COASTAL BEND LOOP
#176 Packery Channel

GPS 27.62, -97.205

ON THE SOUTH END OF MUSTANG ISLAND WHERE TX361 SPLITS

KEY BIRDS
American oystercatcher, long-billed curlew, ruddy turnstone, black-bellied plover

BEST SEASON
All seasons

AREA DESCRIPTION
Grassy salt flats between highway and the water

Following the great war of northern aggression, beef-packing plants were opened at the mouth of the Corpus Christi Pass. A man-made channel was cut and it was called Packers' Channel, and eventually Packery Channel. In the early 1920s, the Corpus Christi Ship Channel was dredged and this caused an irregular water flow through Corpus Christi Pass, which began to silt up.

Packery Channel and its bayside flats hold thousands of shorebirds during a low tide. Watch for American oystercatcher, ruddy turnstone, black-bellied plover, marbled godwit, and the long-billed curlew. Birders will spot snowy plovers scurrying along the edges of the pass. Glass the water for loons, diving ducks, and grebes in the clear waters of the channel.

American Oystercatcher

DIRECTIONS

Continue south on TX 361 close to where it dead ends into PR 22, the road that runs south on Padre Island.

CONTACT INFORMATION

Visitors Office, 403 W. Cotter, Port Aransas, TX 78373
Phone: 361-749-5919
Site open for day use only.

COASTAL BEND LOOP
Padre Island
National Seashore

#177

GPS 27.424, -97.299

BARRIER ISLAND SOUTH OF MUSTANG ISLAND

KEY BIRDS
Peregrine falcon, gulls, terns, white-tailed hawk, and ferruginous hawk

BEST SEASON
All seasons

AREA DESCRIPTION
Sandy and shell-covered dunes and Gulf of Mexico seaside beach, sea grasses, and no trees

The Padre Island National Seashore can provide extremely good birding on this Texas barrier island. Ask for a bird checklist, as well as a map of this 133,000-acre park at the visitor's center.

Padre Island National Seashore plays host to over 380 species of birds each year. Nearly half of all bird species documented in North America may be seen along the national

Sandwich Tern

seashore. The national seashore is a fabulous place for birds and bird-watchers because it is located on the Central Flyway, a major migration route for birds traveling during their migration to and from North, Central, and South America.

The park stretches over 80 miles along the Gulf to the Port Mansfield Cut, dividing Padre Island into North and South Padre Island. This man-made cut was made to allow boats departing Port Mansfield to access the Gulf of Mexico. Most of the beach on the north part of the island is accessible by a four-wheel-drive vehicle.

The paved road ends and travel is good for regular vehicles. From the visitor's center, visitors may drive five miles beyond the end of the paved road before encountering soft sand.

Watch for species such as peregrine falcons that will fly through the park in great numbers during the fall. Migrant land birds use the spring vegetation, as will terns, gulls, and shorebirds on the beaches.

During winter months, watch for raptors perched on the power poles all along Park Road 22. Some raptor species that may be seen are the white-tailed hawk, ferruginous hawk, as well as the white-tailed kite. A tip from a local birder sent me down Bird Basin Road, 2.6 miles north of the visitor's center. A slow drive on the road can be very productive; the road has the right name.

Watch the shallow water marshes on this road to see nesting colonies of colonial water birds such as herons, egrets, terns, and black skimmers. For the best sighting and watching, use your spotting scope from or near the end of the road. Other species to watch for are bitterns, gallinules, and shorebirds. Primitive as well as developed camping facilities are available in the park.

DIRECTIONS
Continue south on TX 361 and turn left on PR 22 to Padre Island National Seashore. TX 361 / PR 22 also continues to the right or west to Corpus Christi. Continue along PR 22 to the entrance and visitor's center which is located about 10 miles after the turn.

CONTACT INFORMATION
Padre Island National Seashore, 9405 S. Padre Island Drive, Corpus Christi, TX 78418
Phone: 361-949-8068
Web site: www.nps.gov/pais/index.htm
This site is open daily with both primitive and developed camping facilities available in the park.

COASTAL BEND LOOP
Packery Channel Park

#178

GPS 27.589, -97.219

BORDERS PACKERY CHANNEL, THAT SEPARATES MUSTANG AND PADRE ISLANDS

KEY BIRDS
Sulphur-bellied flycatcher, gray kingbird, and black-whiskered vireo

BEST SEASON
Winter and migration

AREA DESCRIPTION
Oak mottes, salt and grass flats

The park gives birders a different view of the Packery Channel; and the birds attracted to this waterway to feed and roost. After entering the park, birders should glass the oak mottes to their right. These trees are mostly on private property as well as the housing located here. Please respect the private property by not trespassing.

These trees will pull in migrating land birds in good numbers. Corpus Christi birders consider this one of their most productive spring locations.

Birders should bird along the public road, watching the trees for migrants. A number of rarities have been spotted here in past years, such as the gray kingbird, black-whiskered vireo, and the sulphur-bellied flycatcher.

DIRECTIONS
Return north on the park entrance road and turn left or west on PR 22 toward Corpus Christi. After a short distance turn right into Packery Channel County Park.

CONTACT INFORMATION
Corpus Christi Convention and Visitors Bureau, 1201 North Shoreline Boulevard, Corpus Christi, TX 78403
Phone: 361-881-1888 or 800- 678-6232
Email: members@theccchamber. org
Site open for day use only.

Black-whiskered Vireo

COASTAL BEND LOOP
#179 JFK Causeway Wetlands

GPS 27.654, -97.254

Along the road crossing the Laguna Madre from Mustang Island to Corpus Christi

Key Birds
Black skimmer, reddish egret, pelicans, and shorebirds

Best Season
All seasons

Area Description
Extensive tidal sand flats but little salt marsh vegetation, with sea grass beds on both sides of the causeway

The flats along this causeway are a great place to watch pelicans, shorebirds, herons, and egrets, including the threatened reddish egret.

Other species found here are Wilson's plover, great egret, great blue heron, tri-colored heron, white ibis, laughing gull, brown pelican, great tailed grackle, semi-palmated sandpiper, roseate spoonbill, snowy egret, and least sandpiper.

Located near the west end of the causeway, there is an area of the beach protected for nesting black skimmers. The skimmers and their nests and young may be spotted during the summer months. Birders should also watch for Wilson's plovers and nesting least terns.

Directions
From Packery Channel County Park, return to PR 22 and turn right or west in the direction of Corpus Christi. After traversing the bridge over the Laguna Madre, the JFK Causeway becomes a rather low crossing that offers opportunities to park and view the bay.

Contact Information
Corpus Christi CVB, 1823 N. Chaparral, Corpus Christi, TX 78401
Phone: 1-800-766-2322
Hours of Operation: 10am - 4pm daily. Site open for day use only.

Reddish Egret

COASTAL BEND LOOP

#180 Redhead Pond Wildlife Management Area

GPS 27.639, -97.289

NEAR CORPUS CHRISTI BAY IN CORPUS CHRISTI, TEXAS

KEY BIRDS
Common goldeneye and hooded merganser

BEST SEASON
Winter

AREA DESCRIPTION
Bayside habitats and wetland

Redhead Pond gives birders the chance to view large groups of wild birds very close to downtown Corpus Christi.

It is a joint project of TNCT and TPW. The observation platform here affords a protected and excellent view of the waterfowl that are found in the ponds each winter. As is the case along the Texas middle and upper coasts, rafts of redhead ducks are common, but a number of other duck species as well as grebes and black-crowned night-herons will also winter in this area. Two species that may be difficult to see other places along the coast are the hooded merganser and the common goldeneye.

DIRECTIONS
Drive west on the JFK Causeway that will become South Padre Island Drive west of the Laguna Madre, and then enter Flour Bluff. Exit South Padre Island Drive on Waldron Road; turn left or south under the freeway and return to Laguna Shores Road. Turn right and continue south on Laguna Shores to Redhead Pond WMA.

CONTACT INFORMATION
WMA, Matt Nelson, County Courthouse, Room 101, Bay City, TX 77414
Phone: (979) 323-9553
Site open for day use only.

Hooded Merganser

COASTAL BEND LOOP

South Texas Botanical Gardens

#181

GPS 27.653, -97.404

8545 SOUTH STAPLES STREET
CORPUS CHRISTI, TX 78413

KEY BIRDS
Groove-billed ani, long-billed thrasher, curve-billed thrasher, and pyrrhuloxia

BEST SEASON
All seasons

AREA DESCRIPTION
South Texas scrub brush with garden areas and some virgin mesquite trees and lakeside habitats

This preserve offers birders an assortment of south Texas habitats including an herb-lined bird and butterfly nature trail through the mesquite trees, a cattail-lined "Gator Lake" which can be observed from the birding tower, as well as the open thatched-roof gazebo.

The nature trails at some locations border Oso Creek, offering birders a good chance to experience South Texas scrub birding. Birders should watch for long-billed and curve-billed thrasher, groove-billed ani, pyrrhuloxia, and olive sparrow.

Scan and glass the lake and creek, searching for water and wading birds such as least grebe

Pyrrhuloxia

on the water and Couch's kingbird perched in one of the trees bordering the lake.

The botanical garden staff is in the process of planting more bird attractors in the garden areas, to be used as screen and border shrubs as well as native trees.

DIRECTIONS

Return to Laguna Shores Road and turn right or south and continue to the intersection with Yorktown Boulevard, and turn right or west again. Travel on Yorktown Boulevard to the intersection with S. Staples Street and turn left or south. Continue across Oso Creek on S. Staples to the entrance to the Corpus Christi Botanical Garden on your right.

CONTACT INFORMATION

Phone: 361-852-2100
Open 9:00am to 5:00pm, Tuesday through Sunday.
This site is open for day use only and a fee is charged.

COASTAL BEND LOOP
Oso Bay Park

#182

GPS 27.704, -97.336

ON OSO BAY JUST OFF ENNIS JOSLIN ROAD IN CORPUS CHRISTI

KEY BIRDS
Pelicans, waterfowl, and shorebirds

BEST SEASON
Winter and migration

AREA DESCRIPTION
Saltwater bay with tidal flats and shore areas

A falling tide is the best time at this location for birders. The local papers publish the daily tide tables so, in order to be there at the correct time, check the Corpus Christi Caller Times. While you are visiting this park, watch the bay for pelicans, waterfowl, and shorebirds.

There are a very few coastal flats along the central coast that can beat the numbers that at times will be in the thousands for waterbirds in this area. Birds feeding here in this location and in the shallow waters at sunset are a classic site to remember.

DIRECTIONS
Drive north on Staples Street to South Padre Island Drive, then turn right or east on South Padre Island Drive and continue to the Ennis Joslin Road exit. Turn left on Ennis Joslin Road to Oso Bay Park on your right.

CONTACT INFORMATION
Corpus Christi Convention and Visitors Bureau 1201 North Shoreline Boulevard, Corpus Christi, TX 78403
Phone: 361-881-1888 or 800- 678-6232
Email: members@thecccchamber.org
Site open for day use only.

White Pelican

COASTAL BEND LOOP

#183 Hans A. Suter Wildlife Area

GPS 27.709, -97.338

ON THE WESTERN SHORE OF OSO BAY, ON ENNIS JOSLIN ROAD, NEAR THE PHARAOH VALLEY SUBDIVISION

KEY BIRDS
Pelicans, herons, seagulls, coots, egrets, spoonbills, and many species of duck

BEST SEASON
Winter and migration

AREA DESCRIPTION
Tidal pools, exposed at low tide

I hesitate to write this, but after hearing from the birders who have visited this refuge, it could be considered to be one of the best sea bird watching areas in at least North America.

Some of the birds regularly seen in the refuge are roseate spoonbills, pelicans, egrets, herons, seagulls, coots, and ducks during the winter months.

Use the boardwalk to access the lagoon.

Roseate Spoonbill

Birders should glass the tidal pools all along the boardwalk for shorebirds and rails. There is also a short nature trail connecting the parking lot with the boardwalk, which at times is rich with many species of birds during migrations. Take your time and enjoy the lagoon and its bird populations. The waterbird numbers here are well worth the trip. This is another coastal area where the tides will regulate the numbers and species of birds. Check the local paper for a tide chart and plan your visit accordingly.

DIRECTIONS
Drive farther north on Ennis Joslin Road for a short distance to Hans A. Suter Wildlife Area that will be found on the right.

CONTACT INFORMATION
Padre Island Visitors Information Center, 14252 South Padre Island Drive, Corpus Christi, TX 78418
Phone: 512-949-8743
Site open for day use only.

COASTAL BEND LOOP
#184 Blucher Park

GPS 27.791, -97.399

ADJACENT TO THE CENTRAL LIBRARY, ENTRANCE 100 BLOCK OF CARRIZO STREET

KEY BIRDS
Flycatchers, thrushes, vireos, and warblers

BEST SEASON
Migration

AREA DESCRIPTION
Densely wooded park with a small creek flowing through its center

This location is a major stopover for migrating passerines and hummingbirds. There are guided bird walks each Saturday and Sunday in April at 7:30am, excepting Easter.

This densely wooded park with a small creek flowing through its center attracts migrating land birds. Stroll through the park and check every nook and cranny for flycatchers, thrushes, vireos, and warblers.

Several Blucher family homes have been restored, courtesy of the Corpus Christi Junior League located on N. Carrizo Street. There is an environmental education and information center being established here and should be finished by publication of this book. It was the Blucher heirs who donated the land for Blucher Park to the city.

Great Kiskadee

The Audubon Outdoor Club conducts bird walks every Saturday and Sunday in the spring. Information on these bird walks, as well as a pamphlet on *Birding in the Corpus Christi Area*, may be obtained from the Corpus Christi Convention and Visitors Bureau.

DIRECTIONS

From Texas A & M in Corpus Christi, turn west on Ocean Drive and travel into downtown Corpus Christi. Ocean Drive becomes Shoreline Drive as you enter the waterfront area, and continues north to the downtown business district. Turn left on Williams off Shoreline Drive, and continue up the hill – Williams will make a slight jog to the left and become Lipan – to Carrizo Street. Turn left on Carrizo, and travel a short distance to Blucherville and Blucher Park at the corner of Carrizo and Tancahua.

CONTACT INFORMATION

Corpus Christi Convention and Visitors Bureau, 1201 North Shoreline Boulevard, Corpus Christi, TX 78403
Phone: 361-881-1888 or 800- 678-6232
Email: members@theccchamber.org
Site open for day use only.

COASTAL BEND LOOP
#185 Fred Jones Nature Sanctuary

GPS 27.88, -97.409

ON CR 69E (KOONCE LOOP ROAD) IN PORTLAND, TEXAS

KEY BIRDS
Migrating songbirds as well as hummingbirds, vireos, and warblers

BEST SEASON
Migration

AREA DESCRIPTION
Vegetated with native brush such as mesquite, blackbrush, acacia, brasil, agarita, and Texas olive

Owned and operated by Audubon Outdoor Club of Corpus Christi, this location is considered a "do not miss" spot for birders searching for migrating songbirds. One of the year-round birds is the buff-bellied hummingbird, while other species inhabit the trees and brush found along the creek. This park does not allow vehicles in the park. There are designated parking areas and birders should then walk the area.

To say this location is worth a side trip during migrations is an understatement. Located on upper Nueces Bay, the area is covered with native brush such as mesquite, blackbrush, and acacia, to mention a few.

The best reason this location attracts so many birds is that it is situated in about the middle of many miles of agricultural fields that will, at times, lay fallow.

Birds flying through will be attracted naturally to this wooded area. Birders should watch for several species of vireos and warblers during the migrations.

In order to maintain the location, the club asks for donations. As a personal comment, this area is well worth a donation.

DIRECTIONS
Return to TX 35 / US 181 and continue north to Portland. Exit at Moore Avenue (FM 893), and turn left (west). Travel on FM 893 west approximately six miles until reaching CR 69E. Turn left on CR 69E, and continue for approximately half a mile until reaching the Fred Jones Nature Sanctuary that will be on your left.

CONTACT INFORMATION

Audubon Outdoor Club of Corpus Christi, Inc., PO Box 3352, Corpus Christi, TX 78463
Web Site: http://www.ccbirding.com/aoc/sanctuar.htm
Email: Leah Pummill, president, pumml@juno.com
Portland Chamber of Commerce
Phone: 361/643-2475
Open daily from sunrise–sunset.

Red-eyed Vireo

COASTAL BEND LOOP
Hilltop Community Center

#186

GPS  **27.847, -97.591**

11425 LEOPARD STREET
CORPUS CHRISTI, TX 78410

KEY BIRDS
Groove-billed ani, pyrrhuloxia, olive sparrow

BEST SEASON
All seasons

AREA DESCRIPTION
Native brush habitat

Birders will enjoy the nature trail as it winds through South Texas native brush habitat. Pay close attention (again, walk slowly) in your search for resident birds as well as migrant species. Some of the species found here are pyrrhuloxia, olive sparrow, and the groove-billed ani. While birding along the creek, birders may spot a variety of sparrows during the winter, such as Lincoln's and swamp sparrows. Springtime visitors may hear and see the white-eyed vireo, especially in late spring.

DIRECTIONS
Drive east on I-37 and exit at Violet Road. Turn right or south on Violet, and continue to the intersection with Leopard Street. Turn right or west on Leopard, and drive a short distance to the Hilltop Community Center that will be located on your left.

CONTACT INFORMATION
Phone: 361-241-3754
Site open for day use only.

Groove-billed Ani

#187 Pollywog Pond

GPS 27.523, -97.363

LOCATED OFF OF UP RIVER ROAD NEAR CORPUS CHRISTI

KEY BIRDS
Great kiskadee and groove-billed ani

BEST SEASON
All seasons

AREA DESCRIPTION
Lake and pool habitats

This group of lakes and pools provides habitat for an assortment of ducks and wading birds such as the black-bellied whistling duck. The water department uses these ponds as settlement ponds. Watch for least grebe here as well as least bitterns in the summer.

The willows that line the ponds attract migrants such as white-winged dove and great kiskadee. The low scrub attracts the groove-billed ani.

Tule Lake, located off the 7200 block of Up River Road, is often worth checking for ducks, geese, and wading birds.

DIRECTIONS
Head east on Leopard Street to Violet Road and turn left. Cross I-37 and continue to Up River Road. Turn left on Up River Road and travel approximately two miles to Pollywog Pond, marked by the sign on your right.

CONTACT INFORMATION
Corpus Christi Convention and Visitors Bureau, 1201 North Shoreline Boulevard, Corpus Christi, TX 78403
Phone: 361-881-1888 or 800- 678-6232
Email: members@theccchamber.org
Site open for day use only.

Great Kiskadee

COASTAL BEND LOOP
Hazel Bazemore
County Park

#188

GPS 27.868, -97.642

FARM TO MARKET ROAD 624 AND COUNTY ROAD 69
CORPUS CHRISTI, TX

KEY BIRDS
Hawks, olive sparrow, groove-billed ani

BEST SEASON
Winter and migration

AREA DESCRIPTION
Wetland pond and woodlands

Several major flyways converge at this one location, making Hazel Bazemore Park one of the most unique locations in the nation. This 77.6-acre park located on the Nueces River boasts the highest concentration of migrating raptors in the United States. Hawk enthusiasts have known about this location for more than thirty years, and formal counts have taken place there since 1990.

Ask for a map and bird checklist as you enter the park. Hazel Bazemore County Park is renowned for its hawk migration in September and October. Thousands upon thousands of hawks including Mississippi kites, Swainson's hawks, and broad-winged hawks, will fly the Nueces River and enter the park each year. Birders from around the world travel here to watch the hawks.

Watching the weather report is very important, because hawks like to migrate with the cold fronts of the fall, arriving this far south in late September and early October.

Other species seen here year round are white and white-faced ibis, least grebe, neotropic cormorant, anhinga, buff-bellied hummingbird, roseate spoonbill, black-bellied whistling-duck, mottled duck, Harris's hawk, white-tailed hawk, green jay, long-billed thrasher, olive sparrow, crested caracara, groove-billed ani, pauraque, white-tipped dove, greater roadrunner, golden-fronted woodpecker, and great kiskadee. Watch for least bittern, wood stork, lesser nighthawk, scissor-tailed and brown-crested flycatchers, and Cassin's sparrow during warmer months.

Rough-legged Hawk

Birders hiking along the nature trails should watch for long-billed thrasher, olive sparrow, and the groove-billed ani. Also watch the ponds for various species of ducks and wading birds such as rails.

DIRECTIONS
Continue west on Up River Road (which becomes FM 624 at US 77) to the sign marking the entrance to Hazel Bazemore County Park.

CONTACT INFORMATION
Phone: 361-387-4231
Site open for day use only.

COASTAL BEND LOOP

#189 Wesley Seale Dam and the City of Corpus Christi Wildlife Sanctuary

GPS 28.041, -97.869

ON PARK ROAD 25 NEAR LA FRUTA, TEXAS

KEY BIRDS
Blue-winged teal, gadwall, and American wigeon

BEST SEASON
All seasons

AREA DESCRIPTION
Elm-hackberry forest, along wooded areas and lakeside habitats

This 258-acres sanctuary has a nature trail head that is located to your left as you enter the area. The trail goes through a dense elm and hackberry forest. Watch these trees for several tropical species. Hike across the dam and you will reach the Nueces River.

The water gathers in pools at the base of the dam, often attracting waterfowl such as American wigeon, gadwall, and blue-winged teal. During the winter months, black phoebes have been seen along the rocks. After the dam, birders should continue along the trails and into the trees extending along the river. Osprey may be seen hunting down the river for fish.

The dam has stopped the flooding, that is needed to maintain a good quality bottomland forest. Birders should keep this in mind during a drought.

DIRECTIONS
Stay on FM 624 to the intersection with FM 666, then turn right (north) on FM 666 and continue to Mathis and the intersection with TX 359. Turn left (southwest) on TX 359, and proceed to Park Road 25. Turn right, and after a short distance (0.1 mile) park at the entrance to the City of Corpus Christi Wildlife Sanctuary. Then, continue on Park Road 25 north for 0.5 mile, and park at the north end of Wesley Seale Dam.

CONTACT INFORMATION

Corpus Christi Convention and Visitors Bureau,
1201 North Shoreline, Corpus Christi, TX 78403
Phone: 361-881-1888 or 800- 678-6232
Email: members@theccchamber.org
Site open for day use only.

Blue-winged Teal

COASTAL BEND LOOP
Lake Corpus Christi State Park

#190

GPS 28.062, -97.875

SOUTHWEST OF MATHIS, TEXAS

KEY BIRDS
Curve-billed thrasher, greater roadrunner, and pyrrhuloxia

BEST SEASON
All seasons

AREA DESCRIPTION
Made up of mostly dry chaparral, the areas below the dam offer a more wooded landscape

The present site of Lake Corpus Christi State Park overlooks an impoundment of the Nueces River, which was the disputed boundary between Texas and Mexico following the Texas Revolution.

This 356-acre park is comprised of mostly dry chaparral, a different habitat from the woodlands located below the dam. Below the dam the terrain will be damper, with more humidity, and a better chance of needing insect repellant.

Species such as greater roadrunner, curve-billed thrasher, and pyrrhuloxia are common

Roadrunner

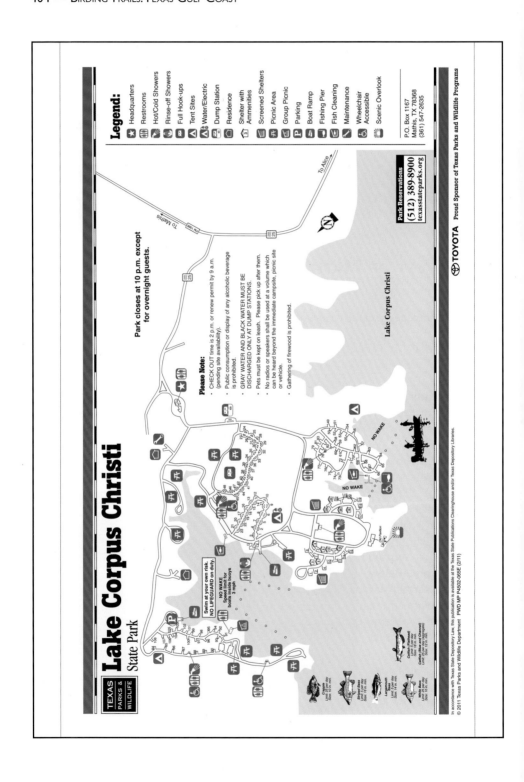

Lake Corpus Christi State Park

Legend:

- Headquarters
- Restrooms
- Hot/Cold Showers
- Rinse-off Showers
- Full Hook-ups
- Tent Sites
- Water/Electric
- Dump Station
- Residence
- Shelter with Ammenities
- Screened Shelters
- Picnic Area
- Group Picnic
- Parking
- Boat Ramp
- Fishing Pier
- Fish Cleaning
- Maintenance
- Wheelchair Accessible
- Scenic Overlook

Park closes at 10 p.m. except for overnight guests.

Please Note:

- CHECK OUT time is 2 p.m. or renew permit by 9 a.m. (pending site availability).
- Public consumption or display of any alcoholic beverage is prohibited.
- GRAY WATER AND BLACK WATER MUST BE DISCHARGED ONLY AT DUMP STATIONS.
- Pets must be kept on leash. Please pick up after them.
- No radios or speakers shall be used at a volume which can be heard beyond the immediate campsite, picnic site or vehicle.
- Gathering of firewood is prohibited.

Park Reservations
(512) 389-8900
texasstateparks.org

P.O. Box 1167
Mathis, TX 78368
(361) 547-2635

To Mathis
To Alice

Lake Corpus Christi

Swim at your own risk.
NO LIFEGUARD on duty.

NO WAKE
Speed limit for boats inside buoys
3 mph

NO WAKE

TOYOTA Proud Sponsor of Texas Parks and Wildlife Programs

here in the plentiful vegetation. The coming of late spring will find birders glassing the grass for Cassin's sparrow. The interesting black-bellied whistling-ducks may be seen on the on the lake, with additional waterfowl species being seen in the winter.

DIRECTIONS

Returning to Park Road 25, travel north for 0.8 mile to the entrance to Lake Corpus Christi State Park.

CONTACT INFORMATION

Lake Corpus Christi State Park, P.O. Box 1167, Mathis, Texas 78368
Phone: 361-547-2635
This location is open daily and offers developed camping with an entrance and camping fee charged.

COASTAL BEND LOOP
Fort Lipantitlan State Historic Park

#191

GPS ⊕ 27.965, -97.818

EAST OF ORANGE GROVE, TEXAS IN NUECES COUNTY

KEY BIRDS
Whooping crane, curve-billed thrasher, vermilion flycatcher, and lark sparrow

BEST SEASON
Winter and migration

AREA DESCRIPTION
Ancient mesquite trees with typical south Texas low brush

Park and walk down to the river below the dam. Watch closely for bitterns, common yellowthroat, and marsh wren along the edges of the marsh. Among some of the species of birds found here and in similar locations are several species of ducks, geese, and seagulls.

Endangered whooping cranes wintering in South Texas are among the most famous and of course, the black skimmer, which is the bird selected to be on the Texas birding signs. The black skimmers, with their interesting feeding method, are found along the entire Texas Coast.

In order to find the curve-billed thrasher, vermilion flycatcher, greater roadrunner, and the lark sparrow, bird the large old mesquites and their surrounding brush. Winter in this location provides habitat for the eastern bluebirds which are found perching on the fences near the entrance of this five-acre park.

Curve-billed Thrasher

For close accommodations, complete with birding on the Nueces River, check out Knolled Farm & Ranch's Bed, Barn & Breakfast, 13016 FM 70, Sandia, TX 78383, Phone: 361-547-2546 / Email: knollefarm@the-i.net, Website: www.knolle.com

DIRECTIONS
Go back on Park Road 25 to the intersection with TX 359, turn right (southwest) and continue across the Nueces River. Immediately after crossing the river turn right at the sign for Camp Shawondasse and continue approximately half a mile to the south end of Wesley Seale Dam. Return to TX 359 and listen for great kiskadee and green jays in the woods along the river. Turn right on TX 359 and proceed west to Sandia. Turn left or south on FM 70 in Sandia, and continue until making an abrupt right. Drive for approximately 2.5 miles and turn left on CR 58. This road will eventually curve to the left, and continue straight to the entrance to Fort Lipantitlan State Historic Park located at the end of CR 101.

CONTACT INFORMATION
Lake Corpus Christi State Park, Mathis, Texas 78368
Phone: 361-547-2635
Primitive camping is allowed.
Site open for day use only and a fee is charged.

BIRDING SIDETRIP
Before you check out Choke Canyon State Park, you may want to wander around in this area for some serendipitous birding. From FM 70, turn right toward Sandia. When the road curves to the left in about 2.5 miles, stay straight ahead on CR 360 toward the Nueces River. This narrow lane winds through picturesque Nueces bottomland country, and eventually curves back northwest to FM 1540. Turn left on FM 1540 and continue to the intersection with FM 70. Turn right and return to Sandia. From Sandia continue southwest on TX 359 to the intersection with FM 534. Turn right on FM 534 and head north toward Dinero. Travel a short distance and turn right on the road marked "Pernitas Point" which is approximately five miles away. Residences in the community of Pernitas Point will attract buff-bellied hummingbird and the groove-billed ani. After birding Pernitas Point, go back to FM 534 and continue to Dinero (look for Harris's Hawk along the way). Continue on FM 534 until reaching I-37 and then turn north on the freeway toward San Antonio.

COASTAL BEND LOOP
Choke Canyon State Park

#192

GPS ⊕ 28.47, -98.338

WEST OF I-37 AND SOUTH OF SAN ANTONIO

KEY BIRDS
Sandhill crane, lesser nighthawk, verdin, Cassin's sparrow, black-throated sparrow, and house finch

BEST SEASON
All seasons

AREA DESCRIPTION
South Texas brush and brasada as well as lakeside habitats

Choke Canyon State Park, consisting of two units – South Shore and Callihan – is located on the 26,000-acre Choke Canyon Reservoir.

Birders should drive slowly on the park roads, watching for lark bunting as well as many species of sparrows. During the winter months, sandhill cranes may be spotted feeding in the open fields.

This area is also a great location to watch for scissor-tailed flycatcher and crested caracara during the summer. Some of the areas bordering the roads are tracts of dry chaparral habitat, so watch for lesser nighthawk, (this is the bird with the shining red eyes on the roads at night) Cassin's sparrow, verdin, and the black-throated sparrow. Birders are well advised to watch for house finch in the brush and on the open slopes.

Choke Canyon Reservoir and Park has been recognized as an important place for birds and bird watchers by the American Birding Association and the Bureau of Reclamation. This distinction was given because of the numbers and varieties of birds supported by the water and the adjacent upland habitats.

The park and lake are also the northernmost range for Mexican species of birds. This is why this has been called one of the finest locations to watch birds in Texas.

Both the Calliham and South Shore units of this park offer exemplary birding opportunities. Ask for a bird checklist and map at the park headquarters.

The Calliham Unit supports populations of wild turkey. Many times around the campsites, Audubon's and Bullock's orioles will be seen in the mesquite trees. Pauraque

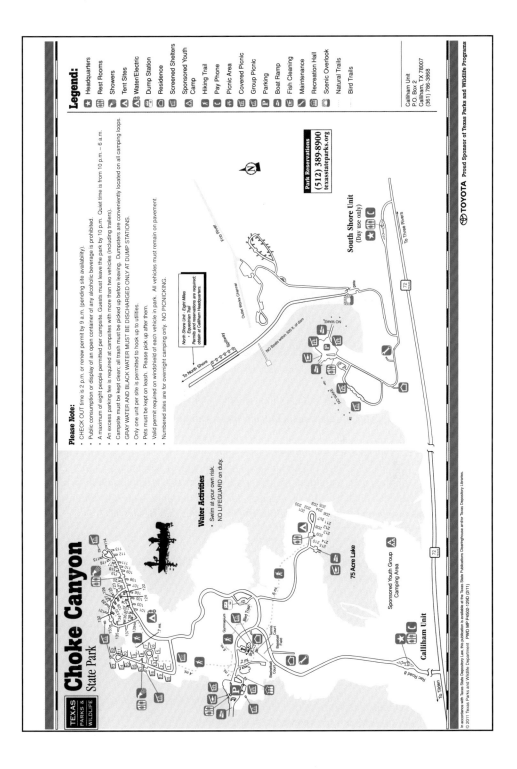

Choke Canyon
State Park

TEXAS PARKS & WILDLIFE

Legend:

- Headquarters
- Rest Rooms
- Showers
- Tent Sites
- Water/Electric
- Dump Station
- Residence
- Screened Shelters
- Sponsored Youth Camp
- Hiking Trail
- Pay Phone
- Picnic Area
- Covered Picnic
- Group Picnic
- Parking
- Boat Ramp
- Fish Cleaning
- Maintenance
- Recreation Hall
- Scenic Overlook
- Natural Trails
- Bird Trails

Please Note:

- CHECK OUT time is 2 p.m. or renew permit by 9 a.m. (pending site availability).
- Public consumption or display of an open container of any alcoholic beverage is prohibited.
- A maximum of eight people permitted per campsite. Guests must leave the park by 10 p.m. Quiet time is from 10 p.m. — 6 a.m.
- An excess parking fee is required at campsites with more than two vehicles (including trailers).
- Campsite must be kept clean; all trash must be picked up before leaving. Dumpsters are conveniently located on all camping loops.
- GRAY WATER AND BLACK WATER MUST BE DISCHARGED ONLY AT DUMP STATIONS.
- Only one unit per site is permitted to hook up to utilities.
- Pets must be kept on leash. Please pick up after them.
- Valid permit required on windshield of each vehicle in park. All vehicles must remain on pavement.
- Numbered sites are for overnight camping only. NO PICNICKING.

North Shore Unit - Eight Miles
- Equestrian Trail
Permits and reservations are required; obtain at Calliham Headquarters.

To North Shore

Water Activities
- Swim at your own risk. NO LIFEGUARD on duty.

75 Acre Lake

Sponsored Youth Group Camping Area

Calliham Unit

South Shore Unit
(Day use only)

To Three Rivers

Park Reservations
(512) 389-8900
texasstateparks.org

Calliham Unit
P.O. Box 2
Calliham, TX 78007
(361) 786-3868

⊕ TOYOTA Proud Sponsor of Texas Parks and Wildlife Programs

In accordance with Texas State Depository Law, this publication is available at the Texas State Publications Clearinghouse and/or Texas Depository Libraries.
© 2011 Texas Parks and Wildlife Department. PWD MP P4502-129D (2011)

To Tilden

Rec Road 8

House Sparrow

(The famous "find Waldo" bird) may be heard calling in the mornings and evenings, and olive sparrows are spotted in the brush. During the summer, watch for Bell's vireo nesting in the lower brush.

Nesting cave swallows are here throughout the summer under the eaves of the picnic shelters. Also watch for vermilion flycatchers around and near the lake.

Camping facilities are provided in the park and many campers will bring their hummingbird feeders. Birders should expect to see a large variety of hummingbirds. Watch especially for Anna's hummer seen in the winter around flowering trees.

DIRECTIONS
Drive north on I-37 and exit at TX 72. Proceed west to Three Rivers. Continue west on TX 72 from Three Rivers to Choke Canyon State Park.

CONTACT INFORMATION
Calliham Unit:
P O Box 2,
Calliham, TX 78007
Phone: 361-786-386
South Shore Unit, P.O. Box 1548, Three Rivers, TX 78071
Phone: 361-786-3538
Sites are open for day use only. However, camping is also available.

COASTAL BEND LOOP
#193 Lake Findley
(the former Lake Alice)

GPS⊕ **27.79, -98.0602**

ONE MILE NORTH OF ALICE, TEXAS

KEY BIRDS
Yellow-billed cuckoo, groove-billed ani, great kiskadee, and green jay

BEST SEASON
Winter and migration

AREA DESCRIPTION
Mostly cleared for city park and lake use but scattered trees provide resting places for birds

Lake Findley has been developed into an 800-acre multi-purpose facility. The bad news is there is very little habitat remaining along the edges of this body of water. There is existing brush remaining on nearby property and the scrub brush near the entrance road at times offers some good birding.

Trees all along the road into the park can be productive for bird watchers and photographers. Birders should scan the trees for northern mockingbird, kingbird, scissor-tailed flycatcher, golden-fronted woodpecker, and mourning dove. Glass or watch the lake shore for several species of egrets and herons.

The park's fishing pier is another spot on the lake where birders should glass the edges for wading birds and other water loving species.

Green Jay

Resident bird species found here include least grebe, great kiskadee, green jay, and the groove-billed ani. Winter month's birders should look for Sprague's pipit in the short grass and the grasshopper sparrow in the taller grasses.

DIRECTIONS
In Alice on US 281, turn left or east on FM 3376 also named Commerce Road. Proceed to North Texas Boulevard (1.5 miles), turn left (north) and continue 0.5 mile to Lake Findley (Alice).

CONTACT INFORMATION
City of Alice,
PO Box 3229
Alice, Texas 78333
Phone: 361- 668-7210
Site open for day use only.

COASTAL BEND LOOP
#194 John J. Sablatura Nature Park

GPS 27.481, -97.496

NEAR BANQUETE, TEXAS, EAST OF CORPUS CHRISTI, ON TX 44

KEY BIRDS
Roadrunners, long-billed thrasher, and several species of warblers during migrations

BEST SEASON
Winter and migration

AREA DESCRIPTION
Mostly cleared, but has some large old mesquite trees as well as some brush

Situated on Agua Dulce Creek, this small 20-acre wooded park is at times during migrations an excellent birding park. Depending upon the weather, check for a variety of migrant landbirds attracted to this out-of-the-way location.

As in many areas, most of the adjoining habitat is now barren and dusty cotton fields. A small amount of brush is located adjacent to the park, and this is where to watch the brush for chaparral-dwelling birds. Don't pass by without devoting a few hours to the park. Some birders have found this to be a great lunch/birding stop on their drive to Kingsville after leaving Choke Canyon State Park.

Yellow Warbler

DIRECTIONS

Drive east from Alice on TX 44 back toward Corpus Christi. Sablatura Nature Park is located on TX 44 between Agua Dulce and Banquete. There are signs for the park.

CONTACT INFORMATION

Scott Cross, Director
Phone: 361-949-8121
Email: nueces.ballipark@co.nueces.tx.us
Site open for day use only.

Great Kiskadee

COASTAL BEND LOOP
#195 Bishop City Park

GPS 27.581, -97.801

ON JOYCE STREET IN BISHOP, TEXAS

KEY BIRDS
Vermilion flycatcher, white-tailed hawk, groove-billed ani, pauraque, great kiskadee

BEST SEASON
Winter and migration

AREA DESCRIPTION
City park with trees and water

Located along Caretta Creek, the City of Bishop is constructing a 0.8 mile nature trail. This greenbelt will, when completed, connect on its southeast corner to the park.

The planned trail will cross Caretta Creek and will have four observation platforms for the purpose of helping visiting birders. This will be in addition to the 0.6-mile trail around a 9.1-acre lake. Birders are encouraged to watch for birds such as vermilion flycatcher during the winter months.

Other species seen around the park and wet areas are the Harris's hawk, least grebe, groove-billed ani, white-tailed hawk, the elusive pauraque, green jay, great kiskadee, long-billed thrasher, hooded oriole, pyrrhuloxia, olive sparrow, and lesser goldfinch.

DIRECTIONS
Drive east on TX 44 to the intersection with US 77, turn right (south) and drive toward Kingsville. When arriving in Bishop continue on Business 77 until reaching the intersection with Joyce. Bishop City Park is located on your left. You will know you are there when you spot the ball fields.

CONTACT INFORMATION
Bishop Chamber of Commerce, 213 E. Main St.
Bishop, TX 78343
Phone: 361-584-2214
Web Site: www.bishoptx.org
Site open for day use only.

COASTAL BEND LOOP
#196 Santa Gertrudis Creek

GPS 27.453, -97.771

ON TX 141 WEST OF KINGSVILLE, TEXAS

KEY BIRDS
Couch's kingbird, green jay, pyrrhuloxia, and Audubon's oriole

BEST SEASON
All seasons

AREA DESCRIPTION
Creekside habitats and the beginning of the true South Texas brasada and its variety of habitats

Over the years I must have crossed Santa Gertrudis Creeks thousands of times. Whenever there was time, I always stopped to see what birds were there, and see if I could capture any of the birds on film. Many times I was rewarded with some great shots.

Santa Gertrudis Creek drops into a sizable pool where it crosses under TX 141, providing a wetland habitat completed by the surrounding brushy draw and some taller trees. Some of the South Texas species that may be seen here are Couch's kingbird, great kiskadee, pyrrhuloxia, green jay, and Audubon's oriole.

This lush oasis, except during drought years, attracts migrating landbirds flying north in the spring. Watch the trees for flocks of lark bunting along the shoulders of TX 141 as you drive back to Kingsville. Take your time and practice patience and you may be able to see a white-tailed hawk, a white-tailed kite, or a Harris's hawk in flight or sitting on a power pole.

DIRECTIONS
Drive south on Business 77 to Kingsville. Turn right (west) on TX 141, and continue west to the crossing with Santa Gertrudis Creek.

CONTACT INFORMATION

Kingsville Visitor Center,
P. O. Box 1562,
Kingsville, TX 78364
Phone: 800-333-5032 or 361- 592-8516
Email: chamber@kingsville.org
Site open for day use only.

Pyrrhuloxia

COASTAL BEND LOOP
King Ranch
#197

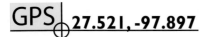

GPS⊕ 27.521, -97.897

ON TX 141 WEST OF KINGSVILLE, TEXAS

KEY BIRDS
Western screech owl, ferruginous pygmy-owl, tropical parula, northern beardless-tyrannulet

BEST SEASON
All seasons

AREA DESCRIPTION
825,000 acres; Varied South Texas brush with oak groves, windmills, and ponds

This sprawling 825,000-acre ranch offers a public bus tour of the King Ranch, as well as birding and nature trips. Both half-day and full-day birding tours are available, especially in the spring and fall. Check the web site for current prices for individuals and groups, and also to download their birding checklist.

Situated at the confluence of several migratory pathways, the ranch is a virtual highway for migrating birds in both fall and spring. The ranch has a bird list of 356 species, and is an International Important Bird Area (IBA). It has the largest known population of ferruginous pygmy owls in the United States.

Some of the birds likely to be seen are the roadrunner, white-tailed hawk, Audubon's oriole, northern beardless-tyrannulet, ferruginous pygmy-owl, Botteri's sparrow, tropical parula, and the green jay.

After visiting the King Ranch, drive east on TX 141 to University Boulevard and the Texas A & M at Kingsville. As you drive through the campus, watch for the hooded oriole and watch for the bird's nests in the tall palms, whether the palms are alive or dead.

Pick up a copy of Kleberg County Birder's Guide and Checklist of Birds at the Kingsville Visitor Center located on US 77.

DIRECTIONS
Return east to Kingsville on TX 141. As you approach Kingsville you will see the entrance to the Santa Gertrudis division of the King Ranch, which is approximately 3.5 miles west of US 77 and the King Ranch Visitor Center.

CONTACT INFORMATION

King Ranch Visitor Center, P.O. Box 1090, Kingsville, TX 78364
Phone: 361-592-8055
Website: www.king-ranch.com/birds
Email: visit@king-ranch.com
This location is access restricted, so please call ahead for reservations. A fee is charged.

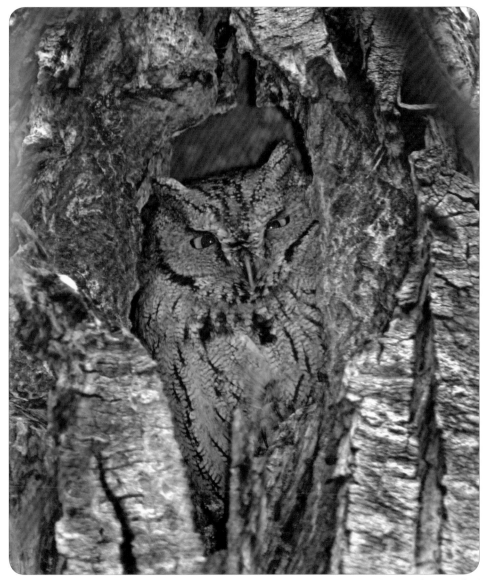

Western Screech Owl

COASTAL BEND LOOP
Dick Kleberg Park

#198

GPS 27.471, -97.86

HWY 77 AND ESCONDIDO
KINGSVILLE, TEXAS

KEY BIRDS
Green jay, great kiskadee, and curve-billed and long-billed thrashers

BEST SEASON
Winter and migration

AREA DESCRIPTION
Creek habitat with large trees and open grassy areas

Hike the trail along the small lake during the winter months to see a variety of waterfowl such as the black-bellied whistling duck, the vermilion flycatcher, and the lark sparrow. During the summer, look under the bridge for nesting cave swallows. This bridge is located at the north end of the lake. The park consists of 184 acres.

Found here year round are species such as curve-billed and long-billed thrashers, golden-fronted and ladder-backed woodpeckers, great kiskadee, and the green jay. Pay close attention to the short grass areas for both pipits, but the Sprague's pipit is not a common visitor.

DIRECTIONS
Return on TX 141 to the intersection with Business 77. Proceed south on Business 77 to the intersection with Escondido and Dick Kleberg Park. Turn left on Escondido to reach the entrance to the park.

CONTACT INFORMATION
Highway 77 and Escondido Road, Kingsville, Texas 78364
Phone: 361-595-8591
Email sivy@klebergpark.org
Site open for day use only.

Brown Thrasher

COASTAL BEND LOOP
#199 Santa Gertrudis Creek Bird Sanctuary

GPS 27.465, -97.83

NORTH OF KINGSVILLE AND JUST OFF US 77

KEY BIRDS
King, sora, and Virginia rails, great kiskadee, and green jay

BEST SEASON
All seasons

AREA DESCRIPTION
Scrub oak and mesquite with a few prickly pear cacti

From the levee, you will be able to view the large, extensive marsh and its residents. Birds that may be seen here are black-bellied whistling duck, least grebe, purple gallinule, marsh and sedge wrens, as well as several species of herons and egrets.

Species that are common here are king, sora, and Virginia rails during the winter. Birders should watch for green jays and great kiskadee in the mesquite wood. The culverts under FM 1717 support nesting cave swallows.

DIRECTIONS
From Dick Kleberg Park, turn right or east on Escondido. Proceed to the intersection with FM 1717. Escondido will veer left on Brahma Blvd. before the intersection, turn right and cross US 77 and continue to the Santa Gertrudis Creek Bird Sanctuary that will be on your left.

CONTACT INFORMATION
Kingsville Visitor Center, Kingsville, TX 78364 / Phone: 800-333-5032 or 361- 592-8516 / Email: chamber@ kingsville.org / Site open for day use only.

Green Jay

COASTAL BEND LOOP
Drum Point & Kaufer-Hubert Memorial Park

GPS | **DRUM POINT: 27.373, -97.707**
KAUFER-HUBERT MEMORIAL PARK: 27.319, -97.683

ABOUT A 20-MINUTE DRIVE SOUTHEAST OF KINGSVILLE

KEY BIRDS
Pyrrhuloxia, painted bunting, bufflehead, lesser scaup, herons, egrets, and shorebirds

BEST SEASON
Winter, migration

AREA DESCRIPTION
Roadside habitats, wetlands, and mudflats at the mouth of Vattmann Creek in the park

BIRDERS WARNING: Be extremely careful on this road during a rain or prolonged wet periods.

Drum Point overlooks Cayo del Grullo, that is a segment of Baffin Bay.

As you drive to Drum Point from US 77, watch for groove-billed ani, long-billed and brown thrashers and the common ground-dove. Other species often seen are painted bunting and pyrrhuloxia along the fencerows.

Drive the unpaved road slowly for about one mile and watch for reddish egrets, herons, pelicans, and ducks such as bluebills and bufflehead as well as several species of shorebirds. Wilson's plover and least tern nest here in summer. Millions of swallows and martins may be seen along this area during September migrations.

When entering the park, watch the Vattmann Creek wetlands and mudflats for egrets, herons, and shorebirds such as Wilson's, snowy, and piping plovers, and species such as pectoral stilt and white-rumped sandpiper.

Glass the ponds in the park for duck species such as black scoter, greater scaup, and surf scoter during the winter months. The brushy areas around the park are great places to watch for green jay, common ground-dove, and olive sparrow.

DIRECTIONS

To Drum Point: Return north on US 77 to the intersection with FM 772, that is about one mile. Proceed east on FM 772 and continue on it as it winds through the brush country to the intersection with CR 2250 E. Turn left (east) and continue to the intersection with CR 1132. Turn left and proceed north down the bluff to where the pavement ends and the caliche begins.

To the Park: Return to CR 2250E, turn left or east and drive to Loyola Beach and FM 628. CR 1132 will veer south before reaching the town. Veer south on FM 628, eventually angling left to Arana Creek and Kaufer-Hubert Memorial Park, watch for the signs.

CONTACT INFORMATION

Kingsville Visitor Center, 1501 Hwy 77, Kingsville, TX 78364
Phone: 800-333-5032 or 361- 592-8516
Email: chamber@kingsville.org
Web Site: http://www.kingsvilletexas.com/index.php/kingsville-birding-birdwatching.html
Developed camping sites available in the park.

Painted Bunting

COASTAL BEND LOOP
#201 Riviera Fishing Pier

GPS 27.301, -97.664

LOCATED JUST OFF CR 2327E IN RIVIERA BEACH

KEY BIRDS
Grebes, pelicans, and waterfowl

BEST SEASON
Winter, migration

AREA DESCRIPTION
Coastal community with some land and birds that are attracted to the water and/or local bird feeders

Located overlooking the mouth of the Laguna Salada, the Riviera Fishing Pier is a great birding location except on windy and cold days. Pelicans, grebes, and several species of ducks are often seen here.

Some of the residents in Riviera Beach put out bird feeders to attract green jays and, at times, groove-billed ani to their feeders. Watch the thick brush along the road for the groove-billed ani.

DIRECTIONS
Retrace your path to FM 628, and turn south toward Riviera Beach. FM 628 will turn right to the intersection with FM 1526, turn left on FM 1526 and proceed to FM 771, then turn left and continue to Riviera Beach and the Riviera Fishing Pier.

CONTACT INFORMATION
Kingsville Visitor Center, 1501 Hwy 77, Kingsville, TX 78364
Phone: 800-333-5032 or 361- 592-8516
Email: chamber@kingsville.org
Web Site: http://www.kingsvilletexas.com/index.php/kingsville-birding-birdwatching.html

Lesser Scaup

COASTAL BEND LOOP
#202 Louise Trant Bird Sanctuary

GPS 27.3, -97.816

LOCATED WITHIN THE CITY LIMITS OF RIVIERA, JUST OFF FM 771

KEY BIRDS
Sora rail, yellow-headed blackbird

BEST SEASON
Winter, migration

AREA DESCRIPTION
Small city park with some trees and marsh habitats

The Audubon Outdoor Club of Corpus Christi maintains this small marsh area.

Sora rails are here during the winter months, and the yellow-headed blackbirds may be seen in the cattails during the spring. Among the unusual species that have appeared here are the red-billed pigeon and masked duck. There has been a lot of development around the sanctuary.

DIRECTIONS
Return on FM 771 west to Riviera. Travel north on US 77 for 0.1 mile, and watch for the Louise Trant Bird Sanctuary just north of the intersection.

CONTACT INFORMATION
Audubon Outdoor Club of Corpus Christi, Inc., P.O. Box 3352, Corpus Christi, Texas 78463
Email: pumml@juno.com
Site open for day use only.

Yellow-headed Blackbird

COASTAL BEND LOOP
#203 Hawk Alley

GPS⊕ 27.257, -97.973

ON TX 285 BETWEEN KINGSVILLE AND FALFURRIAS, TEXAS

KEY BIRDS
Many species of hawk, lark bunting

BEST SEASON
Winter, migration

AREA DESCRIPTION
Patches of native brush, grassy areas, and pastures

This stretch of the highway has been named "Hawk Alley" for the large number of raptor species seen here. This is a favorite spot for local birders.

Some of these species are the Harris's hawk, white-tailed hawk, and crested caracara. Species migrating through have been the broad-winged hawk, Mississippi kite, and Swainson's hawk. Pay special attention to the power poles for perching raptors, and also see them soaring over the grassy areas.

The American kestrel and ferruginous hawk are found in the winter. Also common during the winter months are the lark buntings that are seen mostly along the shoulders of the roads. The red-tailed hawk is a local raptor that is seen many times during the year.

DIRECTIONS
Before driving farther south to the Lower Rio Grande Valley, proceed west on TX 285 toward Falfurrias. This road is Hawk Alley.

CONTACT INFORMATION
Kingsville Visitor Center, 1501 Hwy 77, Kingsville, TX 78364
Phone: 800-333-5032 or 361- 592-8516
Email: chamber@kingsville.org
Web Site: http://www.kingsvilletexas.com/index.php/kingsville-birding-birdwatching.html
This road is open to birders for their day use only.

Red-tailed Hawk

COASTAL BEND LOOP
#204 Sarita/The Kenedy Ranch

GPS 27.219, -97.795

OFF HWY 77, NEAR SARITA, TEXAS

KEY BIRDS
Ferruginous pygmy owl, Audubon's oriole, hooded oriole, Botteri's sparrow

BEST SEASON
All seasons

AREA DESCRIPTION
Wetlands habitat and marsh areas with local brush and trees

The ranch covers approximately 235,000 acres and is mostly grasslands and South Texas brush.

Cave swallows are common in this area. Birders should watch the local feeders for hummingbirds, such as the rufus and buff-bellied hummingbirds. Spend some time and look for hooded orioles nesting in the thick fronds of the palm trees.

Glass the seasonal wetlands to the west of the baseball field, then cross the railroad tracks and go to the end at Garcia Road, less than 0.2 mile.

Information from the ranch at the time of this writing was that the ranch was constructing a picnic area, elevated boardwalk, as well as a watching and photo blind.

Birders should watch for species including least grebes that will breed around the marsh and a variety of local songbirds birds are present year round.

Audubon's Oriole

In the summer months, there will be painted buntings near the marshy areas. Watch closely for Botteri's sparrow, a South Texas species.

DIRECTIONS

Continue south on US 77 from Olmos Creek to Sarita, the seat of Kenedy County, one of Texas' least populated counties (pop. 400). Enter Sarita on La Parra Ave., and continue west two blocks to Mallory St. Go north on Mallory St. to Cueller Ave. and the seasonal wetlands. Return to La Parra and continue to the courthouse. To reach the marsh, turn left on Garcia Rd., continuing about 0.2 mile.

CONTACT INFORMATION

Ranch contact information: Phone (361) 887-6565.
The Kenedy Ranch has arranged with Sanborn's Tours (877-253-6339 or www.kenedy. org) to conduct scheduled trips on a pre-arranged, groups-only basis.
Site open for day use only.

COASTAL BEND LOOP
#205 TXDOT Sarita Rest Area

GPS 27.133, -97.793

ABOUT SIX MILES SOUTH OF SARITA ON HWY 77

KEY BIRDS
Tropical parula, Couch's kingbird

BEST SEASON
All seasons

AREA DESCRIPTION
Grassy areas with area with wild olive and mesquite trees

The tropical parula bird sometimes nests here, so watch closely for this hard-to-see species. Pay close attention to the Texas wild olive trees that attract buff-bellied hummingbirds. These trees are found along the right-of-way on the west side of US 77. This is a busy highway so, like your parents told you, look both ways and then walk across.

Green jay, lesser goldfinch, and Couch's kingbird are common. Watch for scissor-tailed flycatcher, brown-crested flycatcher, and hooded oriole in late spring through the fall months. The palm trees here host several species of nesting birds. Take a restful birding break before driving farther south.

DIRECTIONS
Leaving Sarita, continue about six miles south on US 77 to the Texas Department of Transportation Sarita Rest Area.

CONTACT INFORMATION
No real contact information available. Site open for day use only.

Couch's Kingbird

COASTAL BEND LOOP
#206 Brooks County (Falfurrias) Rest Area

GPS 27.095, -98.146

REST AREA LOCATED ON TX 285 SOUTH OF FALFURRIAS, TEXAS

KEY BIRDS
Summer tanager, tufted titmouse, lesser goldfinch, painted bunting, black-bellied whistling duck

BEST SEASON
All seasons

AREA DESCRIPTION
South Texas brush and trees with a pond and water feature at the end of a nature trail

Featured in this area is a nature trail that winds into and through a stand of oaks to a pond with running water – an attractive feature for birds and birders. This pond attracts a large variety of birds coming to drink and to bathe. The best times here are late afternoons and evenings.

During summer, watch for the brilliant summer tanager, lesser goldfinch, black-crested tufted titmouse, and the colorful painted bunting near and in the water dripper. The palm trees have been the location for hooded orioles to nest and raise their young.

DIRECTIONS
There are two major highways that reach the Valley: US 77 and US 281. Before rushing south on US 77, return to the intersection of TX 285 and US 77 in Riviera (CTC 095), travel west on TX 285 (Hawk Alley) toward Falfurrias. In Falfurrias, go south on US 281 to the TXDOT Brooks County Rest Area, popularly known as the Falfurrias rest stop.

CONTACT INFORMATION
No contact information available except through the Texas Department of Transportation (DOT). Site open for day use only.

American Goldfinch

Ranch Loop

This is the area where men like Capt. Richard King worked to establish ranches in spite of banditos and Indians. Throughout the area, Spanish Land Grants form the outlines of many ranches and coastal areas.

The northernmost location on the Ranch Loop is the town of Port Mansfield. Situated on the Lower Laguna Madre, it is loaded with places to see birds and wildlife.

In the city limits of Port Mansfield during the fall and winter months, large-bodied and antlered whitetail buck browse the yards and parks of the town. The wet areas attract many species of waterfowl, and many wading birds find enough to eat along the shore and many sand bars dotting the bay.

This loop is also home to several State Parks and National Wildlife Refuges welcoming birders during the people migrations of "Winter Texans" and locals alike.

When you add Brownsville, San Benito, Port Isabel, and Harlingen to South Padre Island and Boca Chica Beach you have mile after mile of excellent birding, and birders always ready to help the traveler.

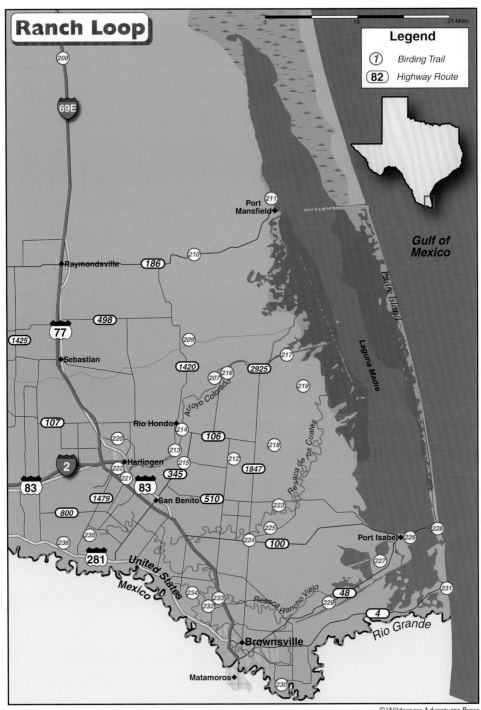

Ranch Loop

0   10   20 Miles

Gulf of Mexico

Padre Island

Laguna Madre

208

69E

211 Port Mansfield

210

Raymondsville 186

498

77 1425

209

Sebastian 1420

207 216 2925

217

219

107

Rio Hondo 214 106

220

218

213

Harlingen 215 212

222 345 1847

221 83

83 1479

510 San Benito

800

235 223

236 225

281 224 100

Port Isabel 226

227

228

United States

Mexico

234 233

232 Resaca Rancho Viejo 48

229

4

Arroyo Colorado

Resaca de los Cuates

231

Rio Grande

Brownsville

Matamoros 230

© Wilderness Adventures Press

Ranch Loop Locations

207.	La Sal Vieja Refuge – East Lake Tract
208.	The Norias Unit of the King Ranch
209.	Santa Monica Wetlands
210.	Sacahuistale Flats
211.	Fred Stone County Park
212.	Las Palomas WMA – Longoria Unit
213.	Port of Harlingen
214.	Rio Hondo - A World Birding Center Site
215.	Mont Meta Cemetery
216.	Las Palomas WMA – Arroyo Colorado Unit
217.	Adolph Thomae Jr. County Park
218.	Cactus Creek Ranch
219.	Laguna Atascosa NWR
220.	Hugh Ramsey Nature Park
221.	Arroyo Park/C.B. Wood Park
222.	Harlingen Thicket
223.	Lon C. Hill (Fair) Park
224.	Los Fresnos
225.	The Inn at Chachalaca Bend
226.	Port Isabel
227.	South Padre Island Locations
228.	SPI Gateway Project
229.	TX Hwy 48 Scenic Drive – Bahia Grande
230.	Sabal Palm Audubon Center and Sanctuary
231.	Boca Chica Beach/The USFWS Boca Chica Tract
232.	TPWD Coastal Fisheries Field Station
233.	Camp Lula Sams
234.	Las Palomas WMA - Resaca de la Palma State Park
235.	Las Palmoas WMA - Ebony Unit
236.	Cannon Road

RANCH LOOP
#207 La Sal Vieja Refuge – East Tract Lake

GPS 26.32, -97.53

NORTHWEST OF RAYMONDVILLE, TEXAS

KEY BIRDS
White-tipped dove, Harris's hawk, crested caracara, and white-tailed hawk

BEST SEASON
All seasons

AREA DESCRIPTION
Marshy area with South Texas brush and wetland species of plants

Without blocking the gate, park along the shoulder of the road and walk in. Birders should consider a daypack with water as well as energy bars if you plan to stay any length of time. Watch for roosting sandhill cranes. Although not found in the large numbers found at La Sal del Rey, this location is well worth the time spent.

Species that birders will find here are white-tailed hawk, white-tipped dove, crested caracara, and Harris's hawk that are common in this location. The right fork of the trail will take you to the lake as well as the wetland near the lake.

Taking the left fork, and then turning to the right where the trails intersect, will take you into an area where you can watch nesting birds on a man-made peninsula extending into the water. Note the signs for closed areas. Please respect these closures in the nesting season.

DIRECTIONS
Return to TX 186 and continue east to FM 1761. Go north on FM 1761 approximately 2.5 miles. FM 1761 will curve dramatically back to the east. Continue north instead and travel on a caliche road, crossing a bridge, until you reach the first road that veers to the west. Go west on this unmarked road to its end and the trailhead entrance to the East Lake Tract.

CONTACT INFORMATION
Santa Ana NWR headquarters at (956) 787-3079. Site open for day use only.

White-fronted Dove

RANCH LOOP

#208 The Norias Unit of the King Ranch

GPS 26.786, -97.774

ON HWY 77, 10 MILES NORTH OF RAYMONDVILLE, TEXAS

KEY BIRDS
Least grebe, white-tailed hawk, crested caracara, vermilion flycatcher and many more

BEST SEASON
All seasons

AREA DESCRIPTION
Brush country with live oak mottes scattered about the ranch, lagoons and windmill-fed ponds, sand hills, and open pastures

Nature tours are a big part of the King Ranch experience, and most birders have been quite satisfied with their experiences. As in most South Texas locations, birders should spot the northern beardless-tyrannulet, tropical parula, and the ferruginous pygmy-owl.

The ranch also hosts many species as well as wintering and tropical south Texas birds. Habitats vary from grassland to wetlands supporting populations of birds such as vermilion flycatcher, least grebe, crested caracara, white-tailed hawk, great kiskadee, as well as the olive sparrow and the south Texas favorite, the green jay.

Least Grebe

DIRECTIONS

Return to the intersection of US 77 and TX 186 in Raymondville. Continue north on US 77 approximately 10 miles to the private King Ranch Norias Unit.

CONTACT INFORMATION

King Ranch Phone: 361-592-8055

Email: krvisitormgmt@interconnect.net, or visit www.king-ranch.com/kingranch/visit.htm. This site is access restricted and an entrance or tour fee is charged.

See Site #197 in the Coastal Bend Trail section for more information on the King Ranch.

RANCH LOOP
#209 Santa Monica Wetlands

GPS 26.366, -97.57

OFF TX 186 JUST WEST OF PORT MANSFIELD

KEY BIRDS
Wood stork, white-faced ibis, roseate spoonbill, migrating waterfowl, and shorebirds

BEST SEASON
Migrations, winter, particularly wet seasons

AREA DESCRIPTION
Basically a small wet area that during drought times can be mostly dry and will cover another large area that may be semi-dry

Birders driving along TX 186 — an elevated road that is 4.7 miles long — will see several oxbow lakes, known in this part of Texas as resacas. These resacas border the highway for a few miles. Drive slowly and watch for anhinga, geotropic cormorant, great chickadee, least grebe, and watch for several species of duck resting and feeding along these resacas.

The brush inside the willows is a productive location to spot warblers and vireos during both migrations. Larger ponds are found a little over seven miles from TX 186 and on the east side of FM 1420. This is a great spot to watch and photograph migrating ducks, including a possible Ross' goose. During dry or drought years these shallow lakes may be dry.

Roseate Spoonbill

Winter wet seasons make these same locations top birding places. Birders may see waterbirds such as the white-faced ibis, wood stork, roseate spoonbill, ducks, geese, and several species of shorebirds. The open fields are known to have attracted aplomado falcons sailing overhead in search of prey species.

The USFWS reports that the aplomado falcons were released on the Laguna Atascosa NWR as part of their reintroduction program. Use your binoculars to identify the different species of raptor.

DIRECTIONS

From the intersection of US 77 and TX 186 in Raymondville, travel east on TX 186 toward Port Mansfield. Continue east on TX 186 to FM 1420 in San Perlita. Go south on FM 1420, and check the pond at 4.0 miles, and a wooded pond (bordered with willows) at 4.5 miles. Continue south on FM 1420 to FM 1018 in Santa Monica. Go east on the dirt road (or on the levee) for about one mile to the largest section of the Santa Monica Wetlands.

CONTACT INFORMATION

No available contact information. This is a public area located off of the county roads. Please respect private property. Site open for day use only.

RANCH LOOP
#210 Sacahuistale Flats

GPS 26.494, -97.559

Located 4.5 miles east of the intersection of TX 186 and FM 1420

Key Birds
Herons, egrets, Botteri's sparrow, ferruginous pygmy-owl

Best Season
All seasons

Area Description
Old mesquites and low brush

Named after the predominant needle-shaped grass, these flats are great places for birders to see nesting species as well as some songbirds that use the grass as a buffer against predators. This grassland begins about 4.5 miles east of the intersection of TX 186 and FM 1420, and is the preferred habitat for wading and shoreline birds. Watch the lower trees for pygmy owls during the nesting seasons.

In the spring, birders should glass shrubs and fence posts that are used by males as song perches. The old mesquites bordering the road between these flats and Port Mansfield are excellent habitat for many of the south Texas birds such as the ferruginous pygmy-owl.

The sacahuista grass is very sharp and the needles will easily go through blue jeans and hiking pants – these grasses are not made for shorts.

Directions
From the intersection of TX 186 and FM 1420, continue east on TX 186 to the Sacahuistale Flats.

Contact Information
Port Mansfield Chamber of Commerce, P. O. Box 75, Port Mansfield, Texas 78598
Phone: 956-944-2354
Site open for day use only.

Cattle Egret

RANCH LOOP
#211 Fred Stone County Park

GPS 26.569, -97.429

IN PORT MANSFIELD, OFF FM 606

KEY BIRDS
Gulls, terns, plovers

BEST SEASON
Migrations, winter

AREA DESCRIPTION
Open bay water, sand bars, open shallow bay, Padre Island, and park habitats

This is the location, a beachfront habitat, where birders can watch and see shorebirds. Located close to the water, birders can see several species of terns and gulls.

Birders of a more adventurous nature should take their boat or charter a boat to take them across the Laguna Madre to the Mansfield Cut. The Mansfield Cut separates North Padre Island from South Padre Island and is a boat channel cut through Padre Island. The algal flats just south of the cut hold the world's largest flocks of piping plovers.

DIRECTIONS
Drive east from the Sacahuistale Flats to Port Mansfield and the intersection of TX 186 and FM 606. Go north on FM 606 to Fred Stone County Park.

CONTACT INFORMATION
Port Mansfield Chamber of Commerce, P. O. Box 75, Port Mansfield, Texas 78598
Phone: 956-944-2354
Site open for day use only.

Herring Gull

RANCH LOOP
Las Palomas WMA – Longoria Unit

#212

GPS 26.192, -97.493

ON 506 JUST SOUTH OF SEBASTIAN, TEXAS

KEY BIRDS
Turkey vulture, mourning dove, red-tailed hawk, Inca dove, rock dove, red-shouldered hawk, greater roadrunner

BEST SEASON
All seasons

AREA DESCRIPTION
South Texas mesquite brush and taller trees of mixed varieties

Las Palomas Wildlife Management Area comprises 18 units, from the Rio Grande Valley to Big Bend of Texas. All of these places within the Las Palomas WMA were bought to provide habitat for white-winged doves in Texas. It has been hunters (again) who paid for these management areas. As the Federal Waterfowl stamp relates to National Wildlife Refuges, the hunters have bought these critical habitats not only for the white-winged doves but a variety of other species. These areas are being restored and allowed to grow. Birders will enjoy these areas throughout South Texas to bird watch at their leisure.

Large and hearty thanks go out to the Texas hunters for helping all wildlife by paying for these locations. The Longoria Unit is being improved with walking trails and viewing areas with feeding and watering stations.

Have you purchased your Public Lands Permit and Federal Waterfowl Stamp?

DIRECTION
From the intersection of US 77 and TX 186, continue south on US 77 to FM 2629 and the town of Sebastian. Go west on FM 2629, and veer south on FM 506. Continue approximately 1.5 miles south on FM 506 from its intersection with FM 2629 to Las Palomas Wildlife Management Area Longoria Unit.

CONTACT INFORMATION
For information about the Longoria Unit, contact Texas Parks and Wildlife.
Phone: 956-447-2704 / Site open for day use only.
Review the public notices posted in the public information kiosks.

Turkey Vulture

WILDLIFE MANAGEMENT AREA NOTES

As TPW properties, the Wildlife Management Areas are open to the public on a fee basis. However, the WMAs lack the staff to collect the fees on site. Birders visit these sites on an honor system. The fees are vital to maintaining these areas that provide important habitat for numerous birds other than game species. Therefore, please take the time to purchase a Texas Conservation Passport ($50), Limited Use Permit ($12), or Annual Public Hunting Permit ($48). These can be purchased at any State Park, TPWD Law Enforcement office, or from merchants selling Texas hunting and fishing licenses. You may also call TPWD Austin headquarters at 1-800-895-4248 to purchase these by credit card.

RANCH LOOP
#213 Port of Harlingen

GPS 26.206, -97.597

LOCATED JUST OFF FM 106, EAST OF HARLINGEN, TEXAS

KEY BIRDS
Ringed and green kingfishers, crested caracara, house finch, American goldfinch, and roseate spoonbill

BEST SEASON
All seasons

AREA DESCRIPTION
The Arroyo Colorado has mostly brush on both banks after you leave the almost park-like habitat of the port

The Port of Harlingen is a barge port providing economic transportation to points as far as the Great Lakes and as close as Corpus Christi by way of the Intracoastal Waterway. Unlike the management at the Port of Brownsville, these people are friendly and most are ready to help the wayward birder. Watch for the grain storage towers, and there are over 150 acres of on-and-off-channel sites.

The Gulf Intracoastal Waterway provides over 1,300 miles of protected waterway.

The Harlingen Channel is maintained to a width of 125 feet and a depth of 12 feet and is supplied by the Arroyo

House Finch

Colorado, a freshwater river. Here again, a boat is a handy thing to use in a slow cruise down the arroyo while glassing the banks for birds. At one time there was a craft that offered tours but has since ceased operation.

The Port of Harlingen is a great place to watch for a Chihuahuan raven, either roosting or on the wing.

DIRECTIONS
Drive to the intersection of US 77 and Loop 499, continue south on Loop 499 to FM 106. Go east on FM 106 to the Port of Harlingen.

CONTACT INFORMATION
Harlingen Area Chamber of Commerce, 311 East Tyler Avenue, Harlingen, TX 78550
Phone: 956-423-5440
Web Site: http://www.harlingen.com/
Site open for day use only.

Red-crowned Parrot

RANCH LOOP
#214 Rio Hondo – A World Birding Center Site

GPS 26.235, -97.585

LOCATED IN RIO HONDO ON THE ARROYO COLORADO

KEY BIRDS
Common pauraque, green and ringed kingfishers, groove-billed ani, long-billed thrasher, olive sparrow, and the endangered red-crowned parrot

BEST SEASON
All seasons, but particularly late spring and summer

AREA DESCRIPTION
Many mesquite trees and other South Texas scrub brush with streamside habitats

Birders have reported green kingfishers nesting under the Rio Hondo bridge. The picnic area is one of the best places in South Texas to watch all three species of kingfishers that are found in North America.

While in Rio Hondo, return to FM 106 and go to South Arroyo Drive. Go south on South Arroyo Drive to the Rio Hondo Cemetery entrance. Here you will find the Texas ebony in profusion. These trees may attract species such as great kiskadee and the green jay.

DIRECTIONS
Go back to FM 106, and continue east to Rio Hondo and the Arroyo Colorado. Rio Hondo is being developed as a World Birding Center satellite location. After crossing the Arroyo Colorado Bridge, leave your car at the picnic area on the north side of FM 106.

CONTACT INFORMATION
City of Rio Hondo
Phone: 956-748-2102
Site open for day use only.

RANCH LOOP
Mont Meta Cemetery

#215

GPS 26.18, -97.588

Located only 4.8 miles from Rio Hondo on TX 345

Key Birds
Black-crested titmouse, ruby-crowned kinglet, orange-crowned warbler

Best Season
Migrations, winter and spring

Area Description
A very well maintained cemetery with large trees that attract many species of bird

Locals and birders alike say that this location is rarely birded. In spite of the small area, it can produce a good number of migrant birds during the spring fallout. The area is the last resting place of many people, so please observe a quiet demeanor while birding.

The Tamaulipan variety of the Texas ebony is common and found here throughout the Valley. The Mont Meta Cemetery has some of the largest ebony trees in South Texas.

During winter months, birders can expect mixed flocks of orange-crowned warblers, ruby-crowned kinglets, black-crested titmice, as well as a few more species of warblers.

A quiet walk along the roads that weave through these magnificent trees will not only restore the soul, but often produce an impressive selection of birds.

Directions
Return to FM 106, and then continue east to TX 345. Go south on TX 345 to the Mont Meta Cemetery.

Contact Information
Mont Meta Cemetery, 26170 Highway 345, San Benito, TX 78586
Phone: 956-399-3097
Site open for day use only.

Black-crested Titmouse

RANCH LOOP

#216 Las Palomas WMA – Arroyo Colorado Unit – World Birding Center Site

GPS 26.321, -97.514

LOCATED JUST OFF FM 2925, NORTHEAST OF RIO HONDO, TEXAS

KEY BIRDS
White-winged dove, mourning dove, green jay, great kiskadee

BEST SEASON
All seasons

AREA DESCRIPTION
Brush-nesting habitat, some farmland and wetlands

This site may be closed during specific times of the year due to the conducting of scheduled hunts. As mentioned earlier, these WMAs were paid for by hunters' funds. Bird watchers have access to these areas during most of the year. At other times, entrance permits are made by special requests only.

The city of Rio Hondo is working with TPW to offer access to the Arroyo Colorado Unit on a controlled basis as part of the World Birding Center complex. A Texas Land Permit may be needed before this book goes to press.

It must be added, this location offers bird and nature watchers one of the most diverse WMAs in the Valley.

White-winged Dove

DIRECTIONS

From Rio Hondo travel east on FM 106 to FM 2925. Travel north on FM 2925 to the Las Palomas WMA Arroyo Colorado Unit.

CONTACT INFORMATION

Steve Benn, 154 B Lakeview Drive, Weslaco, TX 78596
Phone: 956-565-1223 – 956-447-2704
At times this location is access restricted.

RANCH LOOP
Adolph Thomae, Jr. County Park

#217

GPS⊕ 26.349, -97.391

LOCATED AT THE END OF TX 2925 AND SURROUNDED BY MORE OF THE LAGUNA ATASCOSA NWR

KEY BIRDS
Osprey, Harris's hawk, common pauraque, altamira oriole

BEST SEASON
Migrations, and winter

AREA DESCRIPTION
Waterway habitats, with mesquite trees and other South Texas flora

This location does not belong to Cameron County, but is leased from the USFWS and is a part of the Laguna Atascosa NWR. The park offers camping, restrooms, picnic and boating facilities. The entry fee is a daily permit that includes Isla Blanca Park and all other Cameron County parks.

During migration or winter, watch the telephone poles that line the road along the Arroyo Colorado for perched osprey or Harris's hawk. Common pauraque, altamira oriole, and long-billed thrasher are among the species seen here in the park. Watch the roadsides for roadrunners hunting the brushlines.

DIRECTIONS
Continue east on FM 1847 to FM 2925 then drive east on FM 2925 to the end of the road at Adolph Thomae, Jr. County Park.

CONTACT INFORMATION
Adolph Thomae Park Manager: John Todd
Phone: 956-748-2044
This site is open daily with developed camping available for a fee.

Common Pauraque

RANCH LOOP
Cactus Creek Ranch
#218

GPS 26.216, -97.433

LOCATED EAST OF RIO HONDO ON FM 106

KEY BIRDS
American kestrel, American coot, killdeer, black-necked stilt, greater yellowlegs, lesser yellowlegs, common snipe, mourning dove, Inca dove, rock dove, greater roadrunner, ruby-throated hummingbird, belted kingfisher

BEST SEASON
Migrations, winter

AREA DESCRIPTION
South Texas low brush and grassy areas with several ponds

Cactus Creek Ranch is an international learning center for implementing future conservation as well as sharing knowledge about the great outdoors. This ranch was once the Valley Shooting Center, a private trap and skeet facility.

Cooperation with the South Texas Private Lands Initiative has allowed more work to be done and the ranch to be named a Habitat Restoration Site. The ranch is a joint project of the Nature Conservancy and Texas Parks and Wildlife, funded by the National Fish and Wildlife Foundation and private donors.

Begun in 1995, the 400-acre Cactus Creek Ranch was started with only a few blades of grass and local cacti. The ranch has been developed into prime South Texas native habitat, with a commitment to habitat restoration and conservation.

During 1996-1997, the Nature Conservancy along with many volunteers planted over 20,000 native plants on the ranch. The ranch is now a haven for many species of birds, both migratory and indigenous.

As a dedicated partner, the Cactus Creek Ranch has been involved in wildlife habitat restoration under the direction of Wetland Habitat Alliance of Texas and the Texas Nature Conservancy.

Efforts have been made to protect and preserve endangered species and create an environment focusing on the best that Texas has to offer. The ranch's alliances with local, state, and federal organizations demonstrate the strength of working together.

DIRECTIONS

From Rio Hondo, go east on FM 106 to the intersection with FM 2925. Continue east on FM 106 for 2.2 miles. The ranch will be on your left.

CONTACT INFORMATION

Cactus Creek Ranch, Mary Jo Bogatto, P.O. Box 465, Rio Hondo, TX 78583
Phone: 817-201-9697
Site access is restricted.

American Coot

RANCH LOOP
Laguna Atascosa NWR

#219

GPS 26.283, -97.383

LOCATED NEAR THE END OF BUENA VISTA ROAD IN CAMERON COUNTY

KEY BIRDS
White-tipped dove, green jay, plain chachalaca, great kiskadee, olive sparrow, long-billed thrasher

BEST SEASON
Migrations, winter

AREA DESCRIPTION
This landscape is a unique blending of temperate, subtropical, coastal, and desert habitats

This site is open for day use only and a fee is charged. This would be a great place to use your Duck Stamp and save the daily fee. It was Duck Stamp money that bought and paid for this refuge. It is not managed for people, so don't expect a lot of help from the refuge staff.

On the way to the visitor's center, you will pass a five-mile walking loop – the Whitetail Trail – best birded in the early mornings. During the summer months and hot weather, an early start will help you avoid the heat.

There are several locations with feed and water stations for the birds that are maintained by volunteers. There is also a photo blind that has become very popular, and best times are early morning when the grackles will leave the feed alone. This blind is also a good place to see the plain chachalaca walking in with the white-fronted dove.

Birders should be on the lookout for birds such as Bewick's wren and greater roadrunner that are easily seen in this area. Western diamondback rattlesnakes favor this habitat as well, so be cautious.

Most of the refuge trails are open year round; however the visitor's center may be open only October through April during most years, and on a limited basis through the warmer months. Check at the entrance for the exact dates and times the center will be open, or call the refuge.

Plain Chachalaca

Laguna Atascosa NWR comprises over 60,000 acres of coastal Tamaulipan brush, grasslands, lomas, and tidal flats. Much of the refuge is off limits to visitors. Walk the short trails around the visitor's center that have feeding stations and watering sites.

There have been over 369 species of birds spotted on the refuge; of these 42 are accidental, and five are exotic. Don't forget your binoculars, your bird book, and a pencil so you can check them off your list. Birders should make a note of unlisted, accidental, or rare bird species and should report them to refuge headquarters.

Migrations will bring in summer tanagers, orioles, warblers, painted buntings, and other species flying to the birdbath near the visitor's center. Common species such as the great kiskadee, white-tipped dove, plain chachalaca, green jay, olive sparrow, and long-billed thrasher are also observed.

Nesting yellow-green vireos are spotted in this general area. The Mesquite Trail, a 1.5-mile loop, is a great place for birders in the early evenings and mornings.

Beginning at the visitor's center, drive the 15-mile Bayside Drive that will take you through a broad range of habitats. The Paisano Trail crosses into Tamaulipan brush. Watch here for verdin as well as the painted bunting.

Use your spotting scope at the Redhead Ridge Overlook. It is worth the short hike to the top of the hill. A spotting scope is useful to see the many species of ducks. A large percentage of the world's redhead ducks spend the winter on the Laguna Madre. At times, thousands of this species may be seen here.

Birders should be on the lookout for the endangered raptor, the aplomado falcon. These birds are being reintroduced to the refuge, as well as on South Padre Island.

From the visitor's center, follow the signs to the Lakeside Drive. This drive crosses an old resaca where many species of waterfowl may be seen in the winter.

Follow the road to the Osprey Overlook on the Laguna Madre. The fields surrounding this area host large numbers of sandhill cranes and geese in the winter. Always check any large blackbird in the refuge in the summer; it may be a groove-billed ani. Departing the refuge, be sure to watch for sandhill cranes during the winter and grassland shorebirds such as American golden-plover and upland sandpiper during the spring in and along the agricultural fields that border the refuge.

DIRECTIONS

Continue east on FM 106 to Buena Vista Road, trying your best not to tear up your front-end or have your car vanish forever in one of the enormous potholes on FM 106. Turn left or north on Buena Vista Road to its end at the Laguna Atascosa NWR Visitors Center.

CONTACT INFORMATION

John Wallace, Manager, P.O. Box 450, Rio Hondo, Texas 78583
Phone: 956-748-3607

RANCH LOOP
#220 Hugh Ramsey Nature Park
– World Birding Center Site

GPS 26.223, -97.691

OFF LOOP 499 IN HARLINGEN, TEXAS

KEY BIRDS
Brown-crested flycatcher, ringed and green kingfishers, green jay, great kiskadee

BEST SEASON
All seasons

AREA DESCRIPTION
Mostly a Texas ebony woods area, some open grassy areas, and reed-filled bottomlands along the Arroyo Colorado

Another World Birding Center site, Hugh Ramsey Park covers 95 acres with trails and birding blinds winding through Texas ebony woodlands down to the reed-filled bottomlands along the Arroyo Colorado. Partly a nature park and botanical garden, the trails here will take birders through typical chaparral types and developed gardens. Although the park is not fully developed, a visitor's center is scheduled to be built.

Additional trails are being developed providing the opportunity for birders to see South Texas birds such as great kiskadee, green jay, olive sparrow, and brown-crested flycatcher during the summer, and makes this park a welcome center to birders who fly into Harlingen.

Once entering the Hugh Ramsey Nature Park, leave your car in the parking lot and take a slow walk along the nature trail winding through the brush. Birders may also walk to the Arroyo Colorado watching for ringed as well as the green kingfisher. The city of Harlingen is in the initial stages of connecting several parks on the Arroyo Colorado with a paved hike-and-bike trail.

DIRECTIONS
From the intersection of Loop 499 and FM 106, go south on Loop 499 to Hugh Ramsey Nature Park (approximately 0.3 mile), this location is closest to the Valley International Airport.

CONTACT INFORMATION

Harlingen Chamber of Commerce, 311 E. Tyler St., Harlingen, TX 78550

Phone: 956-423-5440

This site is open for day usage only.

Great-crested Flycatcher

RANCH LOOP
#221 Arroyo Park/C.B. Wood Park

GPS | **ARROYO PARK: 26.172, -97.684**
CB WOOD PARK: 26.174, -97.695

SOUTH SIDE OF HARLINGEN, TEXAS

KEY BIRDS
Great kiskadee, several sub-species of kingfishers, curve-billed and long-billed thrashers, and olive sparrow

BEST SEASON
All seasons

AREA DESCRIPTION
Much of the areas in these two parks are open recreational areas with mesquite and some brush

Located inside the Harlingen city limits, the 29-acre Arroyo Park takes in the nine-acre C.B. Wood Park that is a great place for people looking for Valley species. This is a multi-use day-use park containing a nature trail that allows access to the Arroyo Colorado. Birders should watch for the bright yellow markings of the great kiskadee perched on the limbs of the mesquite trees.

The park located on the Arroyo Colorado retains much of its native

Long-billed Thrasher

Tamaulipan brush. Curve-billed as well as long-billed thrashers are found here along with the olive sparrow, a variety of wintering sparrows such as Lincoln's, and nesting flycatchers such as Couch's kingbird and brown-crested flycatcher (summer).

DIRECTIONS TO ARROYO PARK

Continue south on Loop 499 to Hale Ave. Then west on Hale Ave. to New Hampshire, then north on New Hampshire to Arroyo Park.

DIRECTIONS TO C. B. WOOD PARK

From the intersection of New Hampshire and Hale Ave., continue south on New Hampshire to the frontage road of US 77 (about 0.5 mile). Go north on the frontage road to Taft, then east on Taft to 1st Street. Go south on 1st Street to Wilson, then west on Wilson to C. B. Wood Park.

CONTACT INFORMATION

Harlingen Parks & Recreation Department, 900 Fair Park Blvd. Harlingen, Texas 78550
Phone: 956-216-5951
This site is open for day usage only.

RANCH LOOP
Harlingen Thicket – World Birding Center Site

#222

GPS 26.175, -97.688

JUST OFF THE ARROYO COLORADO AND ARROYO STREET IN HARLINGEN, TEXAS

KEY BIRDS
Bewick's wren, olive sparrow, Harris's hawk

BEST SEASON
Migrations, winter

AREA DESCRIPTION
Tamaulipan brush with many native plant varieties

The Harlingen Thicket is being enhanced as a satellite of the World Birding Center. This is a remarkable site, worthy of any amount of time spent here. The habitat here is just a remnant of Tamaulipan brush that was plentiful in urban Harlingen.

An impressive variety of plants here in the center — attracting birds such as Harris's hawk, Bewick's wren, and olive sparrow — are very common in this habitat. Future enhancements at this location will only improve birders chances here in Harlingen.

DIRECTIONS
Return to C.B. Wood Park, and continue east on Harding to 3rd Street. Go south on 3rd Street to Arroyo, then east on Arroyo to its end at the Harlingen Thicket.

CONTACT INFORMATION
Harlingen Chamber of Commerce, 311 E. Tyler St., Harlingen, TX 78550
Phone: 956-423-5440
This site is open for day usage only.

Bewick's Wren

RANCH LOOP
#223 Lon C. Hill (Fair) Park

GPS⊕ 26.119, -97.424

FAIR PARK BOULEVARD AND NORTH J STREET IN HARLINGEN, TEXAS

KEY BIRDS
Hummingbirds

BEST SEASON
Migrations, winter

AREA DESCRIPTION
Open park habitat with trees and some improved birding areas

This park contains a variety of native trees and shrubs and productive butterfly and hummingbird gardens. It is located across from the Municipal Auditorium complex. This is the location of the annual Rio Grande Valley Birding Festival that draws birders from all over the country each November.

The tall trees and wooded habitats are the major attractions to many species of migratory as well as local birds. It must be noted that the park is very popular and can become quite crowed with non-birding park goers who are not very quiet with their activities.

DIRECTIONS
Return on Taft to US 77; remain on the frontage road traveling north. Continue past the intersection of US 77 and US 83 to Fair Park Blvd. and Lon C. Hill Park.

CONTACT INFORMATION
Harlingen Chamber of Commerce, 311 E. Tyler St., Harlingen, TX 78550
Phone: 956-423-5440
This site is open for day use only.

Rufous Hummingbird

Los Fresnos
#224

GPS 26.071, -97.474

LOCATED AT THE INTERSECTION OF TX 100 AND FM 1847, SOUTHEAST OF HARLINGEN, TEXAS

KEY BIRDS
Least grebe, anhinga, neotropic cormorant, black-bellied whistling duck

BEST SEASON
All seasons

AREA DESCRIPTION
South Texas habitats, mesquite, and several resacas wind through the city surrounded by cultivated fields and sugar cane

As you travel TX 100 toward Los Fresnos, there are numerous resacas for the first few miles, all worth glassing for waterbirds. One of the species to watch for is the masked duck that may be found in any of these ponds. Least grebe, anhinga, neotropic cormorant, black-bellied whistling-duck, and a variety of wintering waterfowl also should be found in these lakes.

It was in this city that I spent many years of my adult life gathering birding information and collecting many images of local and migrating species. Except during drought years, the acres of water will provide birders with a vast number of interesting species.

In Los Fresnos, check the city's water treatment ponds on the

Black-bellied Whistling Duck

south side of town. Access is limited, so call ahead to check entry regulations at 956-233-9121. To reach the ponds from US 77/83, drive east on TX 100 for 6.2 miles. Turn south (right) on Nogal opposite a sign for the Ethel L. Whipple Memorial Library.

Continue 0.4 mile to the water treatment plant. Turn right on the dirt road just before the chain link fence and proceed cautiously to the two-diked ponds. Watch for such species as plain chachalaca, Harris's hawk, long-billed thrasher, Bewick's wren, and the olive sparrow.

Several species of ducks and shorebirds are likely to be present. During the summer, birders can watch nesting willets, killdeer, and black-necked stilts energetically defending their spaces.

DIRECTIONS
Starting at the intersection of US 77/83 and TX 100, go east on TX 100 toward FM 1847. At the intersection, you are in Los Fresnos.

CONTACT INFORMATION
City of Los Fresnos, 200 N. Brazil St., Los Fresnos TX 78566
Phone: 956-233-5768
This site is open for day usage only.

RANCH LOOP
#225 The Inn at Chachalaca Bend

GPS 26.087, -97.439

200 CHACHALACA BEND
LOS FRESNOS, TEXAS 78566

KEY BIRDS
Common chachalaca, altamira oriole, green jay, white-winged, mourning, and white-tipped doves, ringed kingfisher, buff-bellied hummingbird, great kiskadee

BEST SEASON
All seasons

AREA DESCRIPTION
South Texas mesquite, ebony brush, resaca (old river) frontage, and landscaped yards and trails

The Inn at Chachalaca Bend is a bed-and-breakfast for visiting birders. It covers 40 acres and is situated only 20 miles from South Padre Island and 12 miles north of Brownsville, near Los Fresnos, Texas. There are nature trails and resacas within these

Altamira Oriole

well-managed acres, allowing for a leisurely birding respite. The inn maintains numerous hummingbird feeders. Green-breasted mango hummingbird appeared here in May 1999!

The inn is operated by Jessie Breedlove and his family – some great people who have been entertaining birders since the B & B's creation. They will go out of their way to be sure your stay and birding adventure is a success and pleasure.

The Inn at Chachalaca Bend presents 40 acres of unspoiled country paradise with beautiful wildlife, natural lake frontage, and luxury accommodations that are popular with year-round birdwatchers.

Birders should watch for birds like the ringed kingfisher, altamira oriole, green jay, buff-bellied hummingbird, great kiskadee, and the roseate spoonbill. The inn is located only a short drive from the Laguna Atascosa National Wildlife Refuge.

DIRECTIONS
From Harlingen, take Highway 77 South, and then take the South Padre Island Exit (Highway 100) – you will be driving east. Drive 7 miles to Los Fresnos. Turn left or north at the light on Arroyo Boulevard or FM 1847. Go 1/4 mile and turn right (east) on Farm Road 2480. Drive 2 miles and turn left or north on Track 43 Road. Go across the resaca and turn right on Chachalaca Bend Drive.

CONTACT INFORMATION
The Inn at Chachalaca Bend, P.O. Box 197, Los Fresnos, Texas 78566
Phone: 956-233-1180 or 888-612-6800
Email: Inn@chachalaca.com
Web: www.chachalaca.com

Cormorant

RANCH LOOP
Port Isabel

GPS 26.042, -97.204

ACROSS THE LOWER LAGUNA MADRE FROM SOUTH PADRE ISLAND

KEY BIRDS
Brown pelican, cormorant

BEST SEASON
Migrations, winter

AREA DESCRIPTION
Bayside city with tall palms and some grassy areas and coastal sand beaches along saltwater bays

A city surrounded by water, Port Isabel is located on the Texas mainland across the Lower Laguna Madre from South Padre Island. Port Isabel can brag of being one of the state's most popular bird watching hotspots.

The climate consists mostly of hot and humid summers and mild, dry winters along this subtropical coastal region. Moving farther inland, the drier landscape is covered mostly by spiny brush. The truth is, if it doesn't have thorns, it bites. This South Texas climate attracts sun followers as well as nature lovers and birders from all over the nation. The climate and the large number of bird species make this area a premier spot for nature parks and birding locations. A large number of Texas birds inhabit the wilds of South Texas.

Birders should walk to the water in Port Isabel from the lighthouse for a great look at the Laguna Madre. Watch for shorebirds, wading birds, gulls, and cormorants. The once-endangered species, the brown pelican, is recovering well and are numerous here. As with several species of waterfowl, drivers are cautioned about the low-flying birds when crossing the bridge to the island. Flashing signs warn drivers of this problem.

Located on South Tarnava Street, the Port Isabel Historical Museum resides in the nearby Champion Building. An impressive collection of historical memorabilia tells the story of the original settling of this once remote area. It must be noted that as a Gulf community, the area experiences tropical storms and hurricanes.

DIRECTIONS
Return to TX 100 and then continue east to Port Isabel. Parking is available near the Port Isabel Lighthouse State Historical Park.

CONTACT INFORMATION
Port Isabel Chamber of Commerce, 421 E. Queen Isabella Blvd., Port Isabel, Texas 78578
Phone: 800-527-6102 or 956-943-2262
Email: info@portisabel.org
Site open for day use only.

Caspian Terns

RANCH LOOP
#227 South Padre Island Locations (SPI)

GPS 26.041, -97.257

ISLAND ON THE SOUTHERN TIP OF TEXAS

KEY BIRDS
Terns, brown pelican, laughing gull, sandpipers, snowy and piping plovers

BEST SEASON
Migrations, winter

AREA DESCRIPTION
Island habitats with saltwater coastal plants that attract birds. Traveling south on the island fresh water pools are found among the dunes.

Located on the southern tip of Texas, this island offers birders several locations starting with the drive south along the beach.

After crossing the causeway turn to the left on Park Road, PR-100 or SPI Boulevard and drive to the end of the pavement. The county has put one of their "disturbing" toll booths charging visitors to keep the beaches clean, which they only manage to do in front of the expensive condos.

Beach goers may get to the beach at Access #6. The soft sand at low tide may require a four-wheel drive vehicle to continue north to the Mansfield Cut. A warning to birders about the sand on this stretch of the beach south of where the pavement ends: The sand can be very soft and deep, and getting stuck should always be kept in mind. Drive as much as possible on the wet hard-packed sand.

In spite of the driving problems along this route, there have been a number of rare pelagic species, gulls, and terns. Watch for peregrine falcons and piping plovers as well as snowy plovers. The plovers are easy to see as they dart along, feeding in the shallow surf.

A location I will bird when on the island is the Valley Land Fund's six-acre birding preserve located on West Sheepshead between SPI Drive and the bay. The Valley Land Fund owns six wooded lots in this area and is improving the property for migratory birds as well as local species. Birders may contact the VLF at P.O. Box 6618, McAllen, Texas 78502 / Phone: 956-686-6429 / Email: info@valleylandfund.com / Web: www.valleylandfund.com.

During the spring migrations, these wooded lots on South Padre may be every bit as productive as High Island near Galveston or Packery Channel near Corpus Christi. Spend at least an hour birding this location. Watch the brush and water features for island birds and migrating dropout species.

The Birding and Nature Center complex is a private, commercial operation located near the SPI Convention Center. It must be mentioned that the Center is not part of the World Birding Center (WBC). The owners of this location have been uncooperative with the South Padre Island birding groups at the Convention Center by blocking off access from the Convention Center's boardwalk. Going South on Padre Island Drive, it's hard to miss the large three-story yellow building. The birder-friendly water features and boardwalk is the next turn to the left after the yellow building.

This location offers an impressive variety of habitats, of which some are man-made, such as the boardwalks and the gardens, which have feeding and watering stations.

The elevated boardwalks give birders a saltwater to brackish as well as a freshwater marsh that is perhaps the best spot in the U.S. to see all of the regularly occurring rails. As many as six species of rails have been seen here at one time, including both yellow and black Virginia and king rails that winter in this marsh; and the clapper rail is also a resident. Depending on the season, watch for marsh wren (year round), the swamp sparrow (winter) and least bittern during the summer months.

Lastly, if you have a few extra dollars, go through the tollbooth into Isla Blanca Park. The entry fee covers a daily permit and you can come and go as you please. There is a circular drive that will take you around the park and very close to the Brownsville Ship Channel and the South Jetties.

The woodlands to the right, just before the park entrance, are excellent locations during spring migration for tanagers, warblers, vireos, buntings, and orioles. Bird from the jetties, near the south end, and glass the offshore waters and the sky for pelagic birds such as northern gannet and magnificent frigatebird.

DIRECTIONS
From Port Isabel, continue east on TX 100 across the Queen Isabella Causeway to South Padre Island (SPI).

CONTACT INFORMATION
South Padre Island Birding and Nature Center, 6801 Padre Boulevard, South Padre Island, TX 78597
Phone: 956-243-8179
For park information, contact Isla Blanca at 956-761-5493 or http://cameron-county-parks.com.
Site open for day use only.

RANCH LOOP
#228 SPI Gateway Project

GPS 26.085, -97.165

PAVED WALKWAYS UNDER AND NEAR THE ISLAND BASE OF THE CAUSEWAY

KEY BIRDS
Osprey, shorebirds, gulls, and terns

BEST SEASON
All seasons

AREA DESCRIPTION
Bay and tidal flats habitat

South Padre Island constructed this concrete trail to access the tidal flats and mangrove trees growing at the base of the causeway. This paved walkway traverses the flats on the south side of the causeway, curves under it, then crosses the flats on the north side to connect with a sidewalk system that continues north on the island.

It never fails to amaze me how the powers that be can build an attraction such as this one and forget to provide parking. Look out across the bay and you will notice half of the "old" causeway falling apart but still standing. The half closest to the island – built at the same time – was torn down with "safety" being the given excuse. Of course the real reason was nothing but county greed; fees are charged for everything.

On both sides of the turnaround are tidal mudflats fringed by black mangrove and some regionally uncommon saltmarsh cordgrass. This

Osprey

is one of the most accessible, and largest, black mangroves growing along the coast in South Texas.

Terns will roost on these flats, as will shorebirds and gulls, making this trail system an excellent opportunity to watch and photograph these species.

DIRECTIONS

Drive to the base of the South Padre end of the causeway. At the turn-around find a parking place and enjoy.

CONTACT INFORMATION

South Padre Island Convention and Visitors Bureau, 600 Padre Blvd., South Padre Island, Texas 78597
Phone: 800-767-2373 or 956-761-3005
Email:info@sopadre.com
Site open for day use only.

RANCH LOOP

#229 TX Hwy 48 Scenic Drive – Bahia Grande

GPS ⊕ **25.973, -97.361**

TEXAS HIGHWAY 48 FROM PORT ISABEL TO BROWNSVILLE

KEY BIRDS
Water birds by the hundreds, herons, egrets, and the roseate spoonbill

BEST SEASON
All seasons

AREA DESCRIPTION
Brushy lomas and grassland habitats, tidal flats and native Tamaulipan brush and cactus

This drive covers over 21,000 acres with 10,000 acres of potential wetlands. The highway has recently been divided and, as you drive toward Brownsville from Port Isabel, you will be passing an extensive area of tidal flats and low hills called "lomas". Lomas are the clay mounds rising above the surrounding tidal flats and are covered with native Tamaulipan

Great Blue Heron

brush, including the locally common Spanish dagger yucca and mesquite.

Due to heavy traffic on TX 48, birders should be very conscious of the car and truck traffic. This goes double for people carrying large cameras or spotting scopes.

The area to the right of TX 48 (driving to Brownsville) is called the Bahia Grande and is being re-flooded by the USFWS. Notice the "Refuge – Keep Out" signs. This seems to be the normal for the USFWS in South Texas: Public land NOT accessible to the public, except by paying a fee.

If you would like to visit this area, which is worth the inconvenience, the refuge offers Tram/Van trips into the Bahia Grande. To book your "Tram Ride", call the refuge at 956-748-3607.

These tidal flats are often covered with shorebirds and water birds such as the reddish egret. Watch for aplomado falcons perched atop the yuccas along this scenic drive.

DIRECTIONS
Drive west on TX 100 to the intersection with TX 48. Go south on TX 48 in the direction of Brownsville. To see the other side, you must drive several miles to the first legal turn-around. Be very wary of drivers along this highway.

CONTACT INFORMATION
John Wallace, Manager, P.O. Box 450, Rio Hondo, Texas 78583
Phone: 956-748-3607
Site open for day use only.

Snowy Egret

RANCH LOOP

Sabal Palm Audubon Center and Sanctuary

#230

GPS 25.853, -97.417

8435 SABAL PALM GROVE RD. BROWNSVILLE, TX 78521

KEY BIRDS
Common yellowthroat and "Lomita" Carolina wrens, gray-crowned yellowthroat, golden-crowned warbler, along with water birds, herons, and egrets

BEST SEASON
Migrations, winter

AREA DESCRIPTION
Palm and heavy brush habitat with wetlands and resacas

At one time, the lower reaches of the Rio Grande had bragging rights on over 40,000 acres of Texas sabal palm forest. This number of palms has now been reduced to less than 100 acres and is managed by the Audubon Society as a sanctuary. According to Audubon, this location is the largest remaining Texas sabal palm fragment in the state.

The magnificent palms are in good company with many species of plants found rarely in the Valley. Avian species here are the Lomita and Carolina wren and the common yellowthroat.

These species are joined at times by the golden-crowned warbler, and gray-crowned yellowthroats have been found here. Neotropical migrants normally wintering in Mexico may remain in the sanctuary throughout the winter months. One of the regular visitors, the buff-bellied hummingbird, is seen at the feeders near the headquarters.

In recent years, the sanctuary staff and volunteers have worked to vegetate surrounding property that had been cleared for agriculture. The sanctuary has a series of walking trails, including one that borders a resaca with observation blinds.

Least grebes as well as many species of ducks and shorebirds may be viewed at close range, especially if water levels are up. It must be noted that the past and present droughts have lowered all water levels. Good rains and a wet year will help this area and South Texas.

DIRECTIONS

Pay close attention to the directions because finding this location is sometimes difficult. Drive south on FM 511. Cross TX 4 and continue to the merger of FM 511 and FM 3068. FM 511 will veer to the right. Continue south on FM 3068 to FM 1419. Turn west or right on FM 1419 and go 0.6 mile to the entrance to the Sabal Palm Audubon Center and Sanctuary, which is on the left.

CONTACT INFORMATION

Audubon Sabal Palm Grove Sanctuary, P.O. Box 5169, Brownsville, TX 78523
Phone: 956-541-8034
Email: jpaz@audubon.org
Web: www.audubon.org/local/sanctuary/sabal and www.sabalpalmsanctuary.org
Site open for day use only.

Osprey

RANCH LOOP

Boca Chica Beach/The USFWS Boca Chica Tract

#231

GPS 25.992, -97.148

EAST OF BROWNSVILLE, TEXAS AT THE END OF TX 4

KEY BIRDS
Aplomado falcon, merlin, peregrine falcon, Harris's hawk, Chihuahuan raven

BEST SEASON
Migrations, winter

AREA DESCRIPTION
Beach and sand marsh habitats including coastal grasslands and lomas

Union and Confederate soldiers fought the final battle of the Civil War at this site in May, 1865 – about a month after the surrender of General Robert E. Lee at Appomattox.

Crossing the miles of coastal grasslands and lomas on TX 4, birders should pay attention to the posts and yuccas for merlins, aplomado falcons, and peregrine falcons during the migrations. Harris's hawk and other hawk species, the Tamaulipas crow, and Chihuahuan raven have been spotted here.

Wilson's plovers, horned larks, and willets have been seen nesting in the flats that border the road. Glass the sacahuista grass and low shrubs for Botteri's sparrows. During winter, watch the telephone poles along the highway for ospreys.

Caution is advised here because, during dry spells, you may find the sand soft and deep. If you turn right or south toward the mouth of the Rio Grande you may encounter a Border Patrol agent watching for illegals crossing the border from Mexico.

Turning left or north will take you to the jetties. Watch for a brown booby seen on rare occasions roosting on the jetty rocks. Piping plovers as well as other shorebirds are often seen on the beach. Spring migrations of hundreds of red knots may be spotted along the beach. Also watch for many of the area's nesting and migrant terns.

A WARNING – Boca Chica Beach may be covered with the Portuguese man-of-war's blue, football-shaped floats with its stinging tentacles. Do not step on or touch. Also, facilities are limited, so please remember to take drinking water, insect repellent, and sun protection. If using a boat to access the USFS tract, be extremely careful and aware of tidal changes.

DIRECTIONS

From the Sabal Palm Sancutary, go back to FM 1419 and go east toward FM 3068. Stay on FM 1419, which eventually curves north back toward TX 4. Go east on TX 4 to Boca Chica Beach and the USFWS Boca Chica Tract. About 10 miles down TX 4 you will notice an historical marker for the Battle of Palmito Ranch. TX 4 continues east to the Gulf of Mexico and Boca Chica Beach.

CONTACT INFORMATION

The Santa Ana NWR: For information or directions, call: 956-784-7500 and/or Brownsville Convention and Visitors Bureau, 650 W. Ruben M. Torres or FM 802, Brownsville, Texas 78520
Phone: 956- 546-3721 or 800- 626-2639
Email: visinfo@brownsville.org
These sites are open for day use only.

Eastern Screech Owl

RANCH LOOP
#232 TPWD Coastal Fisheries Field Station

GPS 25.985, -97.531

95 FISH HATCHERY ROAD
BROWNSVILLE, TX 78520

KEY BIRDS
Eastern screech owl, groove-billed ani, Couch's kingbird, northern beardless-tyrannulet

BEST SEASON
All seasons

AREA DESCRIPTION
Open areas with tall trees and many rearing ponds on the property

The hatchery is inactive, but some ponds will have water. Park in the spaces just past the headquarters. This facility's 20 rectangular ponds may hold cormorants, anhinga, and waterfowl such as whistling-ducks, and even a passing ringed kingfisher.

Summer watchers may see least tern, least bittern, groove-billed ani, and northern beardless-tyrannulet.

In the trees around the facility watch for Couch's kingbird, altamira oriole, great kiskadee, and an eastern screech-owl in its roost hole in a large ash near the headquarters.

DIRECTIONS
From the intersection of US 77/83 and FM 511, drive south on US 77/83 and exit at the Stillman Rd./Old Alice Rd. turnoff. After exiting, remain on the service road, continuing south to Fish Hatchery Rd., then go west on Fish Hatchery Rd. to the TPWD Coastal Fisheries Field Station.

CONTACT INFORMATION
Phone: 956-350-4490
This site is open for day use only.

RANCH LOOP
Camp Lula Sams (Now Private)

#233

GPS 25.989, -97.529

280 N. FISH HATCHERY ROAD
BROWNSVILLE, TX 78520

KEY BIRDS
Ani, greater yellowlegs, lesser yellowlegs, common snipe, mourning dove, Inca dove, rock dove, greater roadrunner

BEST SEASON
All seasons

AREA DESCRIPTION
Low South Texas woodlands and resacas, Texas thorn scrub

Covering 87 acres, Camp Lula Sams is a teaching camp and wildlife refuge and is located on the southern tip of Texas. The diverse habitat and neighboring land including the fish hatchery is maintained by Texas Parks and Wildlife.

These are a few of what birders can expect to see: American coot, black-necked stilt, common snipe, killdeer, greater yellowlegs, lesser yellowlegs, mourning dove, Inca dove, rock dove, greater roadrunner, ruby-throated hummingbird, belted kingfisher.

The site's low woodlands and resacas also contain several cabins that are air-conditioned and with kitchens. The camp has simpler facilities for children or adult groups.

Mourning Dove

The camp also sponsors workshops and nature presentations. Some meals may be arranged for birding groups. This is a great place to see the endangered Texas tortoise. Fees and event schedules will vary depending on the size of the group. Interested parties should call for details.

DIRECTIONS

Drive north on Fish Hatchery Road. It's a half-mile drive to Camp Lula Sams, which is a private wildlife refuge.

CONTACT INFORMATION

Camp Lula Sams, Patrick Burchfield and Carol DeMoss, 280 N. Fish Hatchery Road, Brownsville, TX 78520
Phone: 956-350-9093
Web Site: www.camplulasams.com
This site is open daily with developed lodging available for a fee. An entrance fee is charged.

RANCH LOOP

#234 Las Palomas WMA/Resaca de la Palma State Park – World Birding Center Site

GPS⊕ 25.996, -97.572

1000 NEW CARMEN AVE. BROWNSVILLE, TX 78521

KEY BIRDS
Neo-tropical and nearctic migrants, blue grosbeak, summer tanager, yellow-breasted chat, and American redstart

BEST SEASON
All seasons

AREA DESCRIPTION
Some open areas with old mesquite and other thorny trees and brush

The Las Palomas WMA has 3,311 acres of land purchased to preserve native brush nesting habitat, including farmlands and wetlands for white-winged doves.

Brownsville's Resaca de la Palma – a section of the WMA – boasts the largest tract of native habitat (1,200 semi-tropical acres) in the World Birding Center Site. The oxbow lakes were created by old curves of the Rio Grande. This remote area provides a quiet retreat for all nature lovers as well as birders. These habitats are in stark contrast to the busy border town of Brownsville.

The site contains some very productive mature woodlands, but as it must be mentioned, many of these birding locations are works in progress. Some have just been opened to the general public. Also important to know is that 95 percent of the native habitat has been altered, as is the case in most of this country.

At times resaca levels are regulated for the benefit of wildlife; species like the black-bellied whistling duck, least grebe, various herons, purple gallinule and migrating waterfowl. Birders should watch the ground-level vegetation for species such as the long-billed thrasher, olive sparrow, and white-eyed vireo.

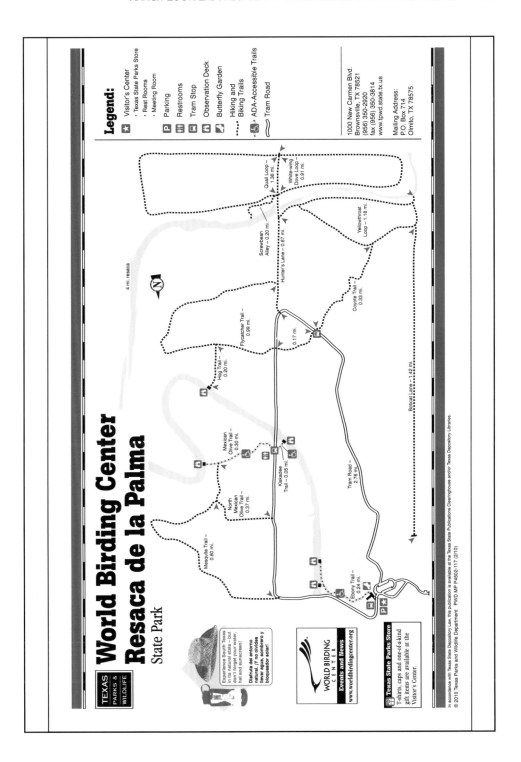

World Birding Center
Resaca de la Palma
State Park

Experience South Texas in its natural state – but don't forget your water, hat and sunscreen!

Disfruta del entorno natural, ¡Y no olvides llevar agua, sombrero y bloqueador solar!

WORLD BIRDING CENTER

Events and News
www.worldbirdingcenter.org

Texas State Parks Store
T-shirts, caps and one-of-a-kind gift items are available at the Visitor's Center.

4 mi. resaca

N

Mesquite Trail – 0.60 mi.

North Mexican Olive Trail – 0.37 mi.

Mexican Olive Trail – 0.30 mi.

Hog Trail – 0.20 mi.

Flycatcher Trail – 0.99 mi.

Kiskadee Trail – 0.05 mi.

Screwbean Alley – 0.20 mi.

Hunter's Lane – 0.67 mi.

Quail Loop – 1.36 mi.

White-wing Dove Loop – 0.91 mi.

Yellowthroat Loop – 1.18 mi.

Coyote Trail – 0.33 mi.

0.17 mi.

Tram Road – 2.76 mi.

Bobcat Lane – 1.42 mi.

Ebony Trail – 0.24 mi.

Legend:
- Visitor's Center
  - Texas State Parks Store
  - Rest Rooms
  - Meeting Room
- Parking
- Restrooms
- Tram Stop
- Observation Deck
- Butterfly Garden
- Hiking and Biking Trails
- ADA-Accessible Trails
- Tram Road

1000 New Carmen Blvd.
Brownsville, TX 78521
(956) 350-2920
fax (956) 350-3814
www.tpwd.state.tx.us

Mailing Address:
P.O. Box 714
Olmito, TX 78575

In accordance with Texas State Depository Law, this publication is available at the Texas State Publications Clearinghouse and/or Texas Depository Libraries.
© 2010 Texas Parks and Wildlife Department PWD MP P4502-117 (2/10)

DIRECTIONS

Drive west on Boca Chica Blvd. until it becomes US 281, known locally as the Military Highway. Drive west approximately 4.5 miles on US 281 to the River Bend Subdivision. The unmarked dirt road across from the River Bend office is the entrance road for Resaca de la Palma WMA.

For the State Park: Drive from Expressway 77/83, exit at Olmito, take FM 1732, follow for 2.5 miles; turn left at New Carmen Ave.; follow for 1.5 miles; at the end of the paved road, turn left to enter the park.

CONTACT INFORMATION

Information about access may be obtained by calling TPW at 956-447-2704. Resaca de la Palma State Park, 1000 New Carmen Ave. Brownsville, TX 78521
Phone: 956-350-2920
This site is open for day use only and a fee is charged.

Blue Grosbeak

RANCH LOOP
#235 Las Palomas WMA – Ebony Unit

GPS 26.083, -97.743

JUST OFF FM 1479, SOUTH OF SAN BENITO, TEXAS

KEY BIRDS
Black-bellied whistling duck and flycatchers such as Couch's kingbird

BEST SEASON
All seasons

AREA DESCRIPTION
Wet areas mixed with south Texas scrub brush and mesquite

Caution when visiting this site: During wet times the roads can be slippery or muddy. An observation platform adjacent to the resaca dominates the site and offers an excellent vantage point for studying the waterbirds that crowd these waters.

Birders should watch for several species of ducks including black-bellied whistling-duck, least grebe, and flycatchers such as Couch's kingbird. Watch the snags and low limbs along the beach for the great kiskadee. Enjoy the variety of both wading birds and those roosting or resting in the trees.

It must be mentioned, all of the Las Palomas WMA units were purchased with funds from hunters. The Ebony Unit continues to be hunted.

DIRECTIONS
Drive west on US 281 to FM 1479. Go north 2.7 miles on FM 1479 to an unmarked gravel road—go east to Las Palomas WMA-Ebony Unit.

CONTACT INFORMATION
Call TPW at 956-447-2704 or check the public information booth for access during hunting seasons.
This site is open for day use only and a fee is charged.
Vieh's B&B is located on FM 675 (0.6 mile north on FM 1479) a short distance from the Ebony Unit. Contact Charlie and Lana Vieh at (956) 425-4651, clvieh@aol.com, or visit their websites: www.vieh.com and www.viehbedandbreakfast.com

Black-bellied Whistling Ducks

RANCH LOOP
#236 Cannon Road

GPS 26.062, -97.785

Located in Cameron County just off US 281

Key Birds
Tropical kingbird, puddle ducks, kingbirds, American white pelican, both species of whistling ducks, Altamira oriole

Best Season
All seasons

Area Description
Brushy expanses with wet areas

USFWS tracts border Cannon Road for much of its length—many South Texas species may be seen along this drive. Driving to near the end of Cannon Road, there will be a power transfer station. This is where Altamira orioles and tropical kingbirds have nested.

It has only been within the past decade that kingbirds have expanded their presence. As the tropical kingbirds have established their nesting to this area, it has become difficult to identify the specific sites. Listen to all tropical/Couch's kingbird calls and songs.

Continue past the power station to where the road ends near a levee and reservoir. This reservoir, in season, supports both species of whistling ducks, puddle ducks, and American white pelicans.

Directions
Return to FM 1479, and then go south to US 281. Go west on US 281 to Cannon Road (marked by a cannon). Travel north on Cannon Rd. (dirt and caliche for most of its distance).

Contact Information
San Benito Chamber of Commerce, 401 N. Sam Houston, San Benito, Texas 78586
Phone: 956-399-5321
Email: info@SanBenitoChamber.com
This site is open for day use only.

Tropical Kingbird

BIRDING TRAILS: TEXAS GULF COAST

South Texas Trail

This trail could be called "Birding the Border" because it follows the Rio Grande from east of Weslaco as it winds its way to Falcon Lake State Park. I would be amiss not to mention there has been trouble along this stretch of the border with disturbing results. However with caution and care birders should not have a problem.

The folks around McAllen are very bird aware and make life extremely good for the birding community with many great locations where your binoculars and spotting scopes will be well used. Go by the Chamber of Commerce in McAllen for list and other locations not mentioned here.

Somewhat North of McAllen off highway 281 on FM 186 is 5,000 acres of the National Wildlife Refuge Sal del Rey. As a walk-in area, it does take some shoe leather to see it all, but the salt lake is well worth the walk and is a major roosting area for migrating waterfowl. Explore this refuge, but watch for rattlesnakes 12 months of the year.

There are nature centers, a location of the World Birding Center, and many other birding attractions along this trail.

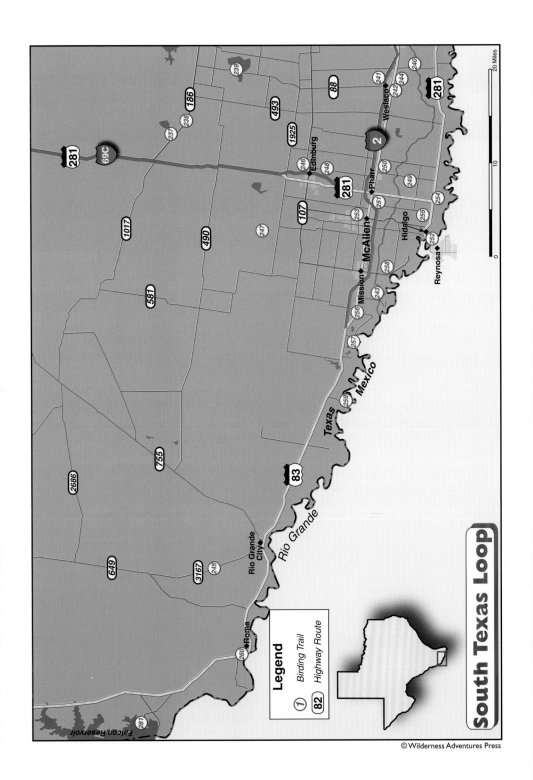

South Texas Loop

Legend
- ① Birding Trail
- 🔲82 Highway Route

© Wilderness Adventures Press

South Texas Loop Locations

237. USFWS La Sal del Rey Tract
238. Brushline Road/Tres Corales Ranch
239. Delta Lake County Park
240. Estero Llano Grande
241. Weslaco Wetlands
242. Valley Nature Center
243. National Butterfly Center
244. Frontera Audubon Thicket
245. Santa Ana NWR
246. Edinburg Scenic Wetlands Trails
247. USFWS Monte Cristo Tract
248. Quinta Mazatlan
249. McAllen Nature Center
250. McAllen Sewage Ponds
251. Williams Wildlife Sanctuary
252. Hidalgo Pumphouse Discovery & Heritage Center
253. The Bird's Nest B&B
254. Anzalduas Dam and County Park
255. Bentsen-Rio Grande Valley State Park
256. Chihuahua Woods Preserve of the Nature Conservancy
257. Las Palomas WMA - Peñitas Unit
258. USFWS Yturria Tract
259. Los Ebanos Ferry Landing
260. Roma Bluffs/The Roma Historic District
261. Falcon State Park

SOUTH TEXAS LOOP
#237 USFWS La Sal del Rey Tract

GPS 26.524, -98.078

ON TX 186, EAST OF LINN, TEXAS

KEY BIRDS
Snow geese, sandhill cranes, long-billed curlews, and Say's phoebes

BEST SEASON
All seasons

AREA DESCRIPTION
Brushy ranchland with open pastures centered around a large saltwater lake and a freshwater pond

This location has been one of my favorite places since well before the USFWS acquired the property as a refuge. At that time it belonged to the Campbell family of Raymondville. During the winter months there can be flocks of lark buntings along the shoulders of TX 186 on the way to this site.

The tract consists of approximately 5,000 acres. La Sal del Rey translates to "the salt of the king" and is named after its principal geological feature – a 530-acre salt lake. Salt has been mined at the lake since aboriginal people occupied the land.

The best birding times at La Sal del Rey are just before and after dawn during winter months. Park at the public information spot on TX 186, where you'll be rewarded by the early

Sandhill Crane

morning exodus of thousands of roosting sandhill cranes, snow geese, and as many as 3,000 long-billed curlews as they leave in the pre-dawn darkness.

Entry points (trailheads) may be accessed off of TX 186, Chapa Road, Brushline Road, and an unnamed dirt road that T's into Brushline Road. The trailheads allow access to an extensive network of trails east of Brushline Road.

In the late afternoon and as dusk approaches, park at the northernmost entry site on Brushline Road and walk to the lake, where you'll be able to see geese, curlews, and cranes as they return to their roosting areas silhouetted against the sunset on the lake.

La Sal del Rey is a good place to find wintering Say's phoebes. During the summer, snowy plovers and other shorebirds nest along the lake's edge, and hundreds of Wilson's phalaropes are often spotted during migration. Crested caracara and white-tailed hawk, are seen in this location year round.

A bird species list covering all the tracts, restoration of native habitat, and other enhancements are planned.

Please note: On all USFWS Tracts, do not block gates. None of the tracts have facilities such as water and restrooms.

DIRECTIONS
Drive south on US 281 to the intersection of TX 186. Go east on TX 186 to the United States Fish and Wildlife Service La Sal del Rey tract of the Lower Rio Grande Valley National Wildlife Refuge.

CONTACT INFORMATION
A map indicating access points may be obtained from the Santa Ana NWR headquarters at 956-787-3079. Additionally, a public information map of this tract is posted 2.3 miles west of Brushline Road on TX 186.

Information about specific tracts is available at the Santa Ana NWR headquarters: 3325 Green Jay, Alamo, TX 78516

Phone: 956-784-7500

Web site: www.fws.gov/refuges/profiles/index.cfm?id=21551

Site open for day use only.

SOUTH TEXAS LOOP
Brushline Road/
Tres Corales Ranch

#238

GPS 26.5, -98.049

BRUSHLINE ROAD OFF OF TX 186

KEY BIRDS
Cactus wren, curve-billed thrasher

BEST SEASON
All seasons

AREA DESCRIPTION
Heavy brush with cactus and other thorn-bearing plants

Brushline Road, which borders both La Sal del Rey and Tres Corales Ranch, is an excellent place for birders. A Texas feature, the prickly-pear cactus, along the road is a great place to see the cactus wren, as well as to watch the barbed-wire fence posts and wires for curve-billed thrashers.

The pond that is visible from the road is a freshwater lake and is easily viewed through a spotting scope. At times there have been thousands of migratory waterfowl, including the black-bellied whistling duck. The road is county property and therefore public, while the ranch is private property. Please do not trespass.

DIRECTIONS
After exploring Brushline Road, go back to TX 186 and go east approximately two miles to the Tres Corales Pond.

CONTACT INFORMATION
A map indicating access points may be obtained from the Santa Ana NWR headquarters by calling 956-787-3079.
Site open for day use only.

Curve-billed Thrasher

SOUTH TEXAS LOOP
#239 Delta Lake County Park

GPS 26.417, -97.946

ON FM 88, NORTH OF MONTE ALTO, TEXAS

KEY BIRDS
Tree swallow, osprey, ringed kingfisher

BEST SEASON
All seasons

AREA DESCRIPTION
A county park with some large trees and mesquite and with channels joining Delta Lake

The lake often hosts numbers of ringed kingfishers. Ospreys are seen at intervals near the lake. This county park is at times in ill repair, but at the last visitation afforded birders restrooms, picnic tables, and some other amenities. Most of the property around the lake is private.

Tens of thousands of tree swallows have been seen at Delta Lake during spring and fall migration, gorging on midges as they swarm over the marshes. The wetlands around the lake are the best place here to glass for rails and other bird species attracted to the water and the water's edge. During spring and fall, migrants will at times flock to the stands of oaks and ash around the picnic areas.

DIRECTIONS
Return to the intersection of TX 186 and FM 493. Go east on TX 186 to FM 88 (immediately east of the third road that accesses the Teniente Tract). Go south on FM 88 approximately five miles to Delta Lake County Park.

CONTACT INFORMATION
Phone: 956-262-6585
Site open for day use only and there is a $2.00 entrance fee.

Tree Swallow

SOUTH TEXAS LOOP
#240 Estero Llano Grande – World Birding Center Site

GPS⊕ 26.124, -97.953

3301 S. INTERNATIONAL BLVD. (FM 1015)
WESLACO, TEXAS 78596

KEY BIRDS
Wood stork, black-crowned night-heron, neotropic cormorant

BEST SEASON
All seasons

AREA DESCRIPTION
Wooded areas, thorn scrub harbor with lakeside and shallow water habitats

This 230-plus-acre refuge is a work in progress as a World Birding Center site. The shallow water location is considered one of the best spots to see a variety of shorebirds and waterfowl. The woodlands as well as the lake are being developed as a major interpretive component of the WBC.

The road borders the southern edge of the Estero Llano Grande. Birders should watch for wood storks that will at times crowd these waters. During the late summers watch for waterfowl, shorebirds, American white pelicans, black-crowned night-herons, and neotropic cormorants feeding here.

The lake also extends to the west side of the FM 1015 bridge. To view this portion of the lake, park on the shoulder of the road located at the northwestern corner of the bridge. You may scope the lake from this high point, or walk down to the lake beside the bridge. Black phoebes have wintered here and in summer, cave swallows nest under the bridge.

Wood Stork

Access to the woodlands north of the Estero Llano Grande is now available. These woodlands host many of the valley specialties, so the Estero Llano Grande WBC interpretive center will offer birders a chance to view both water and land birds within the same property.

DIRECTIONS
From the intersection of US 281 and FM 1015, go north on FM 1015 approximately two miles to Estero (lake) Llano Grande, the headwaters of the Arroyo Colorado.

CONTACT INFORMATION
Estero Llano Grande State Park, 3301 S. International Blvd. (FM 1015)
Weslaco, Texas 78596
Phone: 956-565-3919
This site is open for day use only.

SOUTH TEXAS LOOP
The Weslaco Wetlands

#242

GPS 26.18, -97.978

NEAR THE MID VALLEY AIRPORT IN WESLACO, TEXAS

KEY BIRDS
Vermilion flycatcher, great kiskadee, Couch's kingbird

BEST SEASON
All seasons

AREA DESCRIPTION
Stands of willows and freshwater ponds with some open areas

This is a series of water cleaning ponds for the Weslaco wastewater treatment plant and is owned by the city of Weslaco. The site offers birders the chance to see many varieties of water birds. Some of these species are black-bellied and fulvous whistling-ducks, least grebe, migrant ducks, anhinga, herons, and egrets.

The dikes and land surrounding the pond have grown up with

White Ibis

willows and mesquite. Several species of landbirds, such as great kiskadee, vermilion flycatcher, and Couch's kingbird are fairly easy to see. The neotropical landbirds are attracted here by the lush willows and the fresh water during migrations.

The City of Weslaco is developing this location for better wildlife and bird watching. Parking is available at the end of Airport Drive; please do not block the gate.

The city's plans include building a bridge and observation platform that will allow viewing of the easternmost ponds. As this site develops, it should become one of the better spots in the Valley for viewing waterbirds and migrants.

DIRECTIONS

Return west on BUS 83 about 4 miles to Airport Drive in Weslaco. Go north on Airport Dr. to US 83; continue north on Airport Dr. (veering west) to its end at the Mid Valley Airport and the Weslaco Wetlands.

CONTACT INFORMATION

Weslaco Chamber of Commerce, 301 W Railroad St., Weslaco, TX 78596
Phone: 956-968-2102 or 888-968-2102
This site is open for day use only.

SOUTH TEXAS LOOP
The Valley Nature Center

#242

GPS 26.158, -97.998

301 SOUTH BORDER AVE.
WESLACO, TX 78599

KEY BIRDS
Buff-bellied, ruby-throated, and black-chinned hummingbirds, green parakeet, red-crowned parrot

BEST SEASON
All seasons

AREA DESCRIPTION
Tamaulipan brush land with gardens, trails, and some trees

This is the location where people have a chance to become familiar with the Valley fauna and flora. The Valley Nature Center presents Tamaulipan brush country plants in gardens that can and will attract an array of hummingbirds. Species like the buff-bellied hummingbird and, during migrations, the ruby-throated and black-chinned hummingbirds are rather common.

Located at the rear of Gibson Park, The Valley Nature Center is well vegetated with oaks, hackberry, and ash. Green parakeets and red-crowned parrots will roost in trees. These two species have become well established in South Texas. Large flights of green parakeets are easy to see and hear in many of the surrounding communities such as Brownsville, Harlingen, Mission, and McAllen.

Rather boisterous and less common, the red-crowned parrot is somewhat more difficult to find. Visit a roosting site in late afternoon and listen and look for the parrots. This is the best way to spot these birds. While you are visiting the Valley Nature Center, watch for nesting parrots.

SPECIAL NOTE: For current information about where to find roosting parrots, try contacting the Valley Rare Bird Alert tape at 956-969-2731.

DIRECTIONS

Go back to BUS 83, and then continue west on BUS 83 to FM 88. Go south on FM 88 (Texas Blvd.) to W. 6th Street. Go west on W. 6th Street to S. Border Ave., then north on S. Border Ave. to Gibson Park and the Valley Nature Center.

CONTACT INFORMATION

Phone: 956-969-2475
Email: info@valleynaturecenter.org
Web Site: www.valleynaturecenter.org
The Visitor Center is open Thursday through Sunday 11:00am to 5:00pm. The Nature Park is open Monday through Friday 9:00am to 5:00pm, and Saturday and Sunday 11:00am to 5:00pm.

Green Parakeets

#243 National Butterfly Center

GPS 26.1802, -98.364

3333 BUTTERFLY PARK DRIVE
MISSION, TX 78572

KEY BIRDS
Eastern screech owl, eastern kingbird, scissor-tailed flycatcher, loggerhead shrike, American crow, purple martin, barn swallow, tufted titmouse, eastern bluebird, crested caracara

BEST SEASON
Spring and fall migrations and breeding seasons

AREA DESCRIPTION
Mostly open grassland/pasture with a long stretch of wooded area

In spite of not being as a named birding site, birders will enjoy walking along the woodland trails looking for the many species of native wild birds the area has to offer, and especially those passing through during the migrations. For the last few years there has been an eastern screech owl nesting on the property.

The National Butterfly Center is dedicated to education, conservation, and scientific research on wild butterflies. Its mission is "Growing Connections". The National Butterfly Center connects people to butterflies, which are intimately connected to native plants, which themselves are connected to the earth.

The 100-acre National Butterfly Center is the premier location in the United States to experience the beauty, drama, and emotion of wild butterflies. You will see incredible numbers of kaleidoscopically colored butterflies. The clouds of butterflies are at the National Butterfly Center because, by planting thousands of plants that the butterfly's need for nectar and for caterpillar growth, they have created a butterfly paradise that sustains large populations of hundreds of species of wild butterflies.

DIRECTIONS
On the west side of Mission, from Business or Expressway 83, turn south on Bentsen-Palm Drive. When you reach the entrance to Bentsen Rio Grande State Park and the headquarters for the World Birding Center turn left (east) on "old" Military Road (unmarked). Drive one mile and turn right (south) on Butterfly Park Drive.

CONTACT INFORMATION

Open every day, except certain major holidays: 9:00am to 5:00pm.
Email: nbc@naba.org
Phone: 956-583-5400
Website: www.nationalbutterflycenter.org
Admission: Adults: $10/ Children (4-13): $5/ Children under 4 Free/ Week Pass: $25. The admission fee for those entering the National Butterfly Center with camera tripods or professional video equipment is $50.

Eastern Screech Owl

SOUTH TEXAS LOOP
#244 Frontera Audubon Thicket

GPS ⊕ 26.148, -97.988

1101 S. TEXAS BLVD.
WESLACO, TX 78596

KEY BIRDS
Lesser goldfinch, black-bellied whistling duck, shorebirds, chachalaca

BEST SEASON
All seasons

AREA DESCRIPTION
South Texas brush, mesquite, and pond and lake habitats

Offering 15-acres of opportunities for the birding public, this location attracts birds, butterflies, and those interested in the nature and biodiversity of this area.

The Visitor's Center has a gift shop, meeting room, and is working to renovate a large Mediterranean-style home on the property for future use as a community meeting/gathering place. Improvements and management are by the Frontera Audubon Chapter, one of the most active Audubon chapters.

The landscaped property, with a rich variety of native

American Goldfinch

valley plants including many rare and endangered species, attracts many bird species. Watch for the lesser goldfinch in the sunflowers behind the headquarters. There is also a developed wetland that attracts large numbers of shorebirds as well as the black-bellied whistling-duck.

Green parakeets are known to have nested in the cavities of dead trees bordering the pond, and red-crowned parrots roost in old trees in the immediate neighborhood.

The plain chachalacas have populated the brush and each morning announce their presence with their loud and raspy calling from the roofs of neighborhood homes. During migrations, this thicket is one the better spots to see neotropical migrants away from the coast.

DIRECTIONS

Drive to FM 88 (Texas Blvd.), then go south about 0.5 mile on FM 88 to the Frontera Audubon Thicket.

CONTACT INFORMATION

Frontera Audubon Society
Phone: 956-968-3275
Email: fronteraaudubon@gmail.com
Website: www.fronteraaudubon.org
Call to request permission to visit the sanctuary. This site is access restricted; please call ahead; a fee is charged.

SOUTH TEXAS LOOP
Santa Ana NWR

GPS 26.459, -98.86

3325 GREEN JAY ROAD
ALAMO, TX 78516

KEY BIRDS
White-tipped dove, plain chachalaca, olive sparrow, green jay, and many others

BEST SEASON
Migrations, winter

AREA DESCRIPTION
Riverside habitats and heavy brush with tall old mesquite covered with Spanish moss

This 2,088-acre refuge is located just off of Highway 281 and borders the Rio Grande. It is a Mecca for wildlife.

The Visitor's Center is open seven days a week, all year round, from 8:00am to 4:00pm, excluding major holidays. Beginning the day after Thanksgiving through May, a wildlife tram operates seven days a week, and the wildlife drive is closed to vehicular traffic.

When the tram is not operating, the wildlife drive is open two days a week and the days are subject to change.

At the Visitor's Center, check the sightings list and then pick up a map of the park trail system. There is also information on owl prowls, canoe trips, and other activities that can produce unusual species like the elf owl.

Then birders and photographers should spend a little time at the water features and feeders found near the entrance to the trails. Replenishing the feeders in the mornings makes them magnets for olive sparrow, green jay, white-tipped dove, and the plain chachalaca. Watch for the green kingfisher from the bridge over the irrigation canal.

Walk the trail to Willow Lake to look for waterfowl and the least grebe and red-shouldered hawk in the trees, and a number of shorebirds in the shallow water. Tropical parulas have been known to nest here, although not on a regular basis. The parulas weave their nests in the strands of Spanish moss.

Clay-colored robins have been found along this trail in the past, and also watch for the long pendulous nests of the Altamira oriole. All three kingfishers are found on the refuge except during extremely dry weather.

Unusual hawks, not common to the area such as hook-billed kite, gray hawk, and common black-hawk, which is rare, may be observed as you walk this Spanish-moss-lined trail.

The old headquarters site is a great place to spot buff-bellied, rufous, ruby-throated, and black-chinned hummingbirds. Also watch the old Texas ebony trees for migrant landbirds.

During winter months, tropical parula and rose-throated becards have been seen here in years past. The Pintail Lake Trail leads birders to the largest lake in the refuge, Pintail Lake. Depending on water levels, it is an excellent spot to find large wading birds, a variety of waterfowl, and many species of shorebirds.

Returning to the Visitor's Center via the trail that borders the eastern edge of Willow Lake, pay close attention for marsh wren and the common yellowthroat. Watch the cattails for sora rails.

During the fall migration, stand on the levee bordering the north edge of the refuge and watch the skies for flights of raptors. Thousands of hawks including broad-winged hawk, Swainson's hawk, and Mississippi kite can be seen. Also watch for thousands of broad-winged hawks flying into the refuge to roost for the evening.

DIRECTIONS
Go west on US 281 from its intersection with FM 88 to the entrance to the Santa Ana NWR. Watch for the sign on Highway 281.

CONTACT INFORMATION
Email: jennifer_owenwhite@fws.gov
Web Site: http://www.fws.gov/southwest/refuges/texas/STRC/santaana/Index.html
Phone Number: 956-784-7500
For a schedule and additional information, contact the refuge at 956-787-3079.
This site is open for day use only.

Black-bellied Whistling Ducks

SOUTH TEXAS LOOP

#246 Edinburg Scenic Wetlands Trails – World Birding Center Site

GPS 26.303, -98.141

714 RAUL LONGORIA ROAD
EDINBURG, TX 78542

KEY BIRDS
Green and ringed kingfishers, black-necked stilt, least bittern

BEST SEASON
All seasons

AREA DESCRIPTION
Ponds and park habitats, open woods, thickets

The nature trail, the entrance to the location, is being developed as a unit of the WBC. It consists of 40 acres within the municipal park.

Edinburg has transformed the steady wastewater outflow into a remarkable wetland complex. The water is so clear that visitors may see diamond-backed water snakes in the vegetation that covers the bottom of the ponds.

Birders will enjoy seeing green and ringed kingfishers here as well as the belted kingfisher. Another popular item for birders is the impressive variety of waterfowl, as well as black-necked stilts and least bitterns that nest here in summer.

Black-necked Stilt

DIRECTIONS

Return to FM 907, and go north on FM 907 to US 83. Go west on US 83 to US 281, and then travel north on US 281 to TX 107 (the University exit). Go east on TX 107 to Doolittle Road, and then travel south on Doolittle Road to the Edinburg Municipal Park.

CONTACT INFORMATION

Phone: 956-381-9922
Website: www.edinburgwbc.org
This site is open for day use only.

SOUTH TEXAS LOOP
USFWS Monte Cristo Tract

#247

GPS ⊕ 26.371, -98.255

NORTH OF EDINBURG, TEXAS ON WALLACE ROAD

KEY BIRDS
Plain chachalaca, green jay, great kiskadee, least grebe

BEST SEASON
Migrations, winter

AREA DESCRIPTION
Thicket of native vegetation and several ponds

This tract is composed of 90,000 acres of Texas brushland. The public information point is located along Wallace Road. Walk along the canal and road to access the property that extends to the west of Wallace Road.

During wet years, there will be a number of ponds holding several species of waterfowl. This site is made up of a thicket of native vegetation. This locality is well worth spending some time watching for the several species of waterfowl and land birds spending time here.

Birders should pay special attention and watch for the western diamondback rattlesnakes native to this type of habitat.

DIRECTIONS
At the intersection of TX 107 and US 281, continue north on US 281 to FM 1925. Go west on FM 1925 approximately 7 miles to Wallace Road. Head north on Wallace Road 3.5 miles to the USFWS Monte Cristo Tract.

CONTACT INFORMATION
Edinburg Chamber of Commerce
Phone: 956-383-4974 or 800-800-7214
Email: information@edinburg.com
Web Site: www.fws.gov/refuges/
This site is open for day use only.

Green Jay

SOUTH TEXAS LOOP
#248 Quinta Mazatlan – World Birding Center Site

GPS⊕ **26.288, -98.132**

600 Sunset Drive
McAllen, TX 78503

Key Birds
Plain chachalaca, buff-bellied hummingbird, golden-fronted woodpecker, curve-billed thrasher

Best Season
Migrations, winter

Area Description
Urban oasis, planted with native plants and outlying acres of wild Tamaulipan thorn forest

Quinta Mazatlan is another urban oasis, where quiet trails wind through more than 15 acres of birding habitat located close to McAllen airports & hotels.

This historic mansion with landscaped grounds is owned by the city of McAllen and is being developed as a unit of the WBC. The area has been enhanced with water and bird feeding stations to make them even more attractive to wildlife.

The aged oaks on the property are very attractive to migrant land birds, and the grounds have a large variety of birds – for example, the plain chachalaca, buff-bellied hummingbird, golden-fronted woodpecker, great kiskadee, long-billed thrasher, olive sparrow, and green jay.

Golden-fronted Woodpecker

It has been my pleasure to speak here several times and lead a "bird walk". The grounds are kept very well and the numerous bird species are amazing. The gift shop and people working here are as first class as they come. This is one of my "must make" stops in the McAllen area.

The Quinta Mazatlan has ongoing and year-round programs for young people as well as adults.

DIRECTIONS
Drive south from Edinburg on US 281 to US 83, and go west to McAllen and TX 336 (10th Street). Go south about 1 mile on TX 336 to Sunset. Turn east (left) on Sunset and continue to its end at Quinta Mazatlan.

CONTACT INFORMATION
Phone: 956-681-3370
Web Site: www.quintamazatlan.com
There is an entry fee charged, which is $2.00 for adults and $1.00 for seniors and children.
To make arrangements to bird the grounds, call 956-682-1517.
This site is open for day use only.

Curve-billed Thrasher

SOUTH TEXAS LOOP

#249 McAllen Nature Center

GPS⊕ 26.125, -98.159

4104 WEST BUSINESS US 83
MCALLEN, TX

KEY BIRDS
Cactus wren, curve-billed thrasher

BEST SEASON
Migrations, winter

AREA DESCRIPTION
Managed trails amid South Texas thorny brush and mesquite trees

This is a small park, but it contains an amazing number of native plants and an all-weather trail system. Many of the South Texas bird species may be found at this location. Species such as the cactus wren and curve-billed thrasher can be seen here. Of course, the plantings attract a variety of butterflies.

The visitor's center across from the garden is mostly falling apart. The trails start from here, winding through cactus and Texas ebony. The trails seem to be well-maintained.

DIRECTIONS
From the McAllen Convention Center, go north to BUS 83, then west on BUS 83 approximately 2 miles to the McAllen Nature Center.

CONTACT INFORMATION
McAllen Chamber of Commerce, 1200 Ash Avenue, McAllen, Texas 78501
Phone: 956-682-2871
This site is open for day use only.

SOUTH TEXAS LOOP
McAllen Sewage Ponds
#250

GPS 26.168, -98.274

4100 IDELA AVENUE
McALLEN, TEXAS

KEY BIRDS
Migrant ducks, terns, and shorebirds

BEST SEASON
Wet seasons

AREA DESCRIPTION
Open grassy area with ponds kept reasonably clear of weeds and brush, and a few medium height trees

There is a large sign welcoming birders as you arrive. Drive along the levee to your south to access the ponds, but be very careful after a heavy rain. The water levels in these ponds can change radically, so the birding opportunities can also vary based on the water level.

When the ponds contain water, a variety of water birds and shorebirds may be seen. These shallow ponds in the spring are one of the area's best spots to see migrant ducks, terns, and shorebirds. Both snowy plovers and least terns have nested along the edge of the ponds.

DIRECTIONS
Return east on BUS 83 to Spur 115, and then go south on Spur 115 to Idela Dr. Go west on Idela approximately 1.5 miles to the McAllen Sewage Ponds.

CONTACT INFORMATION
McAllen Chamber of Commerce, 1200 Ash Avenue, McAllen, Texas 78501
Phone: 956-682-2871
This site is open for day use only.

Common Tern

SOUTH TEXAS LOOP
Williams Wildlife Sanctuary

#251

GPS ⊕ **26.189, -98.196**

ON SAM HOUSTON STREET IN PHARR, TEXAS

KEY BIRDS
Great kiskadee, green jay, clay-colored robin

BEST SEASON
All seasons

AREA DESCRIPTION
Heavy south Texas brush, water features, bird feeding stations, and improved pathways

This is a private site that is open only during the day. Williams Wildscapes, Inc. is a specialized landscaping company. Their goal is to plant native and drought-tolerant trees, plants, and shrubs that create an environment to attract birds, butterflies, and other beneficial creatures.

In spite of their busy work schedule, the Williams family is always ready to talk with visiting birders.

Their birding history began in October, 2002 when a blue mockingbird appeared and stayed for two years. In 2003, a slate-throated redstart visited for two days. Then in 2004, a black-headed nightingale thrush was documented in the sanctuary, a U.S. first. It stayed for six months.

This small sanctuary is one of the Rio Grande Valley's most popular places to bird watch.

Clay-colored Robin

DIRECTIONS
From US 83 in Pharr turn on Sam Houston Street and watch for the sign on your left as you are driving south.

CONTACT INFORMATION
Allen Williams, 750 W. Sam Houston, Pharr, Texas 78577
Phone: 956-460-9864
Web Site: http://www.williamswildlifesanctuary.com
This site is open for day use only. This is a private residence. Please call before you go.

SOUTH TEXAS LOOP

#252 Hidalgo Pumphouse Discovery & Heritage Center – World Birding Center Site

GPS 26.097, -98.262

902 S. SECOND ST. HIDALGO, TX 78557

KEY BIRDS
Great blue heron, cattle egret, yellow-crowned night-heron, white-faced ibis, and migrating species

BEST SEASON
All seasons

AREA DESCRIPTION
South Texas brush land, some woods and water

This facility is being incorporated into the WBC, and represents an interesting merger of natural and social history. The USFWS owns a tract of land south of the center, adjacent to the Rio Grande. This area may be birded from the walkway that borders the pumphouse.

Being situated higher than the bordering woodlands, a birder is offered the opportunity to see the canopy as migrants sweep along the river. Future plans include the development of a more extensive trail system that will access the USFWS property.

DIRECTIONS
In Hidalgo, go south one on 3rd Street to Texano, and travel one block west on Texano to 2nd Street. Go south on 2nd Street to the Hidalgo Pumphouse Discovery and Heritage Center entrance.

CONTACT INFORMATION
Hidalgo Chamber of Commerce
Phone: 956-843-2734 - 800-580-2215 – 956-843-8686
Email: yesac956@aol.com
Web Site: http://www.stxmaps.com/go/texas-coastal-birding-trail-the-hidalgo-pumphouse.html
Open 11:00am – 6:00pm Tuesday through Friday and from 2:00pm – 6:00pm on Sundays. There is an admission charge.

Great Blue Heron

SOUTH TEXAS LOOP
The Birds Nest B&B

#253

GPS 26.216, -98.223

ON 6TH STREET IN MCALLEN, TEXAS

KEY BIRDS
Kiskadee, green jay, vireos, orioles, warblers, meadowlarks, and migrating species during the spring and fall

BEST SEASON
All seasons

AREA DESCRIPTION
Large trees and bushes located on a double-sized lot well within the city limits

This is a large private home with several rooms available for birders. The settings and atmosphere make you want to keep your binoculars with you 24/7. The house is built on an extremely large lot with many large trees and palms, with feeders and water features that attract a large number of bird species.

Owner Rhonda makes a comment, "We are birders and our neighborhood is often on the birding festival tours with a well-established area with lots of mature trees and natural habitat. We have a bird condo on the property (essentially a dead palm with holes bored out for bird's nests) that houses innumerable bird species including – swear it – a pair of red-fronted parrots (seasonal), not parakeets. Birders need not venture far to get life lists."

Clay-colored Robin

The official Backyard Bird Count at this location currently stands at over 30 different species – some of which are South Texas specialties like green parakeets, kiskadee, and chachalaca.

DIRECTIONS
Please call for directions in McAllen.

CONTACT INFORMATION
Phone: 956-330-1045
Web Site; http://www.airbnb.com/rooms/127219
Or http://www.airbnb.com/rooms/43709
Blog Site: http://birdmecca.posterous.com/ Also Look at the McAllen CVB Birding
Contests: http://www.mcallencvb.com/uncategorized/2013-spring-birding-contest-register-now
This site is open for guests only.

SOUTH TEXAS LOOP
#254 Anzalduas Dam and County Park

GPS 26.082, -98.194

LOCATED ON **FM 494** A SHORT DISTANCE FROM THE RIO GRANDE IN MISSION, TEXAS

KEY BIRDS
Western meadowlark, hook-billed kite, rose-throated becard, northern beardless-tyrannulet

BEST SEASON
All seasons

AREA DESCRIPTION
Well-manicured multi-use park with one of the most significant stands of mature Rio Grande ash and live oak in the Valley

As you drive in the entrance road, it passes through a grassy area where the western meadowlark often winters along with its eastern variety. Birders, pay close attention to all the sparrows of many species. In addition, a Sprague's pipit has been found in this location.

Western Meadowlark

The park attracts an incredible array of visiting birds such as the nesting gray hawk, rose-throated becard, hook-billed kite, clay-colored robin, northern beardless-tyrannulet, and the tropical parula.

During recent years, a zone-tailed hawk has been sighted, as well as a number of neotropical migrants such as black-throated green, black-throated gray, hermit, and black-and-white warblers.

There is simply no way to predict what new Texas or U.S. species will appear at Anzalduas, so be sure to check it often while you visit the Valley.

DIRECTIONS

From the intersection of Spur 115 and FM 1016, go west on FM 1016 to FM 494. Go south (eventually veering west) on FM 494 to the entrance to Anzalduas Dam and County Park, which is about 3 miles from the intersection of FM 1016 and FM 494.

CONTACT INFORMATION

Phone: 956-585-5311
Website: http://www.allacrosstexas.com/outdoors/mission-anzalduas-county-park-&-dam.htm
This site is open for day use only.

SOUTH TEXAS LOOP

#255 Bentsen-Rio Grande Valley State Park – World Birding Center Site

GPS 26.103, -98.229

2800 S. BENTSEN PALM DRIVE – FM 2062 MISSION, TX 78572

KEY BIRDS
Elf owl, collared forest-falcon, crane hawk, masked tityra

BEST SEASON
All seasons

AREA DESCRIPTION
Rich and fertile alluvial plan with native shrubs, forbs, and shade trees

This park was closed to normal park usage in order to create the World Birding Center headquarters, located near the park entrance. The WBC headquarters offers interpretation and information on the incredible avian diversity of the park.

The headquarters at Bentsen-Rio Grande Valley State Park acts as an anchor to the WBC complex and provides information about what is being seen in the Valley and how to reach additional birding sites.

This location is made up of layers of sediments by centuries of Rio Grande flooding, making the area extremely fertile. There are many native shrubs and forbs that are shaded by Rio Grande ash, cedar elm, anacua trees, and sugar hackberry. The park contains 760 acres and adjoins a 1,700-acre USFW refuge tract off FM 2062.

The park has been a favorite of birders for a very long time, and often hosts a number of species new to the U.S. such as crane hawk, collared forest-falcon, masked tityra, and the stygian owl.

The elf owl breeds in these woods during the late spring and summer. Check with the park staff for the location of a nesting hole that may be visible to the public.

Audubon's Oriole

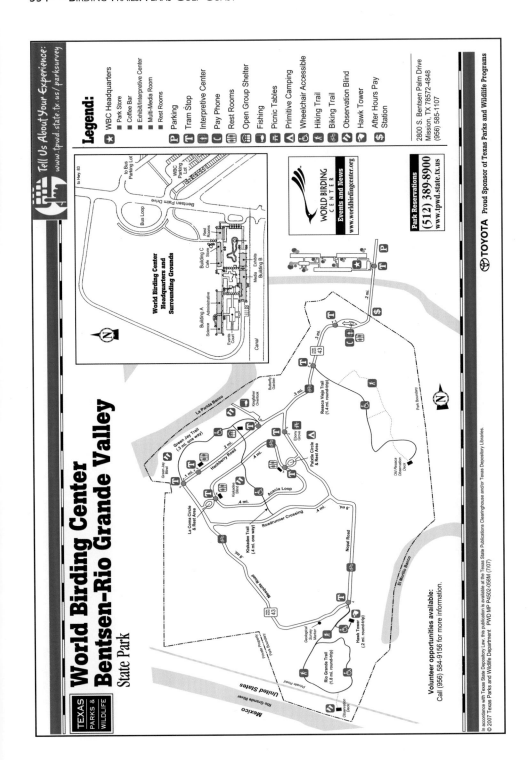

TEXAS
PARKS &
WILDLIFE

World Birding Center
Bentsen-Rio Grande Valley
State Park

Tell Us About Your Experience:
www.tpwd.state.tx.us/parksurvey

Legend:

- ★ WBC Headquarters
- ■ Park Store
- ■ Coffee Bar
- ■ Exhibit/Interpretive Center
- ■ Multi-Media Room
- ■ Rest Rooms
- P Parking
- T Tram Stop
- Interpretive Center
- Pay Phone
- Rest Rooms
- Open Group Shelter
- Fishing
- Picnic Tables
- Primitive Camping
- ♿ Wheelchair Accessible
- Hiking Trail
- Biking Trail
- Observation Blind
- Hawk Tower
- $ After Hours Pay Station

WORLD BIRDING CENTER
Events and News
www.worldbirdingcenter.org

2800 S. Bentsen Palm Drive
Mission, TX 78572-4848
(956) 585-1107

Park Reservations
(512) 389-8900
www.tpwd.state.tx.us

World Birding Center Headquarters and Surrounding Grounds

to Hwy. 83
to Bus Parking Lot
Bus Loop
WBC Parking Lot
Bentsen Palm Drive
Rest Rooms
Building C Cafe Store
Building A Science Administrative
Media Building B
Exhibits
Events Court
Canal

Butterfly Garden
La Parida Banco
Kingfisher Overlook
Green Jay Trail (.3 mi. one way)
Green Jay Blind
Hackberry Road
Ebony Grove
Resaca Vieja Trail (1.4 mi. round-trip)
Parida Circle & Rest Area
3 mi.
4 mi.
La Coma Circle & Rest Area
Kiskadee Blind
Acacia Loop
Kiskadee Trail (.4 mi. one way)
Roadrunner Crossing
Nopal Road
.4 mi.
.8 mi.
Old Resaca Observation Deck
Park Boundary
2 mi.
3 mi.
El Morillo Banco
Mesquite Road
Geological Survey Marker
43
43
Hawk Tower (.2 mi. round-trip)
Rio Grande Trail (1.8 mi. round-trip)

Mexico
United States
Rio Grande River
Private Road
Observation Deck

Volunteer opportunities available:
Call (956) 584-9156 for more information.

🚗 TOYOTA **Proud Sponsor of Texas Parks and Wildlife Programs**

This park was open for camping and fishing but has been closed to those activities so birders can ride on the pre-programed transportation tram, ride bikes, or walk through the park. A two-story observation tower has been constructed that gives visitors a bird's-eye view of the park's canopy and a look into Mexico.

Two enclosed bird blinds and a birding wall allow visitors to see birds up close and watch their behaviors. There are over seven miles of trails with bird feeding stations and water features.

DIRECTIONS

From Anzalduas, return to FM 494, go northwest to La Lomita Mission then continue to the intersection of FM 494 and FM 1016 or Conway Ave. Go west on Conway Ave. until it veers to the north. Instead of continuing north on Conway, veer west on Military Hwy. Continue on Military Hwy. until it dead ends at FM 2062. Turn south (left) into the entrance to Bentsen-Rio Grande Valley State Park and the WBC Headquarters.

CONTACT INFORMATION

2800 S. Bentsen Palm Drive (FM 2062)
Mission, TX 78572
Phone: 956-584-9156
This site is open for day use only.

SOUTH TEXAS LOOP
#256 Chihuahua Woods Preserve of the Nature Conservancy

GPS 26.224, -98.409

JUST OFF BUS US 83, SOUTHWEST OF MISSION, TEXAS

KEY BIRDS
Groove-billed ani, northern beardless-tyrannulet

BEST SEASON
All seasons

AREA DESCRIPTION
Some of the last Chihuahua woods, trees, brush, and cactus

The 349-acre Chihuahua Woods Preserve is a relic of what the Rio Grande Valley once was.

This is a walk-in access during daylight hours. It must be noted that this location is not suitable for children. There are no restroom facilities, the paths are not regularly maintained, and there are numerous thorns, cacti, and poisonous insects and snakes.

Please restrict your birding to the maintained trails, and do not disturb the native vegetation. Many species of South Texas birds reside here such as northern beardless-tyrannulet, groove-billed ani, and at times a red-billed pigeon. During winter months, birders may see a hook-billed kite, a raptor which feeds on the abundant land snails.

DIRECTIONS
Return north on FM 2062 to BUS 83, and then go west on BUS 83 to its intersection with FM 1427. From this intersection, continue west on BUS 83 0.3 mile to where BUS 83 veers to the northwest. Leave BUS 83, and continue straight on the paved road (Old Military Hwy.) that parallels the railroad tracks. This road will turn south across the railroad tracks at 0.2 mile; Chihuahua Woods Preserve of The Nature Conservancy of Texas will be on your left.

CONTACT INFORMATION

The Nature Conservancy of Texas, McAllen, TX 78502-6281
Phone: 956-580-4241
For more information, contact the Conservancy's South Texas Project Office: Patrick Conner, 3409 North FM 1355, Kingsville, TX 78363
Phone: 361-815-7884
Email: pconner@tnc.org.
This site is open for day use only.

Groove-billed Ani

SOUTH TEXAS LOOP

#257 Las Palomas WMA – Peñitas Unit

GPS ⊕ 26.226, -98.455

LOCATED ON THE OLD MILITARY HWY, SOUTH OF LA JOYA, TEXAS

KEY BIRDS
Northern bobwhite, zone-tailed hawk, hook-billed kite

BEST SEASON
Migrations, winter

AREA DESCRIPTION
Grassy fields and South Texas habitats

The Peñitas Unit is one of 13 locations in the Las Palomas WMA. The walking trails in this unit are the roads that serve as access to the native brush within this WMA. The grassy fields near the entrance are a good bet for attracting sparrows during the winter. Listen for northern bobwhite and watch the skies for hawks. Species such as zone-tailed hawk and hook-billed kite may be seen virtually anywhere along the Rio Grande west of Santa Ana NWR.

DIRECTIONS
Go to the intersection of BUS 83 and FM 1427, and then go south (then west) 5.2 miles to Peñitas. Veer left on Old Military Hwy. and then continue west to the Las Palomas WMA Peñitas Unit.

CONTACT INFORMATION
Call TPW or check the information kiosk at the entrance for news about hunting season closures.
Phone: 956-447-2704
This site is open for day use only.

Northern Bobwhite

SOUTH TEXAS LOOP
USFWS Yturria Tract

#258

GPS 26.172, -98.322

LOCATED OFF HWY 83 WEST OF LA JOYA, TEXAS

KEY BIRDS
Varied buntings, long-billed and curve-billed thrashers, white-tailed kite

BEST SEASON
Migrations, winter, and early summer

AREA DESCRIPTION
Upland thorn scrub habitat with mesquite

The well-developed trails on the 1,800-acre Yturria Tract are old ranch roads that go through thick upland thorn scrub habitat. This is a good place to see a mix of Valley specialties and western species.

Green-tailed towhees winter here on occasion and varied buntings have been seen in spring. Long-billed and curve-billed thrashers, verdin, greater roadrunner, white-tailed kite, and other resident birds may be seen all year.

The upland thorn scrub habitat provides excellent bird watching and nature photography. The hiking/walking trails are accessible by foot only. There is a designated parking lot and informational kiosk.

Western species such as black-tailed gnatcatcher, varied bunting, and cactus and Bewick's wrens may be seen at times as you approach the location.

Indigo Bunting

DIRECTIONS
Return to US 83, and continue west about 3 miles to the USFWS Yturria Tract. The tract is located on the north side of US 83, and signs mark its entrance.

CONTACT INFORMATION
USFWS, 325 Green Jay Road, Alamo, TX 78516
E-mail: christine_donald@fws.gov
Phone Number: 956-784-7500
This site is open for day use only.

SOUTH TEXAS LOOP
Los Ebanos Ferry Landing

GPS 26.24, -98.264

LOCATED IN FAR WESTERN HILDAGO COUNTY TWO MILES SOUTH OF HWY 83 ON FM 886

KEY BIRDS
Ringed kingfishers

BEST SEASON
All seasons

AREA DESCRIPTION
Rio Grande habitats and a tree-lined road

This is not what I would call a "hot" birding location, although you may spot a kingfisher perched in a tree by the river or diving for something to eat. It is however a place where you can actually step into the past.

This is the last hand-operated ferry operating on the 1,800-mile length of the Rio Grande, and the last Coast Guard-licensed ferry in the U.S. to be operated by a rope tug. A large Texas ebony tree anchors the three-car barge on the U.S. side. This is private property, but you may walk to the Rio Grande for 25 cents.

Ringed kingfishers are sometimes seen at the landing. At any rate, watching the ferry operate is worth the trip.

DIRECTIONS
Drive west on US 83 to FM 886, then travel south to the Los Ebanos Ferry Landing.

CONTACT INFORMATION
No contact information available.
This site is open for day use only.

SOUTH TEXAS LOOP

#260 Roma Bluffs/ The Roma Historic District – World Birding Center Site

GPS 26.404, -99.018

610 N. PORTSHELLER ST. ROMA, TX

KEY BIRDS
Clay-colored robin, Audubon's oriole

BEST SEASON
All seasons

AREA DESCRIPTION
Sandstone bluffs that extend out toward the Rio Grande, with ash, black willow, and sugar hackberry

Once a thriving steamboat port, today's city of Roma is a birdwatcher's paradise! Roma is the westernmost unit in the WBC complex. It will expand to offer birders access to a number of sites along the Rio Grande in Starr County. The Roma Bluffs and the wildlife viewing area are at the south end of the plaza.

Roma is among the most historic cities in Texas, and is being restored to reflect its glory days as a port on the Rio Grande. From Roma Bluffs - the sandstone bluffs that jut out toward the Rio Grande – there are few

Audubon's Oriole

grander views of the Rio Grande. Watch for Muscovy duck and red-billed pigeon during the early morning and late evenings, as well as all three kingfishers.

In recent years, clay-colored robin and Audubon's oriole have been seen here along the river, and lesser goldfinches are fairly common in the grassy fields.

Directions
Drive west on US 83 through Rio Grande City, and continue west on US 83 to Roma. Go south (left) on Lincoln Ave., then turn east (left) on Estrella and continue one block to the Historic Plaza.

Contact Information
Roma Bluffs World Birding Center, P.O. Box 3405, Roma, Texas 78584
Phone: 956-849-4930
This site is open for day use only.

Northern Cardinal

SOUTH TEXAS LOOP
Falcon State Park

#261

GPS 26.582, -99.144

NORTH OF ROMA, TEXAS ON THE SOUTH END OF FALCON RESERVOIR

KEY BIRDS
Osprey, vermilion flycatcher, Couch's kingbird, white pelican, pyrrhuloxia, northern cardinal, northern mockingbird, red-winged blackbird

BEST SEASON
All seasons

AREA DESCRIPTION
Gently rolling hills covered by mesquite, huisache, wild olive, ebony, cactus and native grasses

The official proclaimed purpose of Falcon Dam was flood control and hydroelectric generation, but a great benefit to wildlife and consequent ecotourism is also a result—especially birding tourists who visit Texas.

Falcon State Park is 572.6 (144 developed) acres located north of Roma at the southern end of the 98,960-surface-acre International Falcon Reservoir in Starr and Zapata Counties.

The woodlands along Falcon Reservoir are worth checking for great kiskadee, vermilion flycatcher, Couch's kingbird, and migrant land birds.

The upland areas are made up of cenizo and should be searched for common pauraque, scaled quail – look around the RV areas in the evening – ash-throated flycatcher, pyrrhuloxia, verdin, and black-throated sparrow.

Caution: It must be mentioned that several visitors as well as residents have been killed on and around the lake. Some say the people were in the wrong place at the wrong time. Caution should be taken, travel in larger groups, and never enter the border areas after dark, which includes the larger and smaller border towns.

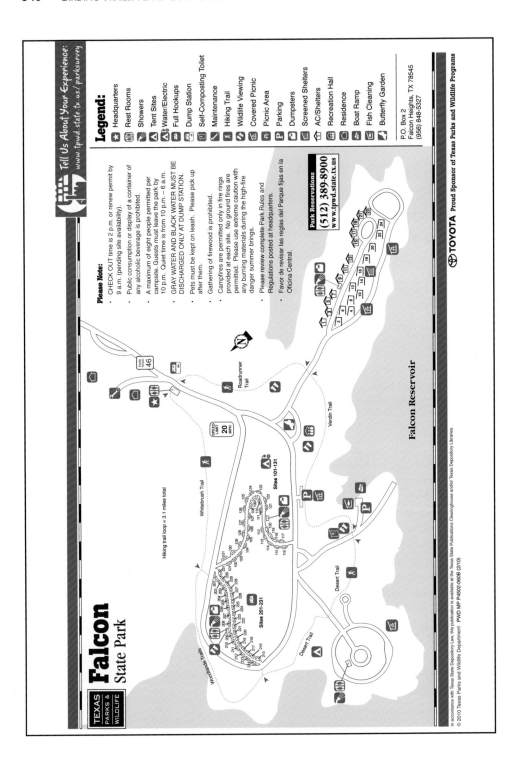

Falcon State Park

TEXAS PARKS & WILDLIFE

Tell Us About Your Experience:
www.tpwd.state.tx-us/parksurvey

Please Note:

- CHECK OUT time is 2 p.m. or renew permit by 9 a.m. (pending site availability).
- Public consumption or display of a container of any alcoholic beverage is prohibited.
- A maximum of eight people permitted per campsite. Guests must leave the park by 10 p.m. Quiet time is from 10 p.m. – 6 a.m.
- GRAY WATER AND BLACK WATER MUST BE DISCHARGED ONLY AT DUMP STATION.
- Pets must be kept on leash. Please pick up after them.
- Gathering of firewood is prohibited.
- Campfires are permitted only in fire rings provided at each site. No ground fires are permitted. Please use extreme caution with any burning materials during the high-fire danger summer brings.
- Please review complete Park Rules and Regulations posted at headquarters.
- Favor de revisar las reglas del Parque fijas en la Oficina Central.

Park Reservations
(512) 389-8900
www.tpwd.state.tx.us

Legend:

- Headquarters
- Rest Rooms
- Showers
- Tent Sites
- Water/Electric
- Full Hookups
- Dump Station
- Self-Composting Toilet
- Maintenance
- Hiking Trail
- Wildlife Viewing
- Covered Picnic
- Picnic Area
- Parking
- Dumpsters
- Screened Shelters
- AC/Shelters
- Recreation Hall
- Residence
- Boat Ramp
- Fish Cleaning
- Butterfly Garden

P.O. Box 2
Falcon Heights, TX 78545
(956) 848-5327

Falcon Reservoir

Roadrunner Trail

Verdin Trail

Whitebrush Trail

Hiking trail loop = 3.1 miles total

Woodlands Trails

Desert Trail

Sites 101-131

Sites 201-231

FARM ROAD 46

SPEED LIMIT 20 MPH

N

TOYOTA Proud Sponsor of Texas Parks and Wildlife Programs

In accordance with Texas State Depository Law, this publication is available at the Texas State Publications Clearinghouse and/or Texas Depository Libraries.
© 2010 Texas Parks and Wildlife Department   PWD MP P4502-060B (2/10)

DIRECTIONS

From Roma, drive north on Hwy 83 to Spur 2098. Follow Spur 2098 to PR46. Go left (north, then west) on PR 46 to Falcon State Park.

CONTACT INFORMATION

Falcon State Park, P.O. Box 2, Falcon Heights, TX 78545
Phone: 956-848-5327
This site is open daily with developed camping available for a fee.

BIRDING TRAILS: TEXAS GULF COAST

Wildlife Management Areas of Texas

The rural landscape of Texas offers a natural beauty and character unsurpassed. Texas boasts some of the most beautiful and abundant populations of plants and wildlife to be found anywhere.

Past generations of Texas families lived in or near rural, natural areas of the state, and understood the value and necessity of healthy natural systems. But today most Texans live near cities and towns, and many of us have lost our connection with the land.

The Wildlife Management Areas (WMAs) of Texas offer a unique opportunity for the public to learn and experience the natural part of Texas and the systems that support life. WMAs are operated by the Wildlife Division of Texas Parks and Wildlife. Today, we have 51 Wildlife Management Areas, encompassing some 756,464 acres of land. WMAs are established to represent habitats and wildlife populations typical of each ecological region of Texas. Today, nearly every ecological region in the state is represented, with the exception of the Cross Timbers and Prairies in north-central Texas.

WMAs were established as sites to perform research on wildlife populations and habitat, conduct education on sound resource management, and to provide public hunting, hiking, camping, bird watching, and a host of other outdoor recreational opportunities - all of which are compatible with the conservation of this valuable resource.

WMAs offer a chance to experience Texas's natural beauty - from the high, wide skies of the Panhandle in the north to the southern tropical thorn forests of the Lower Rio Grande Valley; and from the spectacular western vistas of the Trans-Pecos to the lush green mystery of the Pineywoods in East Texas.

You must have a permit to visit a WMA. The only exceptions are driving tours and special educational events.

Limited Public Use (LPU) Permit - $12

- A $12 Limited Public Use (LPU) Permit is also available which allows an adult to enter these lands, but does not authorize them to hunt.

- The LPU Permit provides entry to Texas Parks & Wildlife Department Wildlife Management Areas at times when they are open for general visitation.
- Only permit holders receive a map booklet listing available areas, facilities, rules, and schedules.

LPU Permits are available at TPWD offices and all license vendors (a place which sells hunting and fishing licenses), or by calling 1-800-TX-LIC-4U (menu choice 1 for license sales) and paying by Visa, Discover, or MasterCard). If the permit is purchased at a TPWD office, the map booklet and supplement will be provided immediately at the time of purchase; otherwise, the publications will be mailed to the purchaser within two weeks of purchase.

Here are five tips to help enjoy Wildlife Management Areas to the fullest:
1. Bring your own drinking water.
2. Insect repellant is recommended for mosquitoes.
3. High heat and humidity in the summer should be taken into consideration when planning a visit.
4. Keep in mind there are no restroom facilities.
5. The WMA is not wheel chair accessible.

Users must have a $48.00 Texas Public Lands Permit available from TPW vendors. This one permit will allow entry to most Texas wildlife management areas.

Texas State Parks

Fee information for specific parks is available on that particular park's website by clicking on the "Fees" link. You can also inquire about specific fees by calling the Park Information line (Monday-Friday from 8am – 5pm) at 1-800-792-1112 (option 3 - option 3). The Central Reservation Center will also give you rates when you make reservations at 512-389-8900. The Reserve America Internet Reservations website (www.reserveamerica.com) also contains fee information for specific parks.

Texas State Parks Pass

The Texas State Parks Pass is an annual pass that offers many special benefits. As a pass holder, you and your guests can enjoy unlimited visits to more than 90 State Parks, without paying the daily entrance fee (card holder and physical pass must be present). You can also receive exciting discounts on camping (restrictions apply), park store merchandise, and recreational equipment rentals, and you are eligible for other specials.

BIRDING TRAILS: TEXAS GULF COAST

Texas Audubon Society Chapters

Arroyo Colorado Audubon

www.arroyocoloradoaudubonsociety.
blogspot.com

Audubon Dallas

PO Box 12713
Dallas, TX 75225
www.audubondallas.org

Bastrop County Audubon Society

Bastrop, TX
www.bastropcountyaudubon.org

Bexar Audubon Society

PO Box 6084
San Antonio, TX 78209
www.bexaraudubon.org

Big Country Audubon Society

PO Box 569
Abilene, TX 79604
325-691-8981
www.bigcountryaudubon.org

Central Texas Audubon Society

1308 Circlewood
Waco, TX 76712
www.centexaudubon.org

Coastal Bend Audubon Society

PO Box 3604
Corpus Christi, TX 78463
361-885-6203
www.coastalbendaudubon.org

El Paso Trans Pecos Audubon Society

PO Box 972441
El Paso, TX 79997
www.trans-pecos-audubon.org

Fort Worth Audubon Society

PO Box 16528
Fort Worth, TX 74162
www.fwas.org

Frontera Audubon

www.fronteraaudubon.org

Golden Triangle Audubon Society

PO Box 1292
Nederland, TX 77627
www.goldentriangleaudubon.org

Houston Audubon Society

440 Wilchester Blvd.
Houston, TX 77079
713-932-1639
www.houstonaudubon.org

Huntsville Audubon Society

PO Box 6818
Huntsville, TX 77342
www.huntsvilleaudubon.org

Llano Estacado Audubon Society

PO Box 6066
Lubbock, TX 79493
www.leas.bizland.com

Monte Mucho Audubon Society

PO Box 200
Realitos, TX 78376
956-764-5701
www.audubon.org/chapters/monte-
mucho-audubon-society

Prairie and Timbers Audubon Society

c/o Heard Natural Science Museum
One Nature Place
McKinney, TX 75069
972-562-5566
www.prairieandtimbers.org

Rio Brazos Audubon Society

PO Box 9055
College Station, TX 77842
www.riobrazosaudubon.org

Rio Grande Delta Audubon Society

8801 Boca Chica
Brownsville, TX 878521
956-831-4653 or 1-866-279-1775
www.riograndedeltaaudubon.org

Texas Panhandle Audubon Society

PO Box 30939
Amarillo, TX 79120
806-656-0036
www.TXPAS.org

Travis Audubon Society

3710 Cedar St.
Box 5
Austin, TX 78705
512-300-2473
www.travisaudubon.org

Twin Lakes Audubon Society

PO Box 883
Belton, TX 76513
www.twinlakesaudubon.org

Tyler Audubon Society

PO Box 132926
Tyler, TX 75713
www.tyleraudubon.org

BIRDING TRAILS: TEXAS GULF COAST

Texas Bird List

The following is a list of bird species accepted for Texas by the Texas Bird Records Committee (TBRC) of the Texas Ornithological Society.

I = Introduced
E = Extinct
u = uncertain origin of introduced/native origin
* = birds expected to be accepted by the TBRC

LOONS

ORDER GAVIIFORMES, FAMILY GAVIIDAE
Red-throated Loon
Pacific Loon
Common Loon
Yellow-billed Loon

GREBES

ORDER PODICIPEDIFORMES, FAMILY DIOMEDEIIDAE
Least Grebe
Pied-billed Grebe
Horned Grebe
Red-necked Grebe
Eared Grebe
Western Grebe
Clark's Grebe

SHEARWATERS, PETRELS AND ALBATROSSES

ORDER PROCELLARIIFORMES, FAMILY PROCELLARIIDAE
Yellow-nosed Albatross
White-chinned Petrel
Black-capped Petrel *
Cory's Shearwater
Greater Shearwater
Sooty Shearwater
Manx Shearwater
Audubon's Shearwater

FAMILY SULIDAE
Masked Booby
Blue-footed Booby
Brown Booby
Red-footed Booby
Northern Gannet

PELICANS, FRIGATEBIRDS

ORDER PELECANIFORMES, FAMILY FREGATIDAE
Magnificent Frigatebird

ORDER PELECANIFORMES, FAMILY PELICANIDAE
American White Pelican
Brown Pelican

CORMORANTS

(ORDER PELECANIFORMES, FAMILY PHALACROCORACIDAE)
Double-crested Cormorant
Neotropic Cormorant

DARTERS

ORDER PELECANIFORMES, FAMILY ANHINGIDAE
Anhinga

BITTERNS AND HERONS

ORDER CICONIIFORMES, FAMILY ARDEIDAE
American Bittern
Least Bittern
Great Blue Heron

Great Egret
Snowy Egret
Little Blue Heron
Tricolored Heron
Reddish Egret
Cattle Egret
Green Heron
Black-crowned Night-Heron
Yellow-crowned Night-Heron

STORM-PETRELS

ORDER PROCELLARIIFORMES, FAMILY HYDROBATIDAE
Wilson's Storm-Petrel
Leach's Storm-Petrel
Band-rumped Storm-Petrel

TROPICBIRDS

ORDER PELECANIFORMES, FAMILY PHAETHONTIDAE
Red-billed Tropicbird

IBISES AND SPOONBILLS

ORDER CICONIIFORMES, FAMILY THRESKIORNITHIDAE
White Ibis
Glossy Ibis
White-faced Ibis
Roseate Spoonbill

STORKS

ORDER CICONIIFORMES, FAMILY CICONIIDAE
Jabiru
Wood Stork

AMERICAN VULTURES

ORDER CICONIIFORMES
Black Vulture
Turkey Vulture

FLAMINGOES

ORDER PHOENICOPTERIFORMES, FAMILY PHOENICOPTERIDAE
Greater Flamingo

SWANS, GEESE AND DUCKS

ORDER ANSERIFORMES, FAMILY ANATIDAE
Black-bellied Whistling-Duck
Fulvous Whistling-Duck
Greater White-fronted Goose
Snow Goose
Ross's Goose
Canada Goose
Brant
Trumpeter Swan
Tundra Swan
Muscovy Duck
Wood Duck
Gadwall
Eurasian Wigeon
American Wigeon
American Black Duck
Mallard
Mottled Duck
Blue-winged Teal
Cinnamon Teal
Northern Shoveler
White-cheeked Pintail
Northern Pintail
Garganey
Green-winged Teal
Canvasback
Redhead
Ring-necked Duck
Greater Scaup
Lesser Scaup
Harlequin Duck
Surf Scoter
White-winged Scoter
Black Scoter
Oldsquaw
Bufflehead
Common Goldeneye
Barrow's Goldeneye
Hooded Merganser
Red-breasted Merganser
Common Merganser
Masked Duck
Ruddy Duck

KITES, HAWKS, EAGLES AND ALLIES

ORDER FALCONIFORMES, FAMILY ACCIPITRIDAE

Osprey
Hook-billed Kite
Swallow-tailed Kite
White-tailed Kite
Snail Kite
Mississippi Kite
Bald Eagle
Northern Harrier
Sharp-shinned Hawk
Cooper's Hawk
Northern Goshawk
Crane Hawk
Gray Hawk
Common Black-Hawk
Harris's Hawk
Roadside Hawk
Red-shouldered Hawk
Broad-winged Hawk
Short-tailed Hawk
Swainson's Hawk
White-tailed Hawk
Zone-tailed Hawk
Red-tailed Hawk
Ferruginous Hawk
Rough-legged Hawk
Golden Eagle

CARACARAS AND FALCONS

ORDER FALCONIFORMES, FAMILY FALCONIDAE

Crested Caracara
Collared Forest-Falcon
American Kestrel
Merlin
Aplomado Falcon
Prairie Falcon
Peregrine Falcon

GUANS

ORDER GALLIFORMES, FAMILY CRACIDAE

Plain Chachalaca

PHEASANTS, GROUSE AND TURKEYS

ORDER GALLIFORMES, FAMILY PHASIANIIDAE

Ring-necked Pheasant (I)
Greater Prairie-Chicken
Lesser Prairie-Chicken
Wild Turkey

NEW WORLD QUAIL

ORDER GALLIFORMES, FAMILY ODONTOPHORIDAE

Montezuma Quail
Northern Bobwhite
Scaled Quail
Gambel's Quail

RAILS, GALLINULES AND COOTS

ORDER GRUIFORMES, FAMILY RALLIDAE

Yellow Rail
Black Rail
Clapper Rail
King Rail
Virginia Rail
Sora
Paint-billed Crake
Spotted Rail
Purple Gallinule
Common Moorhen
American Coot

CRANES

ORDER GRUIFORMES, FAMILY GRUIDAE

Sandhill Crane
Whooping Crane

THICK-KNEES

ORDER CHARADRIIFORMES, FAMILY BURHINIDAE

Double-striped Thick-knee

PLOVERS

ORDER CHARADRIIFORMES, FAMILY CHARADRIIDAE

Black-bellied Plover
American Golden-Plover

Collared Plover
Snowy Plover
Wilson's Plover
Semipalmated Plover
Piping Plover
Killdeer
Mountain Plover

OYSTERCATCHERS

ORDER CHARADRIIFORMES, FAMILY HAEMATOPODIDAE
American Oystercatcher

STILTS AND AVOCETS

ORDER CHARADRIIFORMES, FAMILY RECURVIROSTRIDAE
Black-necked Stilt
American Avocet

JACANAS

ORDER CHARADRIIFORMES, FAMILY JACANIDAE
Northern Jacana

SANDPIPERS AND ALLIES

ORDER CHARADRIIFORMES, FAMILY SCOLOPACIDAE
Greater Yellowlegs
Lesser Yellowlegs
Solitary Sandpiper
Willet
Wandering Tattler
Spotted Sandpiper
Upland Sandpiper
Eskimo Curlew
Whimbrel
Long-billed Curlew
Hudsonian Godwit
Marbled Godwit
Ruddy Turnstone
Surfbird
Red Knot
Sanderling
Semipalmated Sandpiper
Western Sandpiper

Red-necked Stint
Least Sandpiper
White-rumped Sandpiper
Baird's Sandpiper
Pectoral Sandpiper
Sharp-tailed Sandpiper
Purple Sandpiper
Dunlin
Curlew Sandpiper
Stilt Sandpiper
Buff-breasted Sandpiper
Ruff
Short-billed Dowitcher
Long-billed Dowitcher
Common Snipe
American Woodcock
Wilson's Phalarope
Red-necked Phalarope
Red Phalarope

GULLS, TERNS AND SKIMMERS

ORDER CHARADRIIFORMES, FAMILY LARIDAE
Pomarine Jaeger
Parasitic Jaeger
Long-tailed Jaeger
Laughing Gull
Franklin's Gull
Little Gull
Black-headed Gull
Bonaparte's Gull
Heermann's Gull
Mew Gull
Ring-billed Gull
California Gull
Herring Gull
Thayer's Gull
Iceland Gull
Lesser Black-backed Gull
Slaty-backed Gull
Western Gull
Glaucous Gull
Great Black-backed Gull
Kelp Gull

Black-legged Kittiwake
Sabine's Gull
Gull-billed Tern
Caspian Tern
Royal Tern
Elegant Tern
Sandwich Tern
Roseate Tern *
Common Tern
Arctic Tern *
Forster's Tern
Least Tern
Bridled Tern
Sooty Tern
Black Tern
Brown Noddy
Black Noddy
Black Skimmer

PIGEONS AND DOVES

ORDER COLUMBIFORMES, FAMILY COLUMBIDAE
Rock Dove (I)
Red-billed Pigeon
Band-tailed Pigeon
Eurasian Collared-Dove (I)*
White-winged Dove
Mourning Dove
Passenger Pigeon (E)
Inca Dove
Common Ground-Dove
Ruddy Ground-Dove
Ruddy Quail-Dove
White-tipped Dove

PARAKEETS AND PARROTS

ORDER PSITTACIFORMES, FAMILY PSITTACIDAE
Monk Parakeet (I)
Carolina Parakeet (E)
Green Parakeet (u)
Red-crowned Parrot (u)

CUCKOOS, ROADRUNNERS AND ANIS

ORDER CUCULIFORMES, FAMILY CUCULIDAE
Black-billed Cuckoo
Yellow-billed Cuckoo
Mangrove Cuckoo
Greater Roadrunner
Groove-billed Ani

BARN OWLS

ORDER STRIGIFORMES, FAMILY TYTONIDAE
Barn Owl

TYPICAL OWLS

ORDER STRIGIFORMES, FAMILY STRIGIDAE
Flammulated Owl
Eastern Screech-Owl
Western Screech-Owl
Great Horned Owl
Snowy Owl
Northern Pygmy-Owl
Ferruginous Pygmy-Owl
Elf Owl
Burrowing Owl
Mottled Owl
Spotted Owl
Barred Owl
Long-eared Owl
Stygian Owl *
Short-eared Owl
Northern Saw-whet Owl

NIGHTJARS

ORDER CAPRIMULGIFORMES, FAMILY CAPRIMULGIDAE
Lesser Nighthawk
Common Nighthawk
Pauraque
Common Poorwill
Chuck-will's-widow
Whip-poor-will

SWIFTS

ORDER APODIFORMES, FAMILY APODIDAE
White-collared Swift
Chimney Swift
White-throated Swift

HUMMINGBIRDS

ORDER APODIFORMES, FAMILY TROCHILIDAE
Green Violet-ear
Green-breasted Mango
Broad-billed Hummingbird
White-eared Hummingbird
Berylline Hummingbird *
Buff-bellied Hummingbird
Violet-crowned Hummingbird
Blue-throated Hummingbird
Magnificent Hummingbird
Lucifer Hummingbird
Ruby-throated Hummingbird
Black-chinned Hummingbird
Anna's Hummingbird
Costa's Hummingbird
Calliope Hummingbird
Broad-tailed Hummingbird
Rufous Hummingbird
Allen's Hummingbird

TROGONS

ORDER TROGONIFORMES, FAMILY TROGONIDAE
Elegant Trogon

KINGFISHERS

ORDER CORACIIFORMES, FAMILY ALCEDINIDAE
Ringed Kingfisher
Belted Kingfisher
Green Kingfisher

WOODPECKERS AND ALLIES

(ORDER PICIFORMES, FAMILY PICIDAE)
Lewis's Woodpecker
Red-headed Woodpecker
Acorn Woodpecker
Golden-fronted Woodpecker

Red-bellied Woodpecker
Yellow-bellied Sapsucker
Red-naped Sapsucker
Red-breasted Sapsucker *
Williamson's Sapsucker
Ladder-backed Woodpecker
Downy Woodpecker
Hairy Woodpecker
Red-cockaded Woodpecker
Northern Flicker
Pileated Woodpecker
Ivory-billed Woodpecker (E)

TYRANT FLYCATCHERS

ORDER PASSERIFORMES, FAMILY TYRANNIDAE
Northern Beardless-Tyrannulet
Greenish Elaenia
Tufted Flycatcher
Olive-sided Flycatcher
Greater Pewee
Western Wood-Pewee
Eastern Wood-Pewee
Yellow-bellied Flycatcher
Acadian Flycatcher
Alder Flycatcher
Willow Flycatcher
Least Flycatcher
Hammond's Flycatcher
Dusky Flycatcher
Gray Flycatcher
Cordilleran Flycatcher
Black Phoebe
Eastern Phoebe
Say's Phoebe
Vermilion Flycatcher
Dusky-capped Flycatcher
Ash-throated Flycatcher
Great Crested Flycatcher
Brown-crested Flycatcher
Great Kiskadee
Sulphur-bellied Flycatcher
Tropical Kingbird
Couch's Kingbird

Cassin's Kingbird
Thick-billed Kingbird
Western Kingbird
Eastern Kingbird
Gray Kingbird
Scissor-tailed Flycatcher
Fork-tailed Flycatcher
Rose-throated Becard
Masked Tityra

SHRIKES

ORDER PASSERIFORMES, FAMILY LANIIDAE
Northern Shrike
Loggerhead Shrike

VIREOS

ORDER PASSERIFORMES, FAMILY VIREONIDAE
White-eyed Vireo
Bell's Vireo
Black-capped Vireo
Gray Vireo
Blue-headed (Solitary) Vireo
Cassin's (Solitary) Vireo
Plumbeous (Solitary) Vireo
Yellow-throated Vireo
Hutton's Vireo
Warbling Vireo
Philadelphia Vireo
Red-eyed Vireo
Yellow-green Vireo
Black-whiskered Vireo
Yucatan Vireo

JAYS, MAGPIES AND CROWS

ORDER PASSERIFORMES, FAMILY CORVIDAE
Steller's Jay
Blue Jay
Green Jay
Brown Jay
Western Scrub-Jay
Mexican Jay
Pinyon Jay
Clark's Nutcracker

Black-billed Magpie
American Crow
Tamaulipas Crow
Fish Crow
Chihuahuan Raven
Common Raven

LARKS

ORDER PASSERIFORMES, FAMILY ALAUDIDAE
Horned Lark

SWALLOWS

ORDER PASSERIFORMES, FAMILY HIRUNDINIDAE
Purple Martin
Gray-breasted Martin
Tree Swallow
Violet-green Swallow
Bank Swallow
Barn Swallow
Cliff Swallow
Cave Swallow
Northern Rough-winged Swallow

TITMICE AND CHICKADEES

ORDER PASSERIFORMES, FAMILY PARIDAE
Carolina Chickadee
Black-capped Chickadee
Mountain Chickadee
Juniper (Plain) Titmouse
Tufted Titmouse

VERDINS

ORDER PASSERIFORMES, FAMILY REMIZIDAE
Verdin

BUSHTITS

ORDER PASSERIFORMES, FAMILY AEGITHALIDAE
Bushtit

NUTHATCHES

ORDER PASSERIFORMES, FAMILY SITTIDAE
Red-breasted Nuthatch
White-breasted Nuthatch
Pygmy Nuthatch
Brown-headed Nuthatch

CREEPERS

ORDER PASSERIFORMES, FAMILY CERTHIIDAE
Brown Creeper

WRENS

ORDER PASSERIFORMES, FAMILY TROGLODYTIDAE
Cactus Wren
Rock Wren
Canyon Wren
Carolina Wren
Bewick's Wren
House Wren
Winter Wren
Sedge Wren
Marsh Wren

KINGLETS

ORDER PASSERIFORMES, FAMILY REGULIDAE
Golden-crowned Kinglet
Ruby-crowned Kinglet

DIPPERS

ORDER PASSERIFORMES, FAMILY CINCLIDAE
American Dipper

GNATCATCHERS

(ORDER PASSERIFORMES, FAMILY SYLVIIDAE)
Blue-gray Gnatcatcher
Black-tailed Gnatcatcher
(Order Passeriformes, Family Sylviidae)
Blue-gray Gnatcatcher
Black-tailed Gnatcatcher

THRUSHES AND ALLIES

(ORDER PASSERIFORMES, FAMILY TURDIDAE)
Northern Wheatear
Eastern Bluebird
Western Bluebird
Mountain Bluebird
Townsend's Solitaire

Orange-billed Nightingale-Thrush
Veery
Gray-cheeked Thrush
Swainson's Thrush
Hermit Thrush
Wood Thrush
Clay-colored Robin
White-throated Robin
Rufous-backed Robin
American Robin
Varied Thrush
Aztec Thrush

THRASHERS AND ALLIES

ORDER PASSERIFORMES, FAMILY MIMIDAE
Gray Catbird
Black Catbird
Northern Mockingbird
Sage Thrasher
Brown Thrasher
Long-billed Thrasher
Curve-billed Thrasher
Crissal Thrasher

STARLINGS

ORDER PASSERIFORMES, FAMILY STURNIDAE
European Starling (I)

PIPITS

ORDER PASSERIFORMES, FAMILY MOTACILLIDAE
American Pipit
Sprague's Pipit

WAXWINGS

ORDER PASSERIFORMES, FAMILY BOMBYCILLIDAE
Bohemian Waxwing
Cedar Waxwing

SILKY-FLYCATCHERS

ORDER PASSERIFORMES, FAMILY PTILOGONATIDAE
Gray Silky-flycatcher
Phainopepla

OLIVE WARBLER

ORDER PASSERIFORMES, FAMILY PEUCEDRAMIDAE
Olive Warbler

WOOD-WARBLERS

ORDER PASSERIFORMES, FAMILY PARULIDAE
Blue-winged Warbler
Golden-winged Warbler
Tennessee Warbler
Orange-crowned Warbler
Nashville Warbler
Virginia's Warbler
Colima Warbler
Lucy's Warbler
Northern Parula
Tropical Parula
Yellow Warbler
Chestnut-sided Warbler
Magnolia Warbler
Cape May Warbler
Black-throated Blue Warbler
Yellow-rumped Warbler
Black-throated Gray Warbler
Townsend's Warbler
Hermit Warbler
Black-throated Green Warbler
Golden-cheeked Warbler
Blackburnian Warbler
Yellow-throated Warbler
Grace's Warbler
Pine Warbler
Prairie Warbler
Palm Warbler
Bay-breasted Warbler
Blackpoll Warbler
Cerulean Warbler
Black-and-white Warbler
American Redstart
Prothonotary Warbler
Worm-eating Warbler
Swainson's Warbler
Ovenbird
Northern Waterthrush
Louisiana Waterthrush
Kentucky Warbler
Connecticut Warbler
Mourning Warbler
MacGillivray's Warbler
Common Yellowthroat
Gray-crowned Yellowthroat
Hooded Warbler
Wilson's Warbler
Canada Warbler
Red-faced Warbler
Painted Redstart
Slate-throated Redstart *
Golden-crowned Warbler
Rufous-capped Warbler
Yellow-breasted Chat

TANAGERS

ORDER PASSERIFORMES, FAMILY THRAUPIDAE
Hepatic Tanager
Summer Tanager
Scarlet Tanager
Western Tanager
Flame-colored Tanager

SPARROWS, BUNTINGS AND ALLIES

ORDER PASSERIFORMES, FAMILY EMBERIZIDAE
White-collared Seedeater
Yellow-faced Grassquit
Olive Sparrow
Green-tailed Towhee
Eastern Towhee
Spotted Towhee
Canyon Towhee
Bachman's Sparrow
Botteri's Sparrow
Cassin's Sparrow
Rufous-crowned Sparrow
American Tree Sparrow
Chipping Sparrow
Clay-colored Sparrow

Brewer's Sparrow
Field Sparrow
Black-chinned Sparrow
Vesper Sparrow
Lark Sparrow
Black-throated Sparrow
Sage Sparrow
Lark Bunting
Savannah Sparrow
Baird's Sparrow
Grasshopper Sparrow
Henslow's Sparrow
Le Conte's Sparrow
Nelson's Sharp-tailed Sparrow
Seaside Sparrow
Fox Sparrow
Song Sparrow
Lincoln's Sparrow
Swamp Sparrow
White-throated Sparrow
Harris's Sparrow
White-crowned Sparrow
Golden-crowned Sparrow
Dark-eyed Junco
Yellow-eyed Junco
McCown's Longspur
Lapland Longspur
Smith's Longspur
Chestnut-collared Longspur
Snow Bunting

GROSBEAKS AND ALLIES

ORDER PASSERIFORMES, FAMILY CARDINALIDAE
Crimson-collared Grosbeak
Northern Cardinal
Pyrrhuloxia
Rose-breasted Grosbeak
Black-headed Grosbeak
Blue Bunting
Blue Grosbeak
Lazuli Bunting
Indigo Bunting
Varied Bunting
Painted Bunting
Dickcissel

BLACKBIRDS AND ORIOLES

ORDER PASSERIFORMES, FAMILY ICTERIDAE
Bobolink
Red-winged Blackbird
Eastern Meadowlark
Western Meadowlark
Yellow-headed Blackbird
Rusty Blackbird
Brewer's Blackbird
Common Grackle
Boat-tailed Grackle
Great-tailed Grackle
Shiny Cowbird
Bronzed Cowbird
Brown-headed Cowbird
Black-vented Oriole
Orchard Oriole
Hooded Oriole
Altamira Oriole
Audubon's Oriole
Baltimore Oriole
Bullock's Oriole
Scott's Oriole

FINCHES AND ALLIES

ORDER PASSERIFORMES, FAMILY FRINGILLIDAE
Pine Grosbeak
Purple Finch
Cassin's Finch
House Finch
Red Crossbill
White-winged Crossbill
Common Redpoll
Pine Siskin
Lesser Goldfinch
Lawrence's Goldfinch
American Goldfinch
Evening Grosbeak

OLD WORLD SPARROWS

ORDER PASSERIFORMES, FAMILY PASSERIDAE
House Sparrow (I)

Index

Symbols

8-Mile-Road 140–141
40 Acre Lake 242

A

Acadian flycatchers 95
Addicks Reservoir 192–193
Adolph Thomae, Jr. County Park 454
Agua Dulce Creek 413
Alamo 128, 514, 541
Alcoa Birding Tower 308
Alice 411
Allen's hummingbird 185
altamira oriole 291, 454, 469, 470, 483, 492
American avocet 17, 21, 23, 26, 29, 33, 35, 40,
    44, 55, 58, 61, 64, 67, 77, 99, 101, 113,
    119, 126, 127, 134, 138, 140, 146, 155,
    191, 201, 215, 216, 218, 230, 233, 244,
    254, 255, 264, 294, 336, 342
American bittern 24, 28, 33, 43, 90, 98, 106,
    228, 301, 342
American coot 24, 190, 201, 455, 456, 484
American crow 24, 36, 38, 78, 82, 84, 268, 292,
    294, 328, 510
American golden plover 140, 142, 196, 226, 459
American goldfinch 24, 39, 84, 268, 432, 447,
    512
American kestrel 24, 102, 218, 230, 337, 455
American oystercatcher 5, 130, 140, 212, 273,
    308, 313, 350, 360, 376
American pipit 49
American redstart 33, 486
American robin 24, 26, 27, 36, 38, 46, 82, 84,
    135, 236, 268
American white pelican 5, 198, 492, 504
American wigeon 24, 28, 34, 39, 43, 92, 98, 100,
    137, 167, 261, 270, 401
American woodcock 186
Amoco (Chocolate Bayou) Nature Trail
    226–227
AMOCO Settling Ponds 154
Amoco Wetlands Trail 228
Anahuac 98, 100, 106, 108

Anahuac NWR 106–107, 108–109
Anahuac NWR - East Bay Bayou Tract 108–109
Angelina National Forest 22
Angelina-Neches Scientific Area 32
Angelina NF Boykin Springs Recreation Area
    20–21
Angelina NF Upland Island 22–23
Angelina NF Upland Island Wilderness 22–23
Angleton 217, 225, 226, 228, 240, 261
anhinga 30, 49, 62, 74, 77, 96, 112, 296, 297,
    399, 440, 467, 483, 506
ani 484
Anna's hummingbird 410
Anzalduas Dam 530–531
Apffel Park 133–134
aplomado falcon 441, 459, 481
Aransas National Wildlife Refuge 315, 324–325,
    355
Aransas Pass 356, 360
Aransas Pass Wetlands 360–361
Aransas Woods 342–343
Armand Bayou Nature Center 168–169
Arroyo Colorado 6, 447, 449, 460, 464
Arroyo Colorado Audubon 551
Arroyo Park 462–463
ash-throated flycatcher 202, 203, 545
Athey Nature Sanctuary 303–304
Attwater's prairie chicken 159, 160, 181, 264
Attwater Prairie Chicken National Wildlife
    Refuge 264–265
Audubon 3
Audubon Dallas 551
Audubon Outdoor Club of Corpus Christi 426
Audubon Society Chapters 551, 551–552
Audubon's oriole 408, 416, 418, 429, 533, 543
Austwell 324

B

Bachman's sparrow 15, 20, 38, 68
Baffin Bay 373, 423
Bahia Grande 477–478
Baird's sandpiper 273, 274
bald eagle 6, 22, 23, 24, 64, 74, 86, 196, 197, 198,
    246, 331

D

H